# THE LOSER'S BALL

...AND OTHER WINNING STRATEGIES

*Ronnie –*
*Turn your Loser's Balls to*
*"Opportunity Balls.*

**BOB LANNOM**

*Bob Lannom*

**WESTBOW PRESS**
A DIVISION OF THOMAS NELSON
& ZONDERVAN

Copyright © 2024 Bob Lannom.

All rights reserved. No part of this book may be used or reproduced by any means, graphic, electronic, or mechanical, including photocopying, recording, taping or by any information storage retrieval system without the written permission of the author except in the case of brief quotations embodied in critical articles and reviews.

WestBow Press books may be ordered through booksellers or by contacting:

WestBow Press
A Division of Thomas Nelson & Zondervan
1663 Liberty Drive
Bloomington, IN 47403
www.westbowpress.com
844-714-3454

Because of the dynamic nature of the Internet, any web addresses or links contained in this book may have changed since publication and may no longer be valid. The views expressed in this work are solely those of the author and do not necessarily reflect the views of the publisher, and the publisher hereby disclaims any responsibility for them.

Any people depicted in stock imagery provided by Getty Images are models, and such images are being used for illustrative purposes only.
Certain stock imagery © Getty Images.

ISBN: 979-8-3850-2807-8 (sc)
ISBN: 979-8-3850-2808-5 (hc)
ISBN: 979-8-3850-2809-2 (e)

Library of Congress Control Number: 2024912578

Print information available on the last page.

WestBow Press rev. date: 07/05/2024

# Contents

Preface .................................................................................................. ix
Warming Up ........................................................................................ xi

Chapter 1 ............................................................................................... 1
Chapter 2 ............................................................................................... 8
Chapter 3 ............................................................................................. 16
Chapter 4 ............................................................................................. 25
Chapter 5 ............................................................................................. 33
Chapter 6 ............................................................................................. 42
Chapter 7 ............................................................................................. 52
Chapter 8 ............................................................................................. 61
Chapter 9 ............................................................................................. 73
Chapter 10 ........................................................................................... 79
Chapter 11 ........................................................................................... 89
Chapter 12 ......................................................................................... 102
Chapter 13 ......................................................................................... 116
Chapter 14 ......................................................................................... 124
Chapter 15 ......................................................................................... 132
Chapter 16 ......................................................................................... 143
Chapter 17 ......................................................................................... 153
Chapter 18 ......................................................................................... 164
Chapter 19 ......................................................................................... 172
Chapter 20 ......................................................................................... 181
Chapter 21 ......................................................................................... 184
Chapter 22 ......................................................................................... 196
Chapter 23 ......................................................................................... 207
Chapter 24 ......................................................................................... 219

Chapter 25 .................................................................................. 231
Chapter 26 .................................................................................. 245
Chapter 27 .................................................................................. 258
Chapter 28 .................................................................................. 276
Chapter 29 .................................................................................. 289
Chapter 30 .................................................................................. 297

Reviewing Some Interesting Ironies ........................................ 301
Acknowledgements .................................................................. 309
Credits for: References and Resources ................................... 313
Courage and Strength .............................................................. 317
Your Best ................................................................................... 321
The Loser's Ball ......................................................................... 323
My Walk Off .............................................................................. 325

*"I enjoyed reading The Loser's Ball almost as much as I did playing baseball as well as quail and deer hunting with Bob. I just wish that I had a copy of this motivational and inspirational book to give to my players back when I was coaching. I recommend it to any young athlete and even coaches involved in sports as well as in their future business careers."*

- **Pat Lindsey Webb**
Pat Lindsey Webb played baseball in the Navy, and he also played baseball at Austin Peay State University. Pat was a basketball, football and baseball coach. He was a school administrator and served on the Local county commission.

*I can say that I would highly recommend this book to anyone who wants to be entertained by stories about life and not ending up with The Losers Ball.*

- **Jerry Vradenburg**
Belmont University Hall of Fame in basketball and baseball.
Tennessee (TSSAA) Athletic Hall of Fame.
Gallatin HS Hall of Fame.
Nashville Amateur Baseball Hall of Fame.

*I enjoyed reading Bob's autobiographical journey tremendously! He has truly lived a life filled with monumental victories and gut-wrenching defeats. If you love sports, this book is for you. If you want to be inspired, then keep reading. If you need to mend a relationship, that information is here as well. Maybe you just need to know that "The Loser's Ball" allows each reader the motivation to be better tomorrow!*

- **Mark Wilson**
English Teacher/Head Baseball Coach
Gallatin High School (1988-Present)

*"The Loser's Ball" by Bob Lannom is a wonderful personal story of perseverance, positive attitude, and hard work. Along the way, he like all of us, had major disappointments and challenges. "The Loser's Ball" is about how Bob dealt with those challenges and turned them into a life and careers of astounding successes. This is an important read for all ages. I highly recommend it.*

- **Bill Graves**
General Manager (Retired)
Fleetwood Homes

*Bob has hit a "home run" with this book. It has it all; great stories written with sharp humor. He is a storyteller. His faith journey is evident throughout this work. You don't have to be a sports enthusiast to enjoy this read. I have known him for 60 plus years and he has always lived out his faith in all aspects of his life. This is a must read.*

- **Boots Kirby**
Boots Kirby, Belmont University Athletic Hall of Fame in basketball and baseball. Nashville Amateur Baseball Hall of Fame. Sales team for Champion Sporting Goods.

# Preface

Life, just like baseball, is a mental game.

There is no escaping the fact that you will face numerous Loser's Balls. They may start coming your way gradually, maybe with just minor shakeups in your life. Some may come, however, with dramatic impact to knock you off your feet and into the dirt. The battle that must be won is not to waste your time in unsuccessful attempts to block them before they reach you, but to confront each one, not with an immediate undisciplined reaction, but with an appropriate, determined, and opportunistic response to each one.

Don't find yourself dwelling in the loser's bracket, but with a measured and positive attitude, use your energy, courage, strength, stamina, and wherewithal, to execute your responses in the most productive strategies to never give up, but to "give out" utilizing all of your God-given attributes and focus on winning to accomplish your goals.

Throughout my athletic, education, business, church, and family careers, Loser's Balls were and are still thrown to challenge my existence. Life generates them by the thousands. No one is immune to them.

The purpose of this book is to encourage aspiring young athletes and adults as well, who are recipients of them, to turn their Loser's Balls into "Opportunity Balls". Throughout the book I will identify a number of those seemingly, "gotcha" balls and how to turn them into victories, successes, and even championships.

The rare characteristic of a real winner in life is one who possesses those redeeming qualities to accept the initial defeat, pocket the negative, and to adjust decision-making skills to approach a loss as a foundation that is laid, which will support a bigger victory at the next at bat. Often, as you will discover, the ultimate victory or reward may far exceed your original expectations. To God be the glory!......... Phil. 4:13.

# Warming Up

I loved to play the game of baseball. I can't remember when it was not a part of my life while growing up on our little farm near Gladeville, Tennessee. Almost all of the boys who attended Gladeville Elementary School played baseball during our two recess (PE) periods during each day. We devoted the entire time out of classes to choose up teams and play each other with those same teams from Monday through Friday. The next week we would swap up players, creating new teams, and do it over again. That was our routine throughout the school year and every year. We used broken bats that some of us got from chasing foul balls at the Glade games. We used any baseballs whether they had covers on them or not for our games. There were often times when one of us would literally knock the loose cover off of a ball. Some of our game balls were black, having been wrapped with black tape to keep the strings from unraveling.

The Glade, as the locals called it, had a rich history of great baseball teams all the way back to the 1930s. I knew many of those old timers who still lived in or near the Glade, and were regular fans who attended the games on Sunday afternoons during the summer. My daddy had told me many stories about some of the notorious characters and their former Glade baseball exploits. I had decided that one of my goals would be to play for the Glade someday.

Our farm was a typical southern Wilson County farm with an abundance of flat rocks, shallow soil, and loose surface gravel. By the age of ten, I had developed into a pretty good "rock hitter." I spent hours picking up small rocks, pitching them up in the air, and swatting them with either a tobacco stick, or a broken axe handle. I even targeted a couple of large trees across our pond for a triple, or a booming drive into the old oak tree by the spring for a home run. This was my daily batting practice for many years. I even kept a stash of tobacco sticks and a couple of old axe handles stuck behind some bushes between the house and the barn ready for use. I seldom missed my chance at bat going to and from the milk barn every day. Little did I realize my training may just be for nothing.

Neither did I expect that I would be thrown a few Loser's Balls along the way that would jeopardize the opportunity for me to play my game. As a matter of fact, there were no organized youth baseball leagues in the Glade; plus, all of us were denied the opportunity to play Little League or Babe Ruth League baseball in Lebanon, because we did not live in the city limits. Mt. Juliet HS did not have a baseball program, so it didn't look very optimistic for the Glade boys to play any baseball other than our recess games. It was an uphill battle, but you know, there just may be something special over the hill if we keep trying and never give up! I told myself, "If it's there, I would be ready!"

Play Ball!

# Chapter 1

I celebrated my 12$^{th}$ birthday on July 6, 1956, with Mama, Daddy, and my six-year- old brother, Larry. Our little sister, Lugene, who was four months old, was napping during the celebration. Mama had baked me my favorite three-layer chocolate cake covered with a thick layer of chocolate icing. She topped off her work by sticking 12 white candles on top and set it aside ready for the celebration after supper. Daddy and I had just finished milking and were ready to enjoy a delicious meal. Somebody had to guard the cake to keep Larry from sticking his finger in the icing and running off with a sample.

My parents, Wallace and Louise Lannom, with the addition of our new sister, now had a family of five to raise on our 124-acre dairy farm located just two and half miles south of the Glade. The "Glade" was a short name for Gladeville, Tennessee, which was named after its rocky soil and lack of top soil. Wilson County is known for its limestone rock conditions, especially where our farm was located.

Soon after we had cleaned up and ate supper, Mama cleared the table and placed the cake in front of me. She lit all twelve of the candles and told me to make a wish. Daddy grabbed Larry and held on to him to keep him from blowing out the candles before I could think of my wish. Little brothers–but I loved him. Instead of making one, I made two wishes. At twelve years of age, I had missed out on playing four years of little league baseball because the Kiwanis Little League in Lebanon would not permit any players who lived outside the city limits of Lebanon to play. The Lions Club followed the same policy in not allowing boys to play in the Babe Ruth League who lived outside the city limits as well.

I would turn thirteen next year, so my first wish was that the rules would change that would make me eligible to play in the Babe Ruth league in Lebanon. The Glade did not have Little League or Babe Ruth, just the men's team who played in the Cumberland Valley League on Sundays during the summer. My second wish was really more important. It went along with my prayers that I had said for several months. I wish that Daddy Demps would get well and not die from his terrible heart condition. Mama Pearl and Daddy Demps, my daddy's mother and father, were very close to all of us. They lived on their 24-acre farm just across two fields and a woods from our house that Daddy Demps and Daddy had built together when I was two years old. I gathered up a big breath and blew out all twelve candles, hoping that would result in my two wishes being granted. We even lit them again so Larry could blow them out. Maybe his help would work.

Mama couldn't wait. She went into her bedroom and brought out a box wrapped up with a blue bow on top. She was all smiles when she handed it to me and said, "I think you will like it, and it's something you need." I had no idea. The list of things I needed was numerous, but my want list was pretty lengthy too. I let my little brother unwrap the box. There were a lot of things my parents needed, especially with our new addition. Mama was a homemaker and Daddy worked in an airplane factory in Nashville and farmed in the evenings and on the weekends to provide for us.

All of us spent a lot of time together in supporting my grandparents. We didn't take extended vacations because the cows didn't go on vacations. They had to be milked twice every day of the year. There was not a lot of money floating around, but life was the same for most of us kids and families back in the late forties and fifties. I was not much different from nearly all of my friends and classmates.

When the present was opened, I teared up, bigtime. It was a brand-new baseball glove from Jimmy Nokes Sporting Goods in Lebanon. It was an autograph model of Richie Ashburn, an All-Star center fielder for the Philadelphia Phillies. All I remember was that Mama was right. It was something I wanted and needed. My old Western Auto glove daddy had bought me when I was nine, had been mended so many times, taped up, new strings added, and was ready to be retired. What a gift! I was so excited! Maybe the gift of my new glove would go right along with wearing a uniform, and not just at a Glade school recess game. Oh, how I held on to that glove!

I kept it with me pitching up balls in the air, throwing with Daddy, and breaking it in to be ready for my wish to come true. I even recall that it spent several nights beside me while I dreamed of things to happen for me. Some dreams included me catching a line drive for the last out to win a world series. I saw myself in another dream of me jumping up at the outfield fence to rob a home run from the opposing team to win the game.

Friday, August 31, near the end of summer, was a typically hot and dry late summer day. The excitement of my birthday celebration had long subsided. Daddy Demps now lay in his bed struggling to breathe. Everybody was gathered at his and Mama Pearl's house. The doctor had been by to check on him earlier in the morning and had told Mama Pearl, Daddy, and his sisters, Aunt Marie and Maggie Lee (Auntie), that he would probably not make it through the day. It was that bad. When all of us heard the news, it was heart breaking. I walked in the house from the porch and stood by his bed for several minutes thinking of my wish that I had made just weeks ago.

Reality doesn't bow to wishes made or plans we may conjure up to fulfill our wants and desires. It takes its own cruel and unbiased direction regardless of what results come from its eventual closure. I began to think that maybe birthday wishes are more about tradition than reality. It was surely proving that way today, it seemed, unless some miracle was to occur. I loved my grandfather, and seeing him lie there so helpless was hard. I had to go back outside. I knew without a doubt, now, that I would face my first loss of a family relative, my first major Loser's Ball.

Just after lunch, Mary Katheryn, Aunt Marie's daughter, came out on the porch and motioned for my daddy to come inside. I knew from the look on her face that it would not be good news. On Friday afternoon, August 31, 1956, Lee Demps Lannom passed away at the age of 85. My city and country cousins were there. We just moped around not knowing what to say or do. We were quiet and didn't say much, probably the first time in our lives.

A few neighbors from the Vesta Church of Christ were there to be with us. Some of them lived in houses built by Daddy Demps, a fine carpenter in his younger days. There were many homes built by him in the Gladeville and Vesta communities. He was a servant in our little community. Mama Pearl was active earlier as a mid-wife helping to deliver a number of newborns in our community as well. I was fortunate, blessed really, to have Christian parents, two sets of wonderful caring grandparents, relatives, and friends, throughout my early years.

Aunt Maggie Lee (Auntie), daddy's middle sister, had notified the funeral home. They told her that a hearse would soon be on its way to take Daddy Demps to the funeral home in Lebanon. Later, I watched that long black limo pull up beside the front yard fence. Two men got out and started rolling a gurney toward the front door of the house. They soon exited the front door with help from Daddy, Gene, mama's brother, and Uncle Charlie, Auntie's husband. Mama Pearl, along with mama and daddy, Aunt Marie, Auntie, and Mary Katheryn followed the men to the hearse.

Watching them go around the curve and disappear down the old lane with my granddaddy was tough on me to say the least. Losses hurt, some deeply, but my memories of my beloved and talented Daddy Demps will remain forever. During my short life with him he taught me how to read a framing square at ten years of age, how to make airplanes out of dried corn stalks, how to actually draw out and cut a circle using a framing square, how to measure and mark off and saw needed rafters to build a house. I shall never forget when he was confined to sitting in his big chair during his later years, how he would scold me to take it easy on my little brother, saying, "Now Bob, he's little, be nice."

Several hours later, just after about everybody was gone, Daddy walked me under the old sugar maple tree in the yard. As we stood there in the shade, daddy said, "Bobby, I want to ask you to do something for me. Now, if you don't want to, that's okay, but if you don't mind, would you stay with mama now that daddy is gone?" Daddy, instead of barking out commands, would always say, "If you don't mind, hand me that wrench, or go get the cows and bring them to the barn." Or, "If you don't mind do this or that."

I had never seen my daddy cry before today. His blue eyes were glazed and filled with tears as I stood there in complete silence with a big hurt for him. I replied, "Daddy, I will be glad to stay with Mama Pearl. She will be in good hands." My daddy was not a hugger or one to tell you he loved you very often. He was laid back a lot like his daddy. I never saw him angry at anyone. He was always there for others in their time of need. There was no way under the sun that I could have refused to agree to an arrangement that would completely change my life. When I accepted, he put his arm around me and drew me against his chest with a "Thank You!" ..........Suddenly, I grew up that day.

I saw myself as I had never seen before. I fully understood the courage and confidence that my daddy had in his twelve-year-old son to take on the responsibility of helping to take care of his mother. Mama Pearl was seventeen years younger than Daddy Demps. Hopefully, she has a number of years left in her life to enjoy being around her children and grandchildren. It really took a lot of reliance from my daddy to believe that I was mature enough at such a young age to handle the challenge.

On the farm, challenges are nothing new. You are challenged almost daily to perform in situations with no one around but you. The successes you have with God backing you up are won by being able to confront losing situations. Life is full of losses. You get a lot of training in overcoming them. One major loser's ball has now provided me the occasion to deal positively by changing it into an "opportunity ball." I now will sink or swim by how I respond to my daddy's trust he has shown by fulfilling my duties expected of me. I never spent another night in my home with my parents, brother, and sister. I believed in my abilities and was determined to make my daddy and mama proud of me. I never thought negatively of surrendering to failure at all.

I prayed a lot more to God then than that former kid had done before the big change, that's for sure. I have to admit that I was somewhat disappointed that I would not be with my parents, Larry, and Lugene, sharing time together during those nights filled with moments of laughter and family fun. Being six years older than Larry and twelve years older than Lugene didn't help the situation either. I guess that I had convinced myself that this was just a night job. I would be with them many other times throughout the days to come, at church, ballgames, and holidays like Christmas and Thanksgiving. I just forgot about it and looked forward to the future but approached it in a much different way.

I also knew that I was not the only one who was in a similar situation. My cousin, Johnny (Butch), actually lived with and was raised by his grandparents, Uncle Tom Lee and Aunt Kate. We attended the Vesta church together and spent many hours hanging out in the neighborhood. Butch had the first bicycle in the community. I learned to ride a bicycle on his bike. I learned a lot more from him. We just accepted the circumstances and responsibilities given to us and moved on and did the best we could. This was indeed a big change for a twelve-year-old. There were a lot of questions out there as well as concerns. What about the future? How would me and Mama Pearl get along? Would it be more of the same or a bright future filled with excitement and include baseball?

After all, I still had another wish I hope will come true in a year. I will make the most of my assignment with patience and persistence. I do not want to let my daddy or Mama Pearl down. School is about to open. I'm moving to a new room and a new teacher as a sixth grader at the Glade. I feel optimistic and ready to face many new challenges that I'm sure will try me. I just hope that I am prepared to deal with them.

*My little 2-year old brother, Larry, and me at 8, sitting on daddy's new 1952 Chevy truck after our ride home from the dealership.*

# CHAPTER 2

You may have heard someone say that "It takes a village to raise a child". There is a lot of truth to that statement. Mama and Daddy were blessed to have some look-outs in the neighborhood to keep up with their enthusiastic youngsters on the move. Our family always attended church every Sunday morning as well as on Sundays and Wednesday nights. Mama Pearl bought one of the first television sets in the community, but I never got to watch Walt Disney because it came on at 6 pm on Sunday nights. I saw great examples of my mama and daddy as well as Mama Pearl to help right my ship when it started to venture off course.

Mama's parents, James (Boss) Comer and Annie Mai Comer, my other grandparents, attended the church at Corinth down the road as members there. They were super encouragers to me as well. Daddy Boss was talented in woodworking. He even had his own shop beside his beautiful home located at the head of Spring Creek in Rutherford County just across the Wilson County line. I remember the smell of all the cedar shavings he had that covered his shop floor. He was a tinkerer and built a lot of whirligigs or yard art. He taught me the value of making templates that could be helpful in making multiple copies of the same work. I was fortunate to have had two mentors to teach me woodworking skills that would come in handy one day.

I didn't take the opportunity to go too far off course for fear of hurting or embarrassing my support group. That was good. It didn't prevent me from still stretching the limits sometimes with some mild indiscretions committed as acts of just being a little mischievous.

There were several special folks at Vesta that meant so much to me. Mama Pearl's niece, Carrie Harris, taught me in her Bible school class along with her two daughters, Carol, Kay, brother Kenneth, and the other kids about the Lord. Our curriculum materials consisted of one 3x5 index card with the lesson on one side and scriptures on the back. But, she had a pretty good reference book, the Bible, to fortify her teachings from the master teacher. She, along with others like her: Kathryn McCrary, Fritzi Cox, Pauline Sanders, Alice Jones, and Hallie Tuggle, all made a positive impact on my life. Earl Lannom, Unk, as he was called, led singing at Vesta and taught all the boys in Sunday school. With a lot of practice with my mother at the house, I stood beside Earl one Sunday morning at the age of 10 and lead my first song, "Walking In Sunlight". Others who attended there were special to our family as well.

I don't know the reason why he made this statement, but Kay's uncle, Tom Allen Sanders, once said that Kay Harris and Bobby Lannom were the two meanest kids in Vesta. I think that what he really was saying was that we may have earned that crown by being two of the most mischievous kids in Vesta. That, I can agree with. Kay and I still laugh about that distinctive honor we received back then. One of Kay's sons later played football for Tennessee. She and I have made many trips to Knoxville together to watch Big Orange football and baseball games. Both of us were highly engaged in whatever activity was going on at Vesta and the Glade. If we found that things were getting a little boring, both of us were sure to increase its entertainment value to others.

There were two churches in Vesta across from each other, our church and the Methodist church. The only commercial enterprise in the Vesta community was the general store run first by Mr. Will Cox, and later, Mr. Walter Murphy. Unfortunately, Mr. Maxie Trisdale owned a big hay barn next to our church. The church parking lot had an abundance of nice rocks that the boys, after church, used to see how many times we could hit the metal roof on Mr. Trisdale's barn.

If you know the least thing about farming, you learn two rules about barns: no matches inside and rule number two, don't throw rocks on a tin barn roof! That ended when my daddy found out about the rock throwing contest and put an end to that.

The main attraction at Vesta was the world famous, "Boomshaws", which is a Cherokee name that means "deep waters". There are three of them within just a few hundred yards of each other. They are enormous sink holes of at least an acre wide at the top and one hundred feet or more in depth. Two of them flood regularly during heavy rains. The other one, the biggest, has a standing pool of water the year round. The word was that it has no bottom. As a kid, my friends at Vesta and I were determined to find the bottom. Each of us collected baler twine from our barns, met at the Boomshaw, tied about 50 or more twine strings together with a rock tied to one end and dropped it over the edge in the swirling water. That hole of water gobbled up our string and must have carried that rock to China. We gave up. That particular hole was on Kay's Uncle Tom Allen's farm, who later sold it to the Gladeville Utility District for their water supply to its customers.

It didn't take long to tour Vesta. If you blinked while driving through it, you would miss it. I must confess that during the summer Sunday morning sermons, it did cross my mind who was pitching for the Glade that afternoon, and if we had a chance to win the baseball game.

The larger of my two villages was the Glade. The Glade has a lot to be proud of. Two movies have had scenes filmed there. Burt Kennedy directed a film there in 1979 titled, Concrete Cowboys, starring Jerry Reed and Tom Selleck. Mama and Daddy were on location the day that Dobson's Feed Mill was torn down in the opening scenes of the movie. Back then, Tom was known as the "Marlboro Man" doing cigarette commercials. Jerry Reed was famous as a Grand Ole Opry country music star. Mama got to talk to Tom Selleck during that shoot. Lugene, my sister, even had her picture made with him. The old feed mill owned and operated by Ab Dobson and his son Bill, had been vacant for a period of time and was scheduled to eventually be torn down. The movie company wanted to tear it down as part of their movie. It was located directly across from the now standing two-story Masonic Lodge which backed up to the Gladeville baseball field.

There are only two roads that run through the "downtown Glade square". There has never been and still not a traffic light at the intersection, except for a yellow blinking caution light that once hung at the crossing for a short period of time until some of the local snipers in the Glade shot out the glass which was never replaced. The last time I saw it hanging there, it had a bird nest in it and a coon dog asleep directly under it. Laid back is the word! Fortunately, today there are 4-way stop signs at the intersection.

The square has many memories of home owned businesses that were there during my school days. On the north side, the "commercial" side of the square was Mr. Henry Drennon and Ms. Effie's general store. This was a store where you could buy a dollars-worth of regular gas and drive for a week, especially at .19 cents a gallon. Mr. Henry's store was where the school buses met mornings and afternoons to load and unload students to other destinations. You could buy a moon pie and RC cola for ten cents, a pack of Bull Durham tobacco for a nickel, or upgrade to Country Gentleman for a dime. I admit and confess that I learned to roll a cigarette.

Larry and I caught Uncle Edgar's school bus in front of our house to Mr. Henry's store and waited for the high school kids to get off. We ended our route at the Gladeville Elementary School. When we got older, we would get off and ride Mr. Howard Lane's bus to the high school and back to the Glade in the afternoon.

There was Aubrey Towne's feed store, the post office, the bank at one time, and Mr. Tommy Knowles's Auto Repair Shop. Mr. Tommy also drove a school bus, and was an excellent mechanic. He kept our old trucks, cars, and tractors rolling beyond our expectations. He kept the Glade rolling, period! Mr. Ethel Murphy and Mrs. Violet owned the other general store behind Mr. Tommy's garage. Their son, Herb Murphy became a big part of my baseball life.

On the south side of the square stood the Baptist Church.

Next to it was the home of Mr. Otto Beasley, a beautiful home, the only residence right on the square. Further west was Gladeville Elementary. It was rebuilt in 1938, after the original wooden structure burned to the ground. The new school had four rooms surrounding an auditorium that had a stage for special events like chorus productions, or piano recitals. The Grand Ole Opry bluegrass group, The Foggy Mountain Boys, starring Lester Flatt and Earl Scruggs, once performed there. The auditorium was also the site of professional wrestling on several occasions and movies shown on a big screen like "Only The Shadow Knows", and others. The cafeteria was located in the basement.

Mrs. Camellia Sanders taught the first, second, and third grades in one room. My cousin, Mrs. Mattie Bilbro, taught the fourth and fifth in the second room. The third room contained the sixth, seventh, and eighth graders. They were taught by the current teacher/principal. The fourth room was the music room where Mrs. Leona Sloan taught piano lessons to the Glade musical hopefuls once a week. I took piano lessons at the insistence of my mother, who played the guitar and wanted me to become a piano player. Honestly, my real motive was to get out of class. I played one piece at my first and only piano recital on the big stage in the auditorium. I can only tell you now, where middle C is located! I wasn't very good.

There were a couple of houses on the strip across from the school back then. The biggest and most attractive was the home of Ms. Margaret Castleman.

Mr. Tommy Knowles would play a big role in the baseball lives of his son, Tommy Jr., and me as well. Tommy and I were the same age and loved to play baseball. We always tried to play on the same team, when possible, in recess at the Glade. Other boys in my class included, William Dean, Morris, Jimmy, Doyle, Billy, and Eddie. The girls were Emmeline, Betty, Mamie, and Shirlene. Any time someone asked about my class at the Glade that went on to high school together, I told them that there were 7 boys and 4 girls and that we all played football.

It is said that repetition is the best teacher. I agree wholeheartedly.

## The Loser's Ball

I should have been a genius! Since there were three grades in two classrooms and two in the other, that meant that we had to sit and endure the teaching of each grade level two to three times. When we were promoted, we just slid over two rows. All of my teachers at the Glade were good teachers. That plus repetition enabled all the Glade kids to do well later in high school.

The boys, however, lived for recess. We call it Physical Education (PE) now. It was mostly baseball, some football, and a little basketball. There was no gymnasium at the Glade. There were two basketball goals, seldom with nets on them, on a dirt playing surface spaced about 90 feet apart. When it rained one end would always remain wetter than the other, so the boys would take over the dryer goal while the girls complained of being refused to be picked to play on the sides we had chosen. Finally, the principal literally drew a line in the dirt, and divided the area into a boy's end and a girl's end. Any girl or boy caught on the wrong end would have to stay in during recess, the ultimate capital punishment! That was probably the deciding factor to basically eliminate basketball from the boy's agenda.

It had been demonstrated throughout the years that the Glade would turn out to support any sporting event. It was often standing room only at baseball games. There were always huge crowds lining the first base line and standing on the edge of the road down the third base line to watch the men play baseball on Sunday afternoons during the summer in the Cumberland Valley League. Teams from Lebanon, Hartsville, Carthage, LaGuardo, Willette, Tuckers Cross Roads, New Middleton, Sykes, and the Glade made up the league. The Glade had a long history of baseball going back to the 30s. Some of those teams consisted of: John Guethlein, Walter Swain, Henry Drennon, Duncan Ragsdale, Earnest Partlow, Van Dobson, Joe Partlow, John Sanders, Gene Foster, Buck Spickard, Milton Swain, Will Swain, H. Cathy, Owen Drennon, Junior Cook, and Charles Ragsdale. These men played before my time but I came to know many of them growing up. Van Dobson would become a special person to me later.

There was always something going on in the Glade. Attendance was good at all school events. Somebody was once overheard to say that if two dogs got into a fight in the middle of the Glade, in fifteen minutes there would be 50 people choosing sides, cheering them on, and somebody selling hot dogs and drinks from a concession stand. I loved the Glade.

Emotions were often exhibited in close baseball games. Some old timer told me when I was growing up that the Glade always left the field undefeated; if they lost the ballgame, they were sure to win the fight! Those were the days. Baseball during those early years just sparked my interest and desire to push myself in spite of having no team to play with. It was more than just a game. Every player took it seriously. My life as a player, however, was on "hold."

Without much hope of getting to play baseball anywhere, I just guess that I would have to be patient that a birthday wish would come true, or wait until I could play with the men when I turn sixteen. Until then, I will stay on my own work schedule of chopping wood, running after stray cows, digging post holes, hauling hay, cleaning out fence rows and barns, cutting tobacco, milking cows, and hitting rocks over the farm pond with broken axe handles and tobacco sticks. Hopefully it will pay off in the near future. Only time will tell! Just keep on hittin' rocks.

*The "square" at the Glade. It hasn't changed much over the years. Mr. Tommy's Gladeville Motors shop is still in operation by his son, Tommy, my classmate and teammate.*

# Chapter 3

It was a little different that fall when school opened. I had a new bus rider to join me on Uncle Edgar's little cracker box bus. Larry entered the first grade and was a little nervous about starting the adventures of adjusting to life at school. Although Mama had told me to watch out after him his first year there, it was just the normal thing an older brother was expected and willing to do. It didn't change my schedule at home. I still had to be at the barn at 4:30 am to meet Daddy to do the milking. The normal morning routine was the same; finish milking around six, get cleaned up, eat breakfast, and catch the bus at 6:45. Larry and I had about a 200-yard walk down the driveway to the road to be picked up.

Getting away with some of the shenanigans I had previously pulled in school, if repeated, would now be subjected to an extra set of eyes, little brother! Extra caution had to be exercised to escape detection if I intended to stay in good graces at home. I was getting acclimated to my new night address at Mama Pearl's house. She had me all fixed up with a feather bed and quilts she had made. Not only was she a great cook, but was an expert in making beautiful quilts. During my six-year stay at her house, I would accumulate seven quilts.

The adjustment period was very short. It was going to be a good situation for both of us. To arrive at her house to spend the night and have two fried baloney sandwiches waiting wasn't bad at all. She did everything to make it an easy transition. Spoiling may have been a more appropriate description of my stay there.

Things were not quite the same at school, however. I had moved into the "big room." Some of the eighth graders were 15 years old. Some had failed the previous year and had settled into a rebellious attitude in school. Our new teacher was having a difficult time with the older boys who were basically bullying their way and causing problems. It was a tough year. This was not the time for me to cause any more pain for our teacher/principal. The fact was that even though I was now in the big room, I was just a measly sixth grader, under the control of the seventh and eighth grade rulers.

Members of my class had to really avoid giving the big boys a reason to retaliate and show their muscle. I admit that on a few occasions, some of us who had endured about enough, were ready to take them on. Cautious thinking was to prevail in the long run. The better part of valor was to stay cool and hide out! I spent much of my time checking on Larry at recess and making sure that he was not being subjected to any of the issues I saw going on.

All of my classmates were going through the same adjustments, entering an environment that we were not accustomed to seeing. It was time for Bob to lay low, toe the mark, and not to be a part of the problem. Our class stuck together during recess, still playing our baseball games. We made it through the year with just a few bloody noses and torn shirts, but no serious major confrontations. Some of the older boys quit school after Christmas that made the rest of the year much more fun. I was glad that our sixth-grade guys and girls hung in there and supported each other during that year. There were many fun times, so it wasn't a complete loss of a school year.

By the end of the year, I had my assignments at Mama Pearl's home down pat. Not a week went by during the winter that her two wood stoves starved for firewood to keep us warm. Every Saturday during the cold weather, the schedule was to make sure the two stoves in the house had a big pile of firewood near them. In addition, the back porch was stocked with plenty of wood in case it snowed or rained. Each week, two 10-gallon milk cans were filled to the brim with fresh spring water to use for drinking and cooking. I got adjusted to the outside shower and bath facility utilizing the big metal tank that collected rain water from the tin roof of the house. I would bathe at night so I could be ready for school the next morning. Most outside baths during the winter months didn't take very long.

Life was rolling along pretty well. Daddy and I spent a lot of time in the mornings and evenings talking back and forth during the milking process. I guess you could have called it "bonding time". We talked a lot about things that needed to be done on the two farms we were operating. In just about every conversation the topic of baseball came up. It was obvious that he had been paying attention to all of the time that I was spending on my drills to get better. I knew that he felt powerless to be able to make things possible for me to get to play any organized baseball in Lebanon. He mentioned it a couple of times to me to don't give up but stay with it, and maybe things will change.

I still missed being with the family at nights. I missed the nights when I was seven or eight years old when Mama would host her band called the "Pipeliners". She had learned on her own how to play the guitar by just copying the chords. When I was younger, I would listen to them playing with Mama singing many of the country hits like Hank Williams, "Your Cheating Heart" and "Hey Good Looking". Other songs I loved to hear were hits by Loretta Lynn and Patsy Cline, plus two of my favorites by Kitty Wells, "It Wasn't God Who Made Honkie Tonk Angels", and "Silver Haired Daddy of Mine". Mama had a beautiful singing voice. She sounded just like Kitty Wells when she sang her songs. Daddy always asked for her to play his favorite tune on her guitar, "Wildwood Flower".

I remember that she even loaned her guitar to some of the men in the neighborhood who livened up their Saturday nights refreshing themselves with their own special liquid indulgences. She told them that if they put one scratch on her guitar, that they would have to buy her a new one and find another place to borrow one. They always returned it in pristine condition. I had to hand it to her for doing that. That took a lot of trust. I tried to make every moment count when I was with her, Larry, and Lugene. I'm looking forward though, for this year coming to a close. Maybe, just maybe this will be the year that my second birthday wish comes true.

Mama Pearl had already begun to plan out the family garden in February, before school ended. We always had the biggest garden in Vesta. It was more than an acre in size. She showed me one night what would be in our garden for the coming growing season. She had planned for us to plant this year: ten rows of potatoes over 200 feet long, six 200 feet rows of green beans stuck with cedar or locust bean sticks, another six rows of lima beans of equal length, eight lengthy rows of English (bullet) peas, plus rows and rows of cucumbers, cabbage, lettuce, onions, tomatoes, okra, beets, peppers, squash, and the rest in rows of sweet corn, sweet potatoes, and even room to plant cut flowers of zinnias and gladiolas. Whew!

Guess who gets to plant the garden! I asked her, "Mama Pearl, why do we need to plant this much stuff when there is only seven of us in the family?"

"Well honey," she answered, "There are so many people living around us that don't have good help like we do, and don't really know how to raise a garden like we do, and mostly, it's just the Christian thing to do to help them out." She went on to specifically name some of our relatives like Aunt Kate, Aunt Harriett, Uncle Will, several members who attended church at Vesta, and other neighbors who were older, and were not capable of doing the work. I had no response! Who can argue or disagree with an answer like that? I learned that night the meaning of what Jesus said in the Bible, quoted by Paul in Acts 20:35, "It is more blessed to give than to receive". Those were not just words for Mama Pearl, but she practiced them.

I was just glad that my daddy was the main gardener. Mama helped when she could, and Larry was learning to drop seeds and carry bean sticks. Everybody would come together on planting day.

On the back of our farm on Lone Oak Road, was located a nice little two-bedroom house that came with the sale when daddy bought the extra land from family members, expanding the size of our farm. He soon rented it to William Hardy and his new wife. Daddy didn't charge them any rent. William agreed with daddy on a deal. William would work one Saturday a month for us to pay for the rental of the house. It was in great shape. It even had a beautifully hewn stone chimney for a fireplace or wood stove. I remember William living there for a number of years. It may have been unfortunate for him, but daddy would turn him over to Mama Pearl on garden planting days. I loved that arrangement.

I always told my friends that William helped raise me by saving my life on garden planting day. He and daddy together taught me how to plow the garden with our mules, Dick and Kate. I will confess that when plowing crops with our mules, like the garden, corn, and my tobacco crop later, you learn a lot of new words! His father, Mr. Cody Hardy, drove a school bus and was always a big part of our hog killing in the fall. The Hardy family was black. All of the Hardy boys and girls had good jobs and were highly respected in our community. Other black families lived on farms that joined our farm. The Words and Spickards lived north of us. The Lannom kids grew up with Mr. and Mrs. Joe Will Spickard, Mr. Johnny Word, Robert Spickard, and their families. Robert Spickard became a minister and preached my daddy's funeral years later. He and his wife Cassie now run a successful construction business in the Glade just behind Mr. Tommy Knowles's auto shop, now run by his son, my baseball buddy, Tommy, Jr. They are among my best friends still today.

As a twelve-year old, I could not understand why these great friends and neighbors could possibly be subjected to any harsh treatment by anyone. They were not treated that way in our community. That's for sure. We cared for and depended on each other. Race was never an issue.

I tried to talk him out of it, but respected William's decision not to eat lunch with us at the table. Even with insistence from Mama and Mama Pearl for him to eat with us, he always waited till we ate. I finally made the decision that at lunch on the Saturdays William ate with us, I waited and ate with him. When I was a small child, that man carried me for miles on his shoulders. A big brother could not have treated me any better. It was not fair for him or any member of his family to have to do what society at the time forced them to do. Period! Those were the fifties and sixties, however, but our little community respected each person as a creation of God and to treat each other like we would like to be treated. I remember when we celebrated daddy's 80th birthday at the house. Mr. Joe Will Spickard, our neighbor, who was driven over by his daughters, showed up and sat in a wheelchair in our den to be a part of daddy's big day.

How fortunate I was to experience the genuine love and care that all of us should show each other every day. As the Star Wars character Yoda would say, "Blessed, I was". I will add that William and the Hardys suffered no shortages of pork or vegetables for years. Our family saw to that. They were just part of our family!

The weather started to warm up. Spring was on its way. Some of the garden like peas, potatoes, and cabbage were already planted. I cannot remember how daddy or Mr. Tommy Knowles found out the news about the rules of eligibility for Tommy and me to play Babe Ruth baseball in Lebanon. The rules unfortunately, remained the same for the 1957 spring and summer season. No baseball in Lebanon for us again.

When daddy found out and told me at the barn that afternoon, I stopped milking, got up and carried my half-filled bucket of milk out the barn door and sat it on the ground. It all just caved in on me. I broke down and started crying. Daddy saw me go outside, and in a moment, he had his hand on my shoulder. "It's not fair! It's just not fair, daddy! Why? Why? Why won't they let us play? It's just not right!" Daddy said about all he could say at the moment. I could tell it hurt him as well. He just told me, "Don't you quit anything you're doing. One day you'll get to play, and when you do, just show 'em all who is the best, okay?" After a moment of half way recovering from the news that now, both of my wishes didn't come true, I went back in the barn and sat down on my milk stool under Ashes, our milk cow, and started back to milking.

All of that evening in the barn was just a bad dream, a big Loser's Ball, one that I did not see coming and no way to defend it, only to start doing more to make sure when the time comes, if it ever does, I will be the best I can be. Mama already knew and had us a special supper that evening before I went to stay at Mama Pearls. When I got to Mama Pearl's house, already knowing the news, she hugged me and said, "Them folks in Lebanon don't know what they're missing. You keep practicing and show 'em all. Why one day I just believe you'll play in a world series."

As I lay in bed that night, with my window open and the night sounds of crickets filling the dark emptiness, I thought about what she had said. I know she was just trying to make me feel better, but reality set in. I won't even get to play Babe Ruth ball, much less in a world series. I said a prayer to God. My prayer resulted in me remembering a sermon, or part of it, that our Vesta preacher, Brother Darrell Dobson gave one Sunday a few months back. Yes, sometimes, I actually listened to what our preacher said. God has a way of working in mysterious ways.

That sermon just didn't get recalled by accident. Brother Dobson talked about ways God answers prayers. It caught my attention because at the time I was heavily engaged in praying to God about my baseball dilemma. He stated in his lesson, the part that really caught my attention. He said that God answers prayers in three ways: He answers "Yes!" by granting the requests we make to Him. Secondly, He answers "No!" and does not grant the request. The third way He answers prayers is "Not now!"

I lay there hoping that my prayers may be on hold with God. Maybe, "not now" was the answer. That was pretty deep thinking for a kid about to turn 13. God always sees further ahead than we do. Maybe I'm not ready. Maybe something better will come along. I tossed and turned trying to out-guess God with no success and finally drifted off to sleep.

I guess Daddy and Mama called in all of the troops to make my summer without baseball a little more bearable. Once my city cousins, Ann, Earl, and Raymond heard about my ineligibility, especially Auntie and Uncle Charlie, a plan of action was developed. Uncle Charlie, who was one of my very best supporters and fans, asked me to go to Panama City, Florida, with the Bramwell family on vacation. Charlie, Jr., eight years older than me, was in college at UT, living in Knoxville working for the Tennessee athletic department and would not make the trip as the flat tire changer anymore for family vacations. Since I had no baseball games, there was no reason for me to refuse to go. Daddy said he would take care of the milking. I agreed and was excited to go on my first ever vacation, with Uncle Charlie amusingly referring to me as his new designated tire changer.

The Bramwells gave me my 13$^{th}$ birthday party when we were in Panama City on the beach. I had become a teenager in Florida. Seeing the ocean for the first time will remain as one of my best therapies for getting over the loser's ball I received earlier. My cousin, Ann, invited me to attend her 13$^{th}$ birthday party about five weeks later in Nashville where they lived. It was like I had been adopted by them. Auntie was a special lady. She and my mother were like sisters rather than in-laws. Later, Uncle Charlie would play a significant role in my future baseball career.

The huge garden again, provided so much for our family and others in the community. Mama Pearl and I made many illegal trips around Vesta and the Glade delivering garden produce to needy neighbors. The summer passed quickly. Things were about to change around the Lannom household in the next few weeks before school started back. Daddy and Mama had decided to expand the size of our house by adding on a bedroom for Larry. They dug a well, which meant that a bathroom was going to be added, too. We had gone 13 years without one, so it was definitely a tad overdue! In addition, Mama was going to get a utility room added on to make a spot for a new washer and dryer. It also included space for a chest freezer for keeping vegetables and other frozen foods. I was always thankful for Lugene's arrival, which in my opinion, was the catalyst for the needed renovation. She would now claim as her own the old bedroom where Larry and I had stayed.

Mr. Mack Foutch, a carpenter and neighbor who lived near the Vesta church, was hired to head up the construction. Daddy, along with Mr. Foutch, William, me, with Larry handling the scrap wood burning detail, completed the addition in style. Daddy Demps would have been proud. Only until our pump house was completely finished, did I realize that the missing component of my baseball training was now available. The pump house was eight feet square and seven feet high with cement block walls mortared together in a nice flat surface. Before the mortar was dry, I was already throwing hard rubber balls at it working not only on my throwing accuracy and arm strength, but improving my reflexes in fielding the bouncing balls in my new glove. It wasn't long before I had painted black spots on the wall as targets to create line drives, fly balls, and grounders.

The back yard was large enough for all of my creative drills. Inside the pump house, other than the electrical controls, pump, and water storage tank, there was always a bucket with a half dozen or more rubber balls and at least one old baseball with no cover on it. Mama said that she watched me outside her kitchen sink window for hours throwing balls at that pump house wall. Even Larry, at seven years of age, took advantage of that wall. I could see that at his young age he could zip those balls pretty well. Another great bonus regarding the new addition was that I would not have to take another bath using that old tank at Mama Pearl's house in that cattle watering trough in the dark. I love progress!

*"You can't put a limit on anything. The more you dream, the farther you get."*
Michael Phelps.

# Chapter 4

The rest of the summer I attended many of the men's Gladeville baseball team's home games. I saw no need to be concerned anymore about counting on the Lebanon Lions Club changing its rules to make it possible for Tommy and me to get to play Babe Ruth ball anymore. I would turn 16 in three years and maybe play American Legion ball. Hopefully, Tommy and I will get to play together for the Glade on Sundays.

Daddy would drive his 1952 Chevy farm truck taking me to watch the games. I already knew how to change gears, learning to drive it on the farm. I was too young to get a driver's license, but still drove Mama Pearl down the road to deliver gifts of sausage and vegetables to the neighbors. She said if we got stopped by the law, just slide over and she would get behind the wheel. She had it figured out, except she had no driver's license and had never learned how to drive. How is that for confidence?

The Glade roster now consisted of players; Fred Guethlein, Robert Milton Lane, Herbert Powell Murphy, Herbert Sanders and his brother, Willie Rhea, Joel Evans, Sonny Ragsdale, Bill Dobson, Brud Spickard, and others. I remember seeing Bill Dobson, co-owner of Dobson's feed mill, playing shortstop with no shirt on and in overalls and baseball spikes. He was a great ball player. He didn't like wearing that hot wool jersey in the summer heat. Herb Murphy was an outstanding catcher who was another mentor to watch.

The team was managed by Van Dobson, a part of the Dobson family, and a former Glade ball player in the 30s. The games were vigorously contested at the Glade, especially when a ball that was hit struck the electrical wires that stretched from behind first base to the foul pole in left field. It was a ground rule that if the ball struck the wires, it was in play. As far as I know there was not another field anywhere that had electrical wires running over second base. I recall a few shots that were headed for the trees in right field for home runs, but were stopped dead by those wires and the ball dropping into the glove of the second baseman for outs. The Glade was definitely different. I think that is what made it a special place.

All of the boys would hang out around the Glade dugout and hoped to be the recipient of a broken bat or a foul ball. That is where we got our supply of bats for our recess games at school. I got pretty good at taking those broken bats, gluing them back together, driving short nails in the handles, and taping them up with black tape. They were all we needed as kids.

The Glade team of course, like every other team around, operated on a low budget. The baseballs were watched with great care, particularly foul balls. There was no such thing as souvenir balls. The kids would chase foul balls down and return them to the concession stand for a free snow cone, and sign up for a broken bat. Frankly, to me a baseball was a whole lot more valuable than a cup filled with colored ice. I guess that attitude led me to one of my tempting youthful indiscretions at a Glade ball game one Sunday afternoon.

All of us boys were stationed at our usual dugout location waiting for foul balls. A batter fouled off a ball that went sailing over our heads across the road and bounced off the wall of Mr. Book Pickett's store. Naturally, in a flash, we all took off after the ball. Being the fastest, I beat everybody to the building and dove under the front porch head first and grabbed that clean white baseball and crawled out. All the guys just shrugged their shoulders, turned away, and headed back to await the next opportunity. I decided right then that a snow cone was not on my menu. I stuck that ball in my shirt and

## The Loser's Ball

calmly walked to our old Chevy, opened the door and stuck the ball in the glove compartment. I walked back to where the action began earlier and took my place until the game ended.

I don't remember if we won or lost. I just kept thinking about that prize in the truck to take home. Following the game, Daddy soon joined me at the truck and we headed home. Once we got out of the Glade on the road, I opened the door of the glove compartment and took out my prize to play with it in my hands. Daddy immediately looked over and asked me where I got that ball. I told him that it was a foul ball and that I got and put it in the truck.

"Well, I guess you know," he said. "That ball is not yours and you shouldn't have done that, that's stealing." Just as he had finished talking, he slammed on the brakes, turned that blue '52 Chevy truck around in Bill Allen Martin's driveway, and headed back to the Glade. "When we get there," he said, "I want you to take that ball and go over to Van, if he is still there, and give it to him. You understand?" My answer was a quick, "Yes sir."

Van was still there, packing up the bats and catcher equipment near the dugout. Daddy sat in the truck with his arm and elbow stuck out his window. I made, what seemed to be a mile long journey over to return that ball to Van. He looked up and said, "Hey Bobby, what you got there?" I saw him glace over at Daddy in the truck watching the transaction. I felt immediately that Van probably picked up on what was happening. I simply told him that I was returning a foul ball. I was braced to get a lecture on honesty from Van. All that he said when I handed him the ball was, "Thank you, Bobby. I appreciate you getting it for me." As he stuck it in his ball bag, I walked away, the victim of a real "Loser's Ball."

All my daddy said on the way home was, "You did the right thing." We never mentioned it again. I don't think that he even told Mama, for I never heard another word from anybody about that incident. Daddy knew that returning that ball was punishment enough, especially with all of the negatives about not getting to play baseball anywhere.

The news was out about our new teacher/principal at school. It was a man, my first and only male teacher that I had at the Glade. His name was Mr. Charles Davis, a Methodist preacher, who we all thought was sent there to restore law and order after such a horrible sixth grade year. Mr. Davis was a good teacher. I liked him because he liked to play little pranks on us and made school much more fun than last year. It didn't take him long to eliminate any rebellious attitudes. He was a large man and he carried a big stick.

Now that we were in the seventh grade, in the middle of the social status in the big room, I felt a little more at ease. I even felt some degree of comfort returning to committing a few extra-curricular pranks. Larry had done well in Mrs. Sanders's room, getting promoted to the second grade and sliding over his two rows. He now had some buds of his own, so it was a relief for me to not have to spend as much time checking on him.

As seventh and eighth graders, we were given some important jobs during the school day and even before school. Since I arrived on the early bus every morning, a couple of early arrivers and I were given the job in the winter of building a fire in the pot-bellied stove in our classroom. We would get the fire started and take the coal buckets out to the coal pile beside our room, fill them up with coal, and set them inside for use during the day as needed.

One warm afternoon for some reason I can't explain, I thought that if the hand bell Mr. Davis rang to start and end recess should happen to disappear, maybe our ballgames would last a little longer. So, before I left school that evening to catch the bus home, I sneaked that bell off of his desk and stuck it in the old stove that had not been in use that warm day and caught the bus. That particular night the temperature dropped significantly. When I got to school early the next morning to retrieve the bell from the bowels of that stove, one of my other early arrival friends had already started the fire. The stove was hot and glowing by the time I arrived. We have cremated the bell! He didn't know it was burned up. Mr. Davis could not figure out what had happened to it. Bobby sure wasn't going to confess.

## The Loser's Ball

For years that bell's disappearance was a mystery. When I left the Glade and got to high school, I figured that the statute of limitations had expired, so I confessed to my friends. One day several years later, I had some business at the new Wilson Bank at the Glade. I introduced myself to one of the tellers, right after concluding my business. I asked her since she was a local resident, if she had ever heard the story of the school bell disappearing and getting burned up at Gladeville Elementary school years ago. I was shocked when she said, "I do, but I can't remember who it was that did it." I just leaned over her counter and whispered, "Would you like his autograph?"

I guess by escaping detection of my bell incident I gained a little more confidence to proceed with another diversion from the curricular studies. You know, I really just never sat down and planned out these things. It seems that they just materialized at the moment. I just seized the opportunity.

Mrs. Castleman, who lived just across the road from the school had a flock of beautiful peacocks. They regularly traveled around the Glade, often coming on the campus in search of bugs and other foods. One morning during a recess break I happened to be behind the school building and saw that six of those pretty birds had made their way in front of me next to the school making their feeding run. There was a storage building in the middle of the u-shaped school building that afforded a great opportunity to push the birds up a few steps into the open door of Mrs. Sloan's music room. Small kids were hanging around and actually blocked them from escaping on the other side of me. They followed each other right up the steps with me bringing up the rear. Once they were inside, I shut the door and strolled away into the land of innocence.

In about five minutes, the makeshift bell Mr. Davis had made sounded off to end recess. He made his alarm by getting an empty-gallon green beans can from the cafeteria and put a handful of good batting rocks in the bottom. He would hold it high in the air and shake it loud and long. We hustled to class without any more thought about the peacocks in the music room. Our classroom was next door to the captured birds. About 20 minutes into the class period, we heard the sound of these peacocks screaming like distress on steroids. It sounded just like a stadium of high-pitched female voices screaming, "Help…! Help….!" over and over. Mr. Davis jumped out of his chair and rushed out the door to either rescue or recover the victims he had heard next door. We soon heard them in flight before we saw them. All six of them were flying out of an open music room window in a straight-line formation to Mrs. Castleman's house, headed for freedom. Mr. Davis returned shortly and politely asked us, "Does anybody in here know how those peacocks got into Mrs. Sloan's room?" Silence. "Okay," he said, "Guess we'll just have to find out later how they got there."

When I got to school the next morning, Mr. Davis was already there. He kindly asked me to walk over to the music room with him. Apparently, I was the only one identified. It didn't take a rocket scientist to figure out that he had the goods on me. He asked me, "Alright, Bobby, why did you put those peacocks in Mrs. Sloan's room?" Before I took time to think up an excuse that would not amount to much anyway, I fell on the sword and confessed my crime, and simply said, "It just seemed like the thing to do at the time." He told me that since I "fessed up", he would go easy on me. His definition of "easy" wasn't close to mine. He gave me six good licks with his stick, one for each peacock!

I could fill this book with more stories of me and my classmates on stunts we pulled those last two years at the Glade. No property was destroyed. Nobody suffered any pain or anguish. We just had fun. When we get together and talk about our time at the Glade, we still laugh. I guess it really reminded me that maybe Kay's Uncle Tom Allen may have been right after all.

Next year I slide over to the wall! Sadly, Mr. Davis told us that he would not return as our teacher next fall. I don't know if bell burnings, peacocks, Moonie's cave, privy flips, or rock throwing, had anything to do with his decision or not. I just knew that we would have a third different teacher in three years. I have to admit, it was kind of suspicious. Why was it that when I got to the big room, boom! Teachers started leaving the building. It's funny but my Mama and Daddy thought the same thing. I do admit that my arithmetic grades were higher than my conduct grades on my report card. But, I never failed to slide over two rows every year. One more to go and, I will be sitting against the wall next fall. Meanest kid in Vesta? No! Mischievous? Guilty as charged!

*The old Gladeville ball field is still there, the current home of a youth baseball team. The concession stand hasn't changed much, but higher fences and concrete dugouts are modern additions.*

*I spent three years, grades 6-8, in this classroom in the front of Gladeville Elementary School. The cafeteria was located in the basement. This picture could have been taken the day the school bell was burned. Note smoke coming from the old wood/coal stove chimney.*

# Chapter 5

In spite of all of my tendencies to stir the pot a little when it comes to having good fun, I managed to slide over two more rows. I would now be at the "wall". If I make a turn for the better, I may just have a chance to slip the bondage of elementary bliss and attend high school next year. There was still no word on our chances of playing baseball, so I decided to again leave it up to the Lord and keep on trucking. I continued my farming duties as well as collecting a few broken bats to turn into splinters hitting rocks. I had retired my axe handles except to use until I could get another broken bat from the Glade games. I became more active at church and even started leading singing some on Sunday and Wednesday nights. Our youth group there was small but you couldn't beat them. Most of them were kinfolks but the others should have been. We considered them to be that way. I was learning a lot in Bible school and heard some good lessons from the pulpit.

Mama Pearl always had her special seat in the amen corner, of course. She liked to be able to see who missed on Sundays and made it a point to find out the cause of their absence. With only forty or fifty members, nobody could escape her detection. I don't remember her ever threatening them if they didn't come or that she was going to cut off their free garden produce.

When we would have Gospel meetings at Vesta, Mama would always take care of visiting preachers, drawing their lessons on bed sheets, writing scriptures and drawing pictures to make the lessons more attractive. Vesta had no chalkboards or overhead projectors of course. She and Mama Pearl would usually have the gospel meeting preacher, his wife, and kids over for lunch on Sundays after church if the Glade was not playing ball at home, naturally! One Sunday afternoon it was time for Daddy and me to go milk the cows, always early on Sunday evenings in order to get to church on time. We let Mama take care of the preacher and his family.

I loaded up Nelly Belle, our truck, with all the milk buckets and cans and was getting in when Larry ran up screaming bloody murder. I had taken his whistle and had not returned it. Mama and the preacher came running out the back door thinking he had fallen down or that I had slugged him. When I saw the preacher standing there, I felt it necessary to quickly return Larry's whistle in hopes of getting him to stop squalling. When I threw it to him, I hit my elbow on the open truck door and hit the "funny bone" in my elbow. It knocked me completely out and I fell face down on our rock driveway and broke off my two front teeth. I came to with Daddy and the visiting preacher helping me to my feet. Larry took his whistle and disappeared somewhere.

Somebody called our dentist in Lebanon, Dr. Howard, who happened to be at home. He said for somebody to take me to his office and that he would meet us there. What a way to get out of milking! For months I wore silver capped crowns of my two front teeth. There was one consolation. I couldn't whistle with my tongue against my old teeth, but after I finally got my nice permanent caps, I had the loudest whistle around.

We had not heard a lot about our new teacher that was to be the teacher/principal at Gladeville Elementary. Finally, our class of about twelve students made it to the eighth grade in the "big room". We had seen what negative actions that previous students had demonstrated before us. We were an independent and tough group, tough in a positive way. We were very competitive and somewhat territorial in our protection of one another. There was a bond of friendship that seemed to evolve during our maturing process. We had spent seven years together and had weathered the storms. All of us were now more responsible at home helping our parents, farming, working at the store, assisting in the garage, and other duties.

We would be blessed when Mrs. Nell Vaughter showed up to step into a leadership role and corral all of our energies and talents our final year at the Glade. I couldn't have predicted what good things were about to happen that year. Mama Pearl told me when she found out about Ms. Nell, that she was a distant cousin of ours. In a way, I was hoping that she didn't find out that I was kin to her. She was not a pushover. She commanded respect and expected us to treat each other with respect and courtesy.

There were no more lines drawn in the dirt on the basketball court. She had a knack for determining what made each of us tick. Our weaknesses that year would be changed to strengths. She kept the class focused and on target, a great example for a student who one day would become an educator. Bob's life was changing. That lady made a big difference in my conduct as well. She demanded of me things I thought that I could not possibly achieve. She became what all of us in that room needed at that particular time in our lives. She understood us. When I tell others about Ms. Nell, I explain that she taught students, not just subjects. She helped me to focus more on the future than the now.

You would not think that as bold that I seemed to be in pulling pranks on folks that I would have not had a timid bone in my body. I had a weakness. It was a fear of standing alone and speaking before my class or other groups, even at church. I learned later in life that I was not alone with my fear. Psychological studies showed that in ranking fears, the majority of people fear public speaking more than death!

When Mr. Melvin Arnett, our Wilson County Assistant Extension agent and 4-H leader, made his monthly visit to the Glade seeking participants for the county 4-H public speaking contest, Ms. Nell, without my permission, enrolled me on the spot. I had no choice but to put together a speech as one of the representatives of the Glade in the contest. My six-minute speech on "Old Glory" did not win the contest. It instilled in me, however, something of more value, a measure of confidence that would enable me to establish and meet goals that I had previously considered unreachable. We were being groomed and prepared for high school, but didn't realize it.

Mama Pearl, who enjoyed having her television set, made sure that it was ready to watch just a few weeks after I started staying with her. Daddy and I put up the antennae on the roof of her house to get reception for our new black and white TV. Watching Gunsmoke, Hopalong Cassidy, Roy Rogers, Lash Larue, Tim Holt, Tom Mix, and Gene Autry westerns was a treat. When the show, Bonanza, aired in 1959, it became our favorite. The best of all was to be able to watch, starting in 1957, the NBC broadcasts of baseball's Game of the Week. Later, Dizzy Dean and Pee Wee Reese became more famous, broadcasting those games. The highlight, though, was to be able to watch the World Series.

Mama Pearl was a diehard National League fan. She loved the Dodgers and Cardinals. Her brother, Uncle Irve, was a pure Yankee fan. Flies on the wall, as well as everybody there during World Series time were entertained by the banter and rivalries between those two. I loved to watch the "Untouchables". It didn't come on until 8 and lasted an hour. Mama Pearl went to bed with the chickens around 7:30, so I had to turn the TV down and stuff a quilt in the crack at the bottom of the door where she couldn't hear it. Naturally our bed time schedules never matched up.

Watching and listening to the baseball games provided me a learning and educational experience that had been missing. My grandmother was right on target by no accident! I started developing heroes and patterned my swings after some of the greats I saw perform their craft before my eyes. I was all set when school ended in late May. I had baseball games to watch on TV. I had just finished the best year of my elementary school experience. We even had a graduation ceremony on the stage in the auditorium. What a difference one individual can make in kid's lives. I soaked it all up that year. There's just one thing missing........

To play or not to play baseball?

Larry got promoted to the third grade. Lugene was three years

## The Loser's Ball

old and I am still batting rocks, wearing out the pump house wall, cutting wood, milking, hauling hay, working a tobacco crop, putting up new fences, plowing and disking, and still gardening big time. I just turned baseball playing over to the Lord. That is the only option that we have sometimes with problems and hurdles that come our way. You just pocket your Loser's Balls and move on. Stay focused, but keep working and be prepared when your time comes. That was the way I was handling my young life.

Daddy was my greatest inspiration. He was my trainer, my strength coach, my hitting coach, my fielding coach, my fungo hitter, and player psychologist, all rolled into one. Oh, Mama and Mama Pearl were my nutritionists. That was as high tech and up to date as I could have made it. Daddy, along with Uncle Charlie, and a great man and fantastic woman I was yet to meet, would soon become my big-time life changers. I had my faith, my family, and my friends. I was intelligent enough, even at my early age to understand that your success is always dependent on your support group. I don't know of many successful men and women who got that way operating alone. I have carried these lessons that I was so fortunate to have experienced early in life and kept applying them in my professional career.

I shall never forget what happened on that Friday afternoon in early spring of 1958. Mr. Tommy Knowles, our mechanic, Tommy's dad, called the house and asked Daddy and me to meet him at his shop in the Glade. When we arrived, he told us that he had some great news, the news that we had been waiting to hear. The Lebanon Lions Club, sponsor of the Babe Ruth League, in cooperation with the city of Lebanon, agreed, and had changed their eligibility requirements to permit any boy who lived in Wilson County to play in their league. They announced that the first tryouts would be at Baird Park in Lebanon at 9:00 Saturday morning. (Tomorrow!)

My emotions at this point were just plain numbing. To receive this news all of a sudden after at least five years of being on a bubble with nowhere to play just overwhelmed me. I don't know who was the happiest, Daddy, me, Mr. Tommy or my buddy, Tommy. I think all the words I could muster were, "It's about time and Thank you Lord." My "Not now!" has just turned into a "Yes!"

Mama and Mama Pearl were so excited. Mama Pearl started measuring me for sliding pads, to be made from her quilt liners. The trees were greener, the cows seemed to give more milk, the chickens laid more eggs, and my attitude changed overnight. All the work and blisters wearing out axe handles, broken bats, and tobacco sticks hitting rocks, chasing cows, plus the other preparations maybe would work in my favor. I wasn't aware of anyone else who had outworked me. One more step…do well in the tryouts tomorrow.

The five of us, which included my little brother, Larry, in the back seat with me and Tommy, arrived early around 8:30 at Baird Park. The field looked a little bigger than the Glade field and much nicer of course. Tommy and I grabbed a baseball and started warming up, while looking around to check out the competition. We were among the smallest players there. We had hoped that we would get to be on the same team. No other members in our Glade class were very interested in playing baseball other than Jimmy. His parents were new owners of the store across from the ball field next to Dobson's Feed Mill.

Tommy and I did well in the tryouts. Fortunately, both of us were selected to play for the same team sponsored by McDowell Motor Co. Our coaches were Mr. Bud Denny and Mr. Sanford Barrett. Mr. Denny had a son a year older than us named Don, who was our catcher. It was the 13-15 year-old league. The previous rules had prohibited Tommy and me from playing for five years; four years of Little League and our 13-year-old first year of Babe Ruth. We had been working hard for this so long with nowhere to play.

When our coaches asked around if anybody had any little brothers who would like to be our bat boy, Larry immediately raised his hand and got the job. He had just turned 8 and was already going to be in uniform. That meant so much to me beyond measure! There is a picture of us in the picture section of this book with Larry beside me and Tommy on the right end of the first row. Our first team in our first uniforms! It was a dream come true for two young 14-year-olds that had been denied the opportunity for too long. Ironically, I was given the number 14.

Tommy and I were ready to make up for lost time.

The teams that year included: McDowell Motors, Lux Clock, Perfection Ice Cream, Commerce Union Bank, Lea's Butane Gas, and Lebanon Manufacturing. During the season, we met new friends and especially got close to our teammates. I met guys on all of the other teams who had similar stories like me of having to wait to get to play. Many of the 15-year-olds were already playing on their high school teams, mostly with Lebanon and Castle Heights Military Academy in Lebanon. We would play twice a week during the season. Mama and Daddy got to know other parents from all of the teams in the league. The competition was strong. There were some great young players in our League. Why the league waited so long to open up the opportunities for us to play has always remained a mystery. It could have been the lack of sponsors or coaches I suppose. But we are here now. That is in the past.

Mama Pearl quickly found her a place behind home plate and over to the right of the backstop. She brought her own chair and selected that particular location to keep an eye on the calls of the umpires. Usually, the same set of umpires called all the games each week. They got to know Miss Pearl, especially when she let them know when they missed a call. She was not a screamer or one of those fans that umpires wished would get sick the night they were behind the plate. She was polite and even appreciated by the team of umpires because she would let them know when the calls were questionable in a fun way. Most of the time she was right and they knew it. She knew her baseball and was known to do a little coaching on the ride home after games.

Larry did a great job as batboy, but he was known for pulling pranks like putting frogs down the player's shirts or in their gloves. Sometimes he would even bring his own frogs to the games to turn loose. I have no idea why he was like that.

I think that we came in second or third that first season. Lux Clock, with Mike Gannaway, their ace pitcher, won the league title.

Both Tommy and I did well. We hit well in our first year in Babe Ruth. I even pitched a few games but my biggest achievement was very unexpected and not known until the President of the league, Mr. Charlie Escue, approached me and Daddy as we were getting in the car to go home after a game one night. Mr. Escue put his hand on my shoulder and said to my daddy, "Mr. Lannom, I want to let you know that home run that Bobby hit tonight was the first home run to be hit over the fence by a Babe Ruth player in Baird Park. Congratulations!" I don't think that there was ever some marble monument erected out in right field, but the word of Mr. Escue was good enough for us.

Such as was the case in all of baseball back then. Teams didn't hand out participation trophies or many individual awards either. That was still the case in Legion ball and college. As I recall that at bat, I could visualize that rock going over the pond, then over that big tree that stood by our spring at the farm from where Daddy carried our water to the house for 13 years.

I was a changed kid. I didn't know of any event in my life, up to that time, that meant as much to me as my last year at the Glade and my first season of baseball in Lebanon, Tennessee. That entire year was just like icing on a chocolate cake!

That summer, after my first year of getting to finally play my game, passed by so quickly. I stayed busy working on the farm, taking in a lot of the Glade baseball games, always making sure that I got my share of free snow cones. I paid more attention now to the details of the games being played and made mental notes of the good hitters that played for the Glade as well as from opposing teams. I still worked during the summer at the pump house wall, and even took on additional jobs to get stronger for next season. I made many mile-runs to the back side of our farm and to the Cross Roads. Larry was getting old enough to catch and throw balls with me. I watched him and his talents improve from the first time I got to work with him. Daddy and I both agreed that if he got the chance to play earlier than me, he could be special. I know one thing. He could fling a green tomato pretty good. If he's aiming to hit you, you had better duck or run for cover.

*A welcomed addition to our homestead included a new bathroom with water supplied by our well from this pump house. The ivy and vines cover the actual wall where I developed my pitching and fielding skills. Countless hours were spent throwing balls against the wall. I'm surprised it stood up to the practice sessions without being damaged.*

# Chapter 6

Now that I was 14 and a one-year veteran of baseball, I was unofficially appointed as the summer FIC (Farmer In Charge). Daddy and I, while doing the milking in the afternoons, would discuss the next day's assignments for me to complete while he was at work building C130 cargo planes at AVCO. One of my daily assignments was to make sure that the cows were at the barn and all the buckets and cans loaded when he got home from work. I had decided earlier in the summer to use my carpentry skills and build a platform to hook up to the tractor to haul the milk cans and buckets to the barn instead of using the truck. Pouring the milk in the cans would be a lot easier. No lifting was required. My creation was indeed a labor saver.

Daddy was not known to spend a lot of money on maintenance of farm equipment until he absolutely had to. Duct tape and baling wire would suffice for taking care of a lot of repairs. Everybody knew how he was. His sister, Auntie, one Christmas, even gave him a box of gate hinges as a Christmas present. During the last couple of weeks, since the battery in the tractor had about given up the ghost, it would not have enough spark to start our tractor. Instead of buying a new battery, we just parked our little old 20 horsepower Ferguson, "Old Fergie", tractor on a hill behind the yard fence. To start it was just a matter of putting it in first gear, turning on the switch, and letting off of the clutch as it rolled down the hill. This was at first a temporary fix but had developed into a routine! It would run long enough to

## The Loser's Ball

add enough spark to the battery to start it with the starter at the barn and return to the house with our milk cans. Just don't forget to park it on the hill again for the next trip to the milk barn.

One Friday afternoon while I was at the flat rock, a huge span of solid rock, half way between the barn and the house, batting rocks, time slipped up on me. I realized that Daddy would get home soon and find my preparations undone. Thank goodness the cows had already congregated at the barn waiting to get their sweet feed and grain that we used for bait to attract them. I quickly loaded up the empty milk cans and milk buckets on my cart at the rear of the tractor and performed a perfect "jump start" as I coasted down the hill. Suddenly, I remembered that Daddy had told me that the tractor was about out of gas and to be sure and fill it with the gas can in the cooler house before I started it that afternoon. I had forgotten, too late! If I shut off the engine now it won't start. We had some jumper cables, but they had disappeared when Daddy loaned them to a neighbor.

I got off of the tractor and got the full gas can out of the cooler house. I raised the hood to get to the gas tank. After removing the gas cap, I stuck in the funnel and started filling the tank, with "Old Fergie" running. I had just a little gas left to pour in the tank when the funnel slipped. It came out and gas went all over the top of the gas tank and spilled down on the hot engine. Naturally, it caught on fire. Old Fergie was ablaze!

Just as this happened, I see a car that I recognized speedily coming up the driveway and slamming to a stop in front of our barn lot gate. It was Daddy being brought home by his car poolers that worked with him at the airplane plant. I guess that they had seen my smoke signals from the road. I had no way to put out that gas fire except to slam the hood back down and hope to smother out the blaze. That just made things worse.

As Daddy was jumping out of the car, Old Fergie blew up and shot a cumulus blast of fire and black smoke fifty feet in the air with Fergie's hood right on top of it. I just turned around and yelled out, "Welcome home Daddy!" All he said to me was, "Are you alright?" You would think that when your kid blows up the farm tractor, some form of punishment would follow. He was just happy that I wasn't on top of Fergie's hood when she blew.

After his buddies left the fireworks show, we examined the victim. Daddy looked at it and simply said, "Don't worry about it. Gene can fix it!" Gene was Mama's brother who could work magic on most anything that ran that didn't have legs. We just went back to using Nelle Belle to haul the milk. Saturday morning after we milked, I rode with Daddy to the Farmers CO-OP in Lebanon. He bought a new battery.

Tommy and I had made so many new baseball friends during the spring and early summer season of our first year in Babe Ruth. Many of them were going to attend Lebanon High School in the fall. They were very persuasive in talking us into enrolling at Lebanon and play with them on the Blue Devil baseball team. Cumberland University, located in Lebanon, was an NAIA college division baseball power. Many players from Lebanon had played there. Their legendary baseball coach, Woody Hunt would coach 41 years there later, from 1980 to 2021, with six NAIA World Series appearances, one runner-up finish and three national championships.

My daddy graduated from Mt. Juliet High School in 1941. He played football and basketball there. The problem was that although Mt. Juliet still had football and basketball, it did not have a baseball program. Our decision to go to Lebanon was made. William Dean Thompson, one of our Glade classmates, lived several miles east of the Glade toward Lebanon and was zoned to attend high school there. He volunteered to take us to registration in spite of just turning 15. He had no driver's license, but drove his daddy's farm truck to take Tommy and me to Lebanon HS to enroll.

We went inside and looked around and spotted a table with the letters K-L on a card standing up on a table. That had to be the Knowles-Lannom table. A lady at the table asked for our names. When we told her, she started flipping through her papers looking for our names with no success. She finally asked us, "Where did you boys go to elementary school?" We told her, "The Glade". "Are you talking about Gladeville Elementary?" she asked. "Yes mam!", we

## The Loser's Ball

answered. She then threw us a Loser's Ball. "Boys, I'm sorry, but most eighth grade students from the Glade are zoned to attend Mt. Juliet High School. Sorry, you can't enroll at Lebanon. You must be zoned to go to Mt. Juliet."

Well, that was short and not so sweet. Now what? Nothing to do now, but for William Dean to take us back to the Glade. We should have known where we were supposed to go when after his seventh-grade year, our classmate, Eddie Foster, defected to Mt. Juliet a year ago. We always thought that he was getting a head start on scouting out the female population before the rest of us would get there. Tommy and I had no choice. I don't remember who finally drove us to Mt. Juliet to enroll, but we got there a couple of days before the first football practice was scheduled to begin.

Since baseball was out, Tommy and I decided to play football. Although we still were not of magazine cover stature, we were pretty fast, competitive, and had an endurance resume of exposure to the Glade educational culture. Here we are, good old country boys ready to start a new adventure. Once we got registered, we were told, since we wanted to play football, we would have to get a physical. The coaches had made arrangements for some nurses and a doctor from the county health department to conduct physicals on all players. One of the requirements was that all of us must take a blood test. Tommy and I were so country, that when our blood test results came back, they showed up as being 90% pinto bean juice! That must have been good enough. We made the football team.

A lot of the boys in our class from the Glade made the team. Eddie was an end, Perk was a tackle, Jimmy played in the line, Tommy became our center, Doyle and I were running backs. Since there was no baseball team, we made the best of it, making new friends, and adapting to the change of having different teachers for each of our classes. Mrs. Nell Gann, had to be a twin, separated at birth from Mrs. Nell Vaughter, our eighth-grade teacher. She was tougher than nails. I struggled in her class until I figured out that completing homework and a lot of study would be the answer to closing the gap between my puny efforts and her expectations. I would have Mrs. Gann for two years of English. When I graduated from high school and went to college, I came to appreciate her for preparing me to write and express myself during the tough college essay writing classes my freshman year.

Coach Patton, assistant football coach, and girls head basketball coach, was my typewriting teacher. I can still hear him calling out, "a s d f space, semi l k j space." My most favorite class of all was Agriculture. It was taught by a man I came to love and admire. William H. Coley became my mentor, my friend, and was a second daddy to me the next four years at MJHS. I always believed that Mrs. Nell, my eighth-grade teacher, gave him her notes on that country boy from the Glade. Mr. Coley was our Future Farmers of America (FFA) advisor. I bought an FFA jacket with my milk money and pinned on my Green Hand pin. I was as proud of that blue and gold jacket as I was my McDowell Motors uniform. Little did I know that I would wear a number of FFA jackets in the future, later serving our chapter and state. He taught us electric welding, acetylene welding and cutting, electrical wiring, plumbing, tractor overhaul, how to repair lawn mowers, make farm gates, woodworking, how to make rope halters, and how to raise all kinds of crops and livestock. I had found my one class that was self-motivating and loved it.

Agriculture instruction was only half of it. Through the FFA, we learned many leadership skills such as parliamentary procedure and, oh yes, public speaking. All freshman were required to learn the FFA Creed and recite the verses as we stood in front of the class. There were no exceptions. When we got through the entire creed, Mr. Coley told me, "I want you to be our FFA Creed speaker at our district contest in three weeks." I had matured a lot and had gained more confidence to speak as a result of my 4-H speaking and my short time so far in the FFA. I readily accepted.

It was the 1958-59 school year. My district creed winning pennant is still displayed on the Mt. Juliet High School FFA Wall of Fame in the school Ag classroom today. Mr. Coley had a photo made of the year's FFA winners that was on the front cover of our January

1959 FFA calendar. I am in that picture wearing my FFA jacket and holding up my winning pennant.

Tommy and I were off to a booming start with the opportunity to hopefully get to play in some of our Bear's football games. Coaches N.C. Hibbitt, head coach, and Assistant Coach, Elzie Patton, put us through our drills and practices heading into the first game. Mt. Juliet had not had a winning football season in a couple of decades. Our first year was no exception. We went 0 and 9 and a tie with Hendersonville. Losing was not fun, but we kept working. We got to play a lot of defense as freshmen, because a lot of the starting juniors and seniors got all banged up trying to stop runaway trains from Antioch, Bellevue, and other powerful football programs in Nashville. It was a rough year to say the least.

When the football season was over, Coach Patton turned his attention to his girls's basketball program. Naturally, during my first few months I had made some effort to scout out the female members of our freshman class. With football, and having to get home to get the milking done, scouting was limited to class time when we were together, or during lunch.

I had spotted this pretty girl who was on the basketball team. One of my friends had told me her name. I did not have any classes with her and knew very little about her. I finally took a leap of faith one morning before the first bell rang. I walked over to where she was sitting on the first row of the bleachers in the gym, waiting to go to first period class. I sat down beside her, acting as cool as a novice freshman could act and started my spill by introducing myself and waiting for a response. "So, you are Bobby Lannom from the Glade?" she asked. I said "Yep, that's who I am, and your name is Brenda Graves, right?" "Yep, that's my name, but Mr. Patton doesn't want his basketball girls talking to boys right now. He wants us to focus on basketball." Curve ball? No, more like a sinker! Taking my cue to leave now, I got up and said, "Well, I guess I'll see you later." and walked away.

I couldn't believe that conversation. I had just stepped up to the plate and got called out on the first pitch! A big time Loser's Ball!

Rejected in the top of the first. I must be doomed with the damsels! Well, at least she knows my name and will not be calling me, "Hey you!"……….. I hope.

I think Uncle Tom Lee, Mama Pearl's brother, who was a county commissioner, arranged for my cousins, Carol and Kay to be able to catch the Glade bus and then transfer to another bus to attend Mt. Juliet. Carol happened to land a job as one of the managers on the girls's basketball team. Kay, Carol's younger sister, was two years younger than us. Kay would later become an outstanding basketball player for the Bears as well as a successful girls basketball coach and administrator. Now, that Carol is basketball manager on Brenda's team, I may get a break!

The Glade had a pretty good record of sending several good athletes to Mt. Juliet. Vesta and the Glade kids were making their way onto the athletic teams at MJHS. Although the freshmen were the bottom statue on the totem pole, all of us were adjusting pretty well. My time was consumed in developing my farm projects for my agriculture class. Each student was required to have some type of ag-related work experience project at home or after school as part of earning advanced degrees and awards. I had no trouble with that. As part of my income from helping out on the farm, Daddy game me a couple of pigs, a cow, and turned the tobacco crop completely over to me. Mr. Coley helped me find three registered Guernsey cows to buy and add to my herd.

By the end of my freshman year, I had my own milk check coming in every other week and had sold my first pig crop of finished hogs at the market. I learned to keep all the records of expenses and income in my FFA record book. Earning advanced degrees was no problem. I now had assumed a lot more of the farm responsibilities. Larry was now able to drive the repaired version of old Fergie hauling hay and picking corn. I felt like a big farming land baron!

In April, I found out that I would be attending the 1959 Tennessee Association FFA State Convention in Memphis, along with the juniors and seniors in the "calendar picture". Allen Graves, who was a senior and a cousin of Brenda's was in the Mt. Juliet group. While

## The Loser's Ball

at convention, he and I talked about the Graves family. Allen and his brothers, Larry and Joe, lived on a dairy farm just like me. We hit it off just great. That's when I found out more about his cousin, Brenda. Allen and Brenda's dads were brothers. They all attended the same church together. I'm beginning to think that the fox is now finding a way to get into the hen house.

The upper classmen moved in their assigned rooms together, while I as a lowly freshman was sharing a room with Mr. Coley. Those three or four nights we were together my future was planned. We would sit up at nights, sometimes past midnight, with Mr. Coley advising me on what classes to take, and what contests to prepare for and enter. Public speaking events always topped our discussions. He wanted me to compete in every public speaking contest available. He told me, "Whatever you do, Bob, be sure and take as many college prep classes at school as you can so you can go to college." He enhanced what he had just said by saying, "By going to college, I mean, the University of Tennessee!" I assured him that I had already made that decision. Listening to George Mooney and Bob Fox broadcasting Tennessee football games on our truck radio, while we were picking beans or doing other work, had won me over. I told him that I wanted to play baseball there too. Many goals were sat that week in Memphis. I was fortunate and blessed to have achieved many of them. That week was when I decided that I wanted to become a state FFA officer and an agriculture teacher/FFA advisor.

I developed a close friendship and appreciation for my new classmates, teachers, teammates, and other students that I met that first year in high school. All of them were starting their new journeys just like me, not sure of what the future would hold or what direction we would go. One consolation was that we were here and making our journeys together. I had learned already in my brief record of competing in team sports, that the team is bigger than any individual. A lot of talented kids are so interested in their own personal ambitions and victories that they fail to understand that it is the team that enables you to stand in the winner's circle or walk to the podium and receive a trophy. Learning the skills of teamwork is an often-forgotten trait that is so necessary in sports and in business. Later in my life I would be blessed to experience success in both. It is rare indeed, for an athlete or business executive to get to the top of his/her profession without the support and influence of others.

There was still a big hole in my life that needed filling. It seemed that my big Loser's Ball was following me into every new episode of my journey. I finally came to the realization that MJHS was not going to have baseball as a sport for me. I didn't have time to play basketball because of working on the farm. It was a sport that I was certainly not prepared to play, anyway. It looks like football is going to be my game.

Now that our first year of high school had come to an end, Tommy and I shifted our thoughts to the 1959 baseball season ahead in Lebanon. This would be our final year to play in the Lebanon Babe Ruth League. We had a lot of good players returning on our McDowell Motors team and couldn't wait for the first pitch. Every available minute that I had that spring before the season was spent preparing for that final season. I would be ready!

*I did not know that this picture of me, back left, holding up my 1958-59 FFA Creed winning pennant along with other Mt. Juliet HS FFA members, would be displayed beside our advisor, Mr. Bill Coley, in his Wilson County Agriculture Hall of Fame recognition booth at the Ward Ag Center. Allen, back right, Brenda's cousin, is holding his winning Dairy Judging pennant as well.*

# Chapter 7

I had pitched several games last year for McDowell and was now a 15-year-old. New head coach, Sanford Barrett let me know that I would be the starting pitcher this season. My time on the pump house wall, and having Daddy to serve as my catcher, increased big time. I began to get ready to assume my new role. I asked Daddy if some of the Glade men's pitchers would be willing to give me some good lessons on pitching. He told me that our neighbor, Mr. Billy Thornton, who lived next door to our farm, was either a minor leaguer or outstanding amateur pitcher at one time.

It wasn't long that I was sitting on his front porch, ball and glove in hand, listening to him talk of his old baseball career. Here I am now, at my own neighbor's house listening to this man right under my nose. How convenient! He would catch with me and help me with my windup, stretch, and delivery. He even showed me how to check runners and make pick-off throws to first. He told me to be sure to get my legs in the best shape I could because you thrust your body off of the pitching rubber with your feet and legs with your lead foot pointed directly at your target. He showed me how to grip a fast ball, a curve, change up, and a drop ball, now called a sinker ball. He showed me how to hide the ball so that I could keep the hitters from knowing what was coming. He emphasized follow through, how to strengthen my arm, how to protect it, even making sure not to sleep on my throwing arm at night. Always, he emphasized, finish your delivery in a good defensive posture to be able to field your position as pitcher.

During each visit with him, I was a huge sponge, soaking up all of his teachings I could. The time that I spent there with Mr. Thornton and following his training was priceless. There is no doubt that with me improving, our team would have a better chance to play for a championship. I couldn't wait to share his knowledge with my teammates, especially those who would be pitching as well. After all, there was Mike Gannaway, Lux Clock's ace pitcher returning to win it all again. Even my daddy had said at our supper table one evening during some losses to Lux with Mike pitching, "All Gannaway has to do to beat yall, is to throw his glove on the mound and you are beaten before the game starts!" I was determined that he would not be saying that again this year. My daddy was a psychologist sometimes, I think.

We started practice with several new players. George Summers, returned as our "sneaky" first baseman. When I was pitching some last year, George and I would have these little conferences near the mound and I would slip the baseball in his glove without the runner on first or his coach seeing the exchange. He would pat his glove and I would act like the ball was still in my glove but following mound procedures to not get a balk called by the ump. As the runner would take his lead, George would simply say, "Mr. Ump!" and tag him out. It was good for two or three times a year.

Doug Raines returned. Doug was a good hitter and had an attitude worth catching. Jesse Russell was our assistant coach. His son, Phillip played for us. Our veteran batboy, my 9-year-old brother returned and did a fantastic job. We saw fewer frogs this time around. Of course, Tommy was back and ready to play a great second base again this year.

As the season progressed, it was evident if nothing changed, that McDowell Motors and Lux Clock were going to fight it out for the championship. Mama Pearl stepped up her interactions on questionable calls with the umpires. By now, Miss Pearl was in her prime and showed no let up as the season went forward. Mike continued to be a great pitcher for Lux. I could tell from my training from Mr. Thornton that he knew how to pitch and do it well. He also had one year of high school ball at Castle Heights behind him. That season went by so fast. It was a lot of fun. George and I even managed a couple of hidden ball pick offs, too. Tommy hit the ball well that year. I had gained a lot more strength than I had as a 14-year-old and hit well. Even the new guys contributed many runs to our victories.

Occasionally on Saturday mornings when we would go to town (Lebanon) to get groceries, I would take in a movie at either the Princess or Capitol theaters near the square. Color movies were a treat since all we had was that little B and W version at Mama Pearl's house. 3-D movies were the best! I remember watching a popular 3-D movie, "The Charge at Feather River" starring Guy Madison. If I failed to get a hit at the game on Saturday night, Mama Pearl would forbid me from watching any more movies at the theater on game day, thinking it affected my eyes. Who was I to argue?

Once Mama Pearl saw that our team was looking pretty good, she was into it at her position behind home plate. The season ended in a tie between McDowell Motors and Lux Clock Co. The championship game was scheduled for a Saturday night. I did not go to the movies that day!

Another superstition or belief that Mama Pearl had was that I never played well if I laid around a lot on game day. She concluded that if I was riding Old Fergie, either plowing all day or disking ground, that I would have a good game at the plate and pitching. I couldn't argue with that either. Before the games that I was to pitch, our players' parents would yell over to her and ask her. "Did Bobby plow today?" Somehow it seemed to work. Why and how? I have no clue. It may be just like what Yogi Berra was quoted as saying about the game of baseball, *"Baseball is 90% mental and the other half physical"*. I do believe that relaxation for pitchers as well as players means something, and to free your mind of what lies ahead is helpful. I learned early to be relaxed at the plate. It made a big difference. That Saturday night, she was asked that question if I had plowed today. She responded, "He plowed about all day. He's ready!"

Maybe I should have plowed a little longer. Lux took an early

## The Loser's Ball

lead, but we came back to tie the game at 2 runs apiece. I don't have a score book of that game to show the box scores and how the game went through the seventh and last inning. It was a tough game, just two good teams in youth baseball going after each other. Mike pitched well. His teammates, led by shortstop, Mike Dixon, and others played well. Our guys hung in there and matched them run for run to the end. I finally managed to pitch a complete game giving up 4 runs. McDowell Motor Co. scored, finally pulled ahead.

The final score was McDowell Motors 5, Lux Clock 4. Tommy and I along with a bunch of gritty little country boys had won our first baseball championship. If we received trophies, I have no idea where mine went. The only team championship picture that I have was taken from a newspaper article that appeared in the Lebanon Democrat. The actual headline print above the picture wasn't even about our win! It is unclear because of its age and being just a newspaper article. I would have loved to include it in this book, but unfortunately, it really is unprintable.

Coach Barrett received the championship trophy from Mr. Charlie Eskew, president of the league, and a long-time friend and supporter of youth baseball in Lebanon. Members of that championship team of 1959, other than Tommy and me, included: Phillip Parkerson, Phillip Russell, Chuck Jones, Charles Huffine, Clayton Birdwell, Joe Ferrell, George Summers, and Carl Jones.

Several of my friends and I made the All-Star team. Practice began just a few days after our last game with Lux Clock. Now, my opponents have nearly overnight become my teammates. Our team went up against a great team from Nashville. Our game was played in Nashville. The Nashville team had a left-handed pitcher that started against us and threw a no-hitter. We did not last as long as two practices. We had never faced a left-hander who was that good. I thought about that game and how he controlled us from the start. I was happy that I hit a line drive to center even though the center fielder made a diving catch on it. I spent no more than 15 minutes thinking about that game. I was glad to mentally stick that

Loser's Ball in my pocket and remember it no more. We were just overmatched. I guess that win just wasn't meant to be!

I am so thankful that our all-star coaches decided after losing that game would not be our last contact with baseball in the summer of 1959. What happened next was a giant highlight of my baseball career while not playing and winning a big game.

Our team was going to get to attend a Nashville Vols minor league game at Sulphur Dell in Nashville. Believe it or not, I had never attended a professional baseball game anywhere, so this was going to be a treat. Sulphur Dell was the home of the Vols. The team had been known in years past as the Blues, Tigers, Seraphs, and Centennials. In 1908, Grantland Rice, editor of the Nashville Tennessean newspaper, named the team the Volunteers. It was later shortened to the Vols.

It was a field like no other in baseball. There was a 45-degree embankment around the outfield against the wall. The outfield fence was 16 feet high and was on top of the embankment. The right field fence was only 262 feet from home plate. The bottom of the fence was 22 ½ feet above the surface of the playing field. On top of the fence was a screen that was 30 feet high, so a hitter had to hit a ball a height of 52 ½ feet to clear the fence for a home run. Right-fielders have actually fielded sharply hard-hit line drives off of the wall and thrown some runners out at first. When Babe Ruth played at Sulphur Dell in an exhibition game, he refused to play in the outfield. It was often called the "Dump". Some visiting outfielders referred to the field as "Sulphur Hell".

Our team arrived that afternoon in time to watch batting practice and infield. I looked around taking in the sights and ballpark smells and wondered how in the world had I missed out on this before. We had great seats just down the right field line watching missed home runs slam against the large screen and fall straight down to the 22 ft high embankment. I paid special attention since I was a left-handed hitter. I sat imagining seeing my towering home run clearing the fence and screen then finally landing on the ice plant roof. Once I had taken in the stands, the vendors walking up the aisles yelling out,

## The Loser's Ball

"Popcorn! Get your popcorn here!", and checking out the hitters and fielders, I now made it official. I want to play baseball and maybe one day, be out there on the field doing my thing, the game I love.

When Nashville took the field and started their infield, hitting to the outfield who was making their catches and throws to second, third, then home, I was amazed at the arm of the center fielder. He was one-hopping throws to home plate from center field and nailing his bullets to second and third right on target. His name was Buddy Gilbert. The Vols were a minor league team of the Cincinnati Reds. I kept wondering, why is this guy still in the minor leagues, especially with a right arm like that? I was now 100 % sold on the idea that this player is now my idol. I contained my commitment until I could get to see him at bat. Once the game started and I was hot dog fed, popcorn supplied, and coke refreshed, I got to see him at the plate. He hit left-handed just like me. During one of his at bats he hit a booming high fly ball over the right field screen and landed on top of the Noel Cold Storage building for a home run. Now, I have my idol to watch for the next few years. I intend to come back and watch him play again.

All of us thanked our coaches for this great day at the ballpark. I left that old stadium that day with a new enthusiasm and motivation to work even harder to become a better ball player. I can't explain it any other way except to say that the providence of God works in people's lives to put you and people in each other's lives for a special time or moment that you never imagined. This has happened to me many times. I would not get to see Buddy play again at Sulphur Dell. He would be called up to play in the majors with Cincinnati. I want to thank Bill Traughber for writing his book, "Nashville Baseball History, From Sulpher Dell to the Sounds". His research is phenomenal.

One summer I was visiting my cousins, the Bramwells in Nashville. I always enjoyed the visits there, except the time Earl, Raymond, and I were playing around in their back yard and I decided to climb this old elm tree that was beside the famous "alley" that ran beside their home. It was the fastest way to escape pursuers who chased us after stunts we pulled on them and had to get back to the basement to hide. Uncle Charlie and Auntie were gone somewhere this particular day and had taken Daddy and Mama with them. It had been raining that morning leaving the old elm tree wet and pretty slippery. I decided to climb the tree and look at their "treehouse." As I neared the entrance to a contraption they called their treehouse, I slipped and fell head first hitting the edge of the concrete of the roadway in the alley. Blood was going everywhere. Osie, who was cleaning the Bramwell house that day came out screaming. The cousins were yelling for their older brother, Charles, to come. Charles, who happened to be home that day, loaded me up in his car and took off with his friend, Anthony in the back seat, holding a rag on my head to stop the bleeding. We made it to the emergency room where the doctor cleaned me up and put a bunch of stitches in the "C" shaped wound in the top of my head. I still wear that scar as a reminder to be "C"areful. The rest of my city cousin visits were much better.

A couple of weeks passed since my trip to the ballgame to watch the Nashville Vols. Daddy and Mama took our family down to Nashville to visit the Bramwells as we often did. After lunch, Uncle Charlie made a phone call and told Daddy and me that he wanted to take us over to a friend's house for a visit. You could see that he was more than a little excited about his phone call. We loaded up in his car and drove to the home of Mr. Jim Turner. By now, it was evident that Uncle Charlie has taken a special interest in my baseball pursuits and me personally. He knows that everything I do is done to get better in my game.

We were welcomed at the door by Mr. Turner, who invited us into his den in the rear of the house. I don't know how long my bottom jaw stayed on my chest when I looked around and thought that I was in Cooperstown, at the Hall of Fame. I was in the home of Jim Turner, the former pitching coach of the New York Yankees. He had recently retired after being with the Yankees from 1949-1959, coaching under the legendry Yankee manager, Casey Stengel. During that time the Yankees had won 7 World Series championships. His past uniforms were hung in glass cases. Autographed baseballs hung six inches apart on brass chains from the ceiling to the floor. Helmets, gloves, and other items were displayed. On one wall hung copies of his World Series checks framed and in perfect line.

He had coached Whitey Ford, hung around Mickey Mantle, Yogi Berra, Bobby Richardson, Elston Howard, and others. Wow! He reminded us of the good times that he had coming with Uncle Charlie to our farm in the Glade several times to rabbit hunt. I was too young to remember, but if I had known him back then, his hunting time would probably have been reduced by answering questions from me about the Yankee players.

In Joe Traughber's book, he writes that Jim Turner's wife, after Sulphur Dell had earlier closed in 1963, would later show up along with 35 others in 1969, at the demolition of the old historic ball park, filming with her home video camera the stadium prior to its demise by wrecking balls and heavy equipment.

*"In baseball and in business, there are three types of people; Those who make things happen, Those who watch things happen, and Those who wonder, what happened?"*

Tommy Lasorda

Personally, I felt fortunate to have surrounded myself with folks who made things happen. Meeting Coach Jim Turner was such an honor and a privilege, especially for a Glade boy like me. I began to realize with the support of Uncle Charlie, that my life could be headed in an almost unbelievable direction if I made the commitment and determination to improve my game. He would not let me be one of those who sat around and "wonder what happened?"

Our 1959 Lebanon Lions Club Babe Ruth League Championship photo only appeared in a Lebanon Democrat newspaper article, too poor of an image to copy. This picture, I am so proud to include, was taken of the 1958 McDowell Motors team, my first year to wear a baseball uniform at 14 years of age, coincidently, my uniform number! My silver front teeth caps also shined with my smile. Tommy, my Glade buddy, is number 8. I was so excited as was our batboy, little brother Larry to my right, to be on this team which won the league championship a year later.

# Chapter 8

*"If you are afraid of failure, you don't deserve to be successful."*
Charles Barkley

After winding up the summer, I was pumped as I started back to high school as a sophomore. The first days are always the best, seeing your old classmates and teammates again. Football practice is always a hot time in September, especially dressed out in pads. I am glad that I spent a lot of time running from the front of our farm to the back of it all summer. It is about a mile round trip. I also ran from our house to the "crossroads" down where our road meets the main highway. That distance is exactly a half mile from our mailbox. I still managed to include a lot of work in my baseball training. My pitching skills had really improved after my visits to Mr. Thornton's training sessions.

During the summer, Mr. Coley, my Ag teacher made some visits to our farm to help me in clipping my cows to show in the county and state fairs. We didn't have a truck big enough to haul them, but Robert Guethlein, a neighbor down the road, showed cattle and volunteered to take mine to the shows and fairs along with his. He just backed up to the pond bank where my three girls marched right in his truck.

We almost got arrested in Macon County at their county fair showing our cattle. You always want to feed your cattle as much as they will eat just minutes before the show to make them look bigger. That's a show technique. Ours were about full when we noticed some great grass next to the fairgrounds in front of the high school. Robert and I led a couple of our cows over there and let them graze to their heart's content. We both were sitting on the ground leaning up against some trees and went to sleep while our champions fed. We were awakened by a Lafayette city police officer tapping us on the shoulder with his baton. We had no excuse but to confess our crime and pleaded for his redeeming graces. He finally asked us to kindly lead our animals back to the fairgrounds and not come back. Salvation!

I would miss Robert since he had graduated last year. He was always a great friend of our family. One of my classmates later married Robert and moved to the Glade on his farm. I had named my three Guernsey show cows, Faith, Hope, and Charity. Faith was my best. She actually won the blue ribbon in a show competing against a cow owned by Dr. Sam McFarland, a doctor in Lebanon, who had a huge farm. I couldn't have made all of those shows without Robert's help.

Several days before school actually began, we were on the practice field getting ready for the season. The schedule did not show any better hopes for victories than last year. We were basically playing the same teams again. It did not look good. My Mt. Juliet teammates who saw a lot of action last year; Bob and Pat Hackney, Wayne Wright, Leslie Earheart, Mike Hedgepath, and the Glade boys; Eddie Foster, Tommy Knowles, Billy Pickett, Doyle Sanders, and Bob Lannom, were ready to make a difference this season. I can quickly summarize the 1959-60 MJHS football season. Again, we went 0-9 and tied Hendersonville for the second straight year. Loser's Balls on steroids. In two years, the Bears were 0-18 and 2 ties, still looking for our first win. Patience may be a virtue. I guess you could say that we were one of the most patient and virtuous teams around!

My teachers were fantastic and always tried to help us maintain some degree of confidence in spite of our depressing losses. I had a great time that year in my agriculture class. So did all of Mr. Coley's boys. Girls were not yet permitted to take agriculture classes and join the FFA. I was elected to a chapter office. I placed second in my first district prepared public speaking contest. We won numerous district awards as individuals and teams that year. Without ag, we would probably not have won anything.

Bob, Pat, Tommy, and Eddie played a lot on the basketball team. School after football was a great experience. I wasn't ready to quit at all, just glad I still had my head on after two tough years. In an attempt to comfort us our history teacher said that Abraham Lincoln lost 18 elections before being elected president of the United States. I just hope I don't have to wait much longer to finally win a football game. Be patient with our 18 losses, yet Persistent!

I had a rule. Never have a girlfriend at Christmas time! I didn't have the money to afford presents for them. I was never a cheap guy, just practical. No, I was cheap! After Christmas I began to start looking around for prospective candidates to which I would offer my affections. I had ruled out that basketball girl, Brenda, especially since she had made no attempt to correct her poor judgement of character when she ran me off last year in the gym. There were some cute freshman girls who just might be available. I couldn't rush the progress since I didn't have a driver's license yet. All of my dates would have to be in the hall or during classes.

I finally made the decision to just work on the farm, take care of Mama Pearl and my three girls in the milk barn. Mr. Coley took me to the state FFA convention again where I met so many great guys around the state. It was beginning to look like ag was my thing at school. I bought another jacket that had my name and chapter office on it, practically wearing it every day to school. The FFA was molding me into a new person. I was falling right in line.

By the end of my sophomore year in high school, I was making enough money from my farming operation to set aside money to buy me a car next year. I had no intention of buying a new one, but take my time and find a nice one that didn't break down twice a week. Mama Pearl kept on frying baloney sandwiches and BLTs, plus providing me with her delicious fried peach pies. I heard an old resident in the Glade, who never had much, say that he was raised on fried peach pies. He said that he made three meals out of them: ate a couple for breakfast, drank water for dinner, and swelled up for supper!

Watching old westerns and baseball games on TV got better. I got ready to sell my old sow, but Daddy recommended that instead of selling, slaughter her and sell the meat to the neighbors, keeping the hams for myself. Mama Pearl and I made some more illegal runs up and down Vesta road. I made exactly $111 on the deal and kept the hams. I was selling three calves a year for roughly $750, plus my tobacco crop was bringing in $800 annually. I also sold feeder pigs from my other two sows returning nearly $1,000 per year. Making money on the farm, but losing football games was just me.

I called it the "Big League." I was now an official member of Lebanon's Post 15 American Legion Team. Uniting with former opposition players was a blessing. Each of us were baseball players having fun going on road trips to places such as Tullahoma, Columbia, Hartsville, Sparta, Springfield, Clarksville, and other towns. We had a great season our first year. What a beginning! I will never forget the bus rides with Charles Dedman leading the song, "Does Your Chewing Gum Lose Its Flavor On The Bedpost Over Night?" I had a good year hitting several home runs and hit over .400 that season. Post 15 even won the Middle Tennessee American Legion championship that year, but lost in the state finals. Tommy had decided not to play Legion ball that year. I think that he preferred making money as his dad's assistant in the garage.

I celebrated my long-awaited sixteenth birthday with another chocolate cake and within a few days received my driver's license. No more illegal produce deliveries. Mama Pearl can now stay in her seat if she sees flashing lights.

Another bonus to turning 16 was that I could now play on the Glade men's team. Mr. Van Dobson was still the manager of the team and asked both me and Tommy to join the team in the summer of 1960. Tommy played second base and I played shortstop. Now I am getting in a lot of baseball. I have told this story many times that I was making up for lost time not getting to play Little League and high school ball. Now Mama and Mama Pearl had two uniforms to wash, two Legion games during the week and Sunday afternoon with the Glade. I was as happy as a lost hog in a corn patch.

Tommy and I had played three or four games with the Glade. After we had just won a home game against Hartsville, Van, the manager, who I hoped had lost his memory about that foul ball I returned to him about four years ago, told me to stick around a few minutes that he wanted to talk to me. I told Daddy to hang around that I had to meet with Van about something he wanted to talk to me about. He said he would wait in the truck for me. Sounds familiar. I walked back over to where Van was loading up the bats and equipment, but this time he reached in his ball bag and handed me a white box. He said, "Go ahead. Open it up." I wasted no time in opening it up to see a brand new "white" baseball, wrapped in the manufacturer's protective tissue paper. Without mentioning the incident that happened years ago when I returned that stolen Loser's Ball to him, he just said, "This one is yours. Take it home with you and wear it out this week. Next Sunday you are pitching for us." It is still hard to write about this story without shedding a tear. It was then that I found out that Van knew exactly what had taken place at the same spot years ago. All I could do was give him a hug and a big "Thank You!" for the trust and faith he had in me not only as a player, but as a person, a kid who had grown up learning valuable lessons on a baseball field.

I don't remember the score but we won the next Sunday at the Glade with Herb Murphy as my catcher. Herb was a Yogi that Sunday. When he saw me getting in trouble, he would call time out, walk out to the mound with a calming voice as he did at many other games later, which helped shape my skills and mentality playing the good old game. Mama Pearl, by the way, found her spot behind home plate evaluating every call by the umpires. I felt that my battery, unlike old Fergie's, was now on full charge.

After putting it off for far too long, I made the decision along with two of my cousins, Kay and Butch, and a friend, Brenda Faye, to obey the gospel. Johnny Brown, a visiting preacher who was conducting our gospel meeting at Vesta, did the baptismal honors. All four of us began our new birth as young Christians the same day. From then on, I knew that I had another Father that I could call on many times to guide me in the way that I should go. Our Bible school teachers, friends, and neighbors at Vesta overwhelmed us with hugs and congratulations. I shall always be grateful to all of those caring and encouraging supporters in my home community.

Today, three of us that remain, often get together, remembering those wonderful times growing up in Vesta. Brenda Faye's mother, Mrs. Kathryn (Ma) McCrary, had her 100$^{th}$ birthday, September 29, 2023. What a lady and one of my best ever sports supporters. "Ma", as she has been called for years, still attends and sits in her reserved seat at most of the new Green Hills High School basketball games. She is a big Tennessee and San Francisco Forty Niners fan since her adopted great grandson, Jauan Jennings of Tennessee fame, now plays for the Forty Niners.

I was fortunate to get the opportunity to sit with Ma during the recent district tournament basketball games in Gallatin. We sat from 3 pm to 9 pm watching four tournament games. She is the only fan that I know of who has a free pass to all TSSAA district, regional, sub-state, and state championship games. She is loved by so many and to see even opposition players, coaches, and fans greet her at games, is powerful evidence of what kind of person she is. She turns 101 in September.

I received a call from one of the former Gladeville residents and baseball stars of the past. His name was Brud Spickard. Brud had a younger brother, Beverly, who was a year older than me and played on our football team. I had grown up watching Brud play for the Glade men's team. He was a great athlete and friend. Their dad, Mr. Johnny Spickard, was the Wilson County Register of Deeds. Beverly later served in the same position as his dad before retiring. Brud called me to ask if I would be interested in attending a three-day try out conducted by the St. Louis Cardinals in Columbia, Tennessee. That was an easy decision. I stayed with Brud and his wife, Ann, at their house during the tryouts. Brud was in charge of the city ball park maintenance as part of his summer duties as well as an assistant baseball and football coach at Columbia High School.

I had met many of the Columbia baseball players during Legion games. Brud assigned two of his players, Region Peebles, a talented running back with Columbia, and Hal Wantland, who was the team's starting quarterback, to show me the sights of Columbia at night. Region was trying out with the Cardinals as a pitcher. Hal also proved to the Cardinals scout, Buddy Lewis, that he had great skills as a catcher. Each evening after the tryouts, Region, Hal, and I would go to different places to eat and visit with their friends and players. They were great hosts. We became good friends rather than mortal enemies playing for different teams.

I tried out as an infielder, playing my position at shortstop. During one session that I shall never forget, Region was pitching when I took my turn at bat. In our attempts to impress the scout, neither of us was engaged in friendship sports at the moment. Region threw me a nice fast ball down the middle of the plate that I hit over the right field fence for a home run. Later that evening, he asked me, "Why did you do that?" I replied with a little caustic humor, "Why did you throw it down the middle?" We would recall this moment again later.

After one of the sessions, I had a chance to talk to Coach Lewis, the scout conducting the tryouts. I asked him to give me the best advice he could on hitting. He being a good diplomat, complimented me on my performance during the tryouts. Obviously at my young age I had thoughts of signing next week. He gave me some great advice about hitting that I filed away in the "better hitting tips" section of my brain. His advice was, "Remember that there is a strike zone for one reason. It is called the "strike zone". That is the zone where you without exertion, reaching, or golfing at a baseball, contain your swing. Stay within the 17-inch home plate width and let the less desirable pitches go by you for balls." He went on to tell me," The goal of pitchers is to get you to change your swing by reaching for outside pitches, chasing balls in the dirt, or high pitches that result in a miss or "worm killer" ground balls. Stay relaxed and restrain your temptation to go after bad pitches. If you have to work or reconfigure your swing away from your relaxed and normal attempt to hit the ball, you will lose."

Later, one of my favorite baseball coaches reminded me of the same thing and added another term for reaching for high, out of zone pitches. He referred to hitters going after these high pitches as being called "apple knockers." I could relate to that since I had often done that, using tobacco sticks, to knock apples off the lower limbs of Mama Pearl's old apple tree. Great advice from two former pros of the sport!

I had experienced a lot so far that summer. I became a Christian, got my driver's license, played for two baseball teams, made new friends, renewed old friendships, watched a young pro selected as my idol at the beginning of his new baseball career, and met a retired baseball legend who was completing his fabulous career with the Yankees, plus hitting a home run while trying out with the St. Louis Cardinals. Summer was not over yet.

With about three weeks to go before school started, Uncle Charlie let me know that I was again to be the designated tire changer to go with the Bramwells on their summer vacation. This year we were headed for Chicago, Illinois. Auntie packed up her traditional fried chicken, baked beans, potato salad, and of course, plenty of cokes. We left Nashville for Chicago on the morning of August 11, 1960 for a 10-day trip. Once we arrived, again with no flat tires, Uncle Charlie let us know that tomorrow night on the 12th, we would be attending the College All Star football game at Soldier Field in Chicago, and watch the college all-stars play the current back-to-back NFL Champion Baltimore Colts.

The Colts were my favorite team. They featured the top NFL quarterback by the name of Johnny Unitas and his favorite receiver, Raymond Berry. I suggest that you google the hardships that these two Hall of Famers went through to get to this point in their careers. Loser's Balls were nothing new to these two, who by luck or providence ended up playing together and becoming legends.

Unitas was considered too small to play pro ball. He was 6'1 and weighed 145 pounds. He grew up in Pittsburg, who finally drafted him in their 120th pick as an extra quarterback. Pittsburg had four quarterbacks and released him before his first season began. Unitas spent a year searching for a team that would take him. The Colts finally picked him up, and the rest is history, as they say. He won his first NFL Championship beating the New York Giants at Yankee Stadium in 1958 in sudden death, which is still considered the greatest NFL football game ever played. Unitas was as tough as they came. His former teammate, Bubba Smith, tells the time that Unitas had been sacked and his face pushed in the dirt by the rushing linebacker. Unitas called the same play and the same linebacker charged in. Unitas threw the ball in his face and broke his nose. Bubba stated, "That's my man!" He retired, having won three NFL titles and one Super Bowl. Johnny Unitas was inducted into the NFL Hall of Fame in Canton, Ohio in 1979. His number "19" was retired by the Colts.

Berry was so geekie looking with his black rimmed glasses he wore because he was nearsighted. It appeared by his walk that he had one leg shorter than the other. He actually had a miss-aligned back that required him to always wear a back brace. His lanky frame of 6'1 and 154 pounds often mislead observers to think that he was the equipment manager, rather than a player. He never played at any school that threw the ball very much. He was the most hard-working, persevering player of the decade. He was what I call, a "rock hitter." He was always getting someone to throw him passes before and after practices. He was the first one on the practice field and the last one to leave. He even carried around rubber balls to his classes, continually squeezing them to increase the strength of his grip.

A story is told that while Berry was playing his first year at Shriver College, there was a 220-pound bully of a linebacker who liked to pick fights. One day the lanky Berry was chosen as the potential recipient of his practices. The coaches found out but arrived too late. Both of his eyes were swollen and closed and blood everywhere. He was rushed to the hospital and followed by his players to check on him. When they entered the hospital and stood at his bed, it was not

Berry, but the bully lying in the bed. One of Berry's coaches replied, "He ran into the wrong one to pick a fight with."

Berry did okay but not brilliant at SMU, where passing at the time was not a big part of the offense. Berry worked on his skills continually, hoping one day to get the chance to prove his worth in the pros. Raymond Berry's name was not called in the NFL draft of 1954, until the 20th round by the Baltimore Colts. Raymond Berry partnered with his buddy, Johnny Unitas, to become the best passing/receiving duo in the NFL. The slow, near-sighted, back-braced Berry with his 13-year career with the Colts, caught more passes in the NFL than any other receiver. He was inducted into the NFL Hall of Fame in 1973 as one of the greatest receivers to ever play the game. That night I got to watch the Colts as my two favorite football players defeated the College All Stars 32-7 behind outstanding performances by Johnny Unitas and Raymond Berry. Thanks to Google and the profootballhof.com.

There are many stories like this about Loser's Balls delivered to athletes, businessmen, and others who tucked them away and turned them into "Opportunity Balls." You may be one of those young and aspiring athletes, who one day will find out that your persistence and dedication to improving your skills, may put you in the winner's circle much like many legends of the past, in spite of the Loser's Balls that come your way.

Go to Google and check out the stories of Wilma Rudolph, Jim Abbott, and Charlie Boswell. These heroes were thrown major Loser's Balls that would have made most people give up and live their lives in the "Loser's bracket of life." There is no reason that you are any different.

Wilma Rudolph was the twentieth of 22 children born in her family in Saint Bethlehem near Clarksville, Tennessee. She contracted scarlet fever and infantile paralysis, caused by polio, at the age of five. She was told that she would never walk again. She wore a leg brace until she was twelve years old. Her parents sought treatment in Nashville, receiving treatments up to four times a day. She finally overcame her illness and started running to strengthen her weakened legs. Her speed was noticed by Ed Temple, Tennessee State University track coach. She became a lady "Tigerbell", setting records at many track meets. Wilma ran in three events in the 1960 Summer Olympics in Rome, Italy, winning a gold medal in all three events. She broke the world records in the 100 meters, the 200 meter run, and finally in the 4x100 relay. Wilma Rudolph was considered to be the fastest woman on earth. She became an icon as one of the most popular athletes, white or black in the country.

Permit me to move the calendar forward a few years. I was teaching agriculture classes at Gallatin High School around 1971, when several other teachers and I decided to get our Master's degree in Agricultural Education at Tennessee State University, located a few miles away in Nashville. When our graduation day arrived, we sat in our caps and gowns in the bleachers of the football stadium on the campus to receive our diplomas. Our commencement speaker was none other than Wilma Rudolph. After the ceremony she made it a point to shake our hands and congratulate us on receiving our Masters. We were blessed that day to meet such a lady of class and distinction and to be challenged by her commencement address.

My next hero is Jim Abbott. Jim was born without a right hand. His Loser's Ball did not slow him down in preventing him from playing college and professional baseball. He became a great left-handed pitcher, adapting by shifting his glove under his right arm while throwing and moving it back to his left hand to receive the throws from his catcher. While at the University of Michigan, he led the Wolverines to two Big 10 Championships, and was selected the nation's best amateur athlete in 1987, and winning the Golden Spikes Award the same year. Abbott, representing the United States in the 1988 Summer Olympics in Seoul, Korea, pitched against Japan to win the Gold Medal. He was drafted in the first round of the 1988 draft and went to the majors playing for the California Angels in 1989. One of his highlights, while pitching for the Yankees, included pitching a no-hitter against Cleveland in 1993.

He played for the Angels, Yankees, White Sox, and Brewers during his 10-year career in the major league. Jim Abbott's statement he made about his trials to meet his goals, should be the same guidelines for our success. He said, *"I truly believe that difficult times and disappointments can push us to find abilities and strengths we wouldn't know existed without the experience of struggle."* Wikipedia.org.

Another one of my heroes is Charley Boswell. Charley was a former Alabama football player and a minor league baseball player for the Atlanta Crackers in 1941. He was drafted into the US Army and promoted to captain. He was permanently blinded when a tank exploded during his attempt to rescue a comrade trapped inside. During his rehabilitation, he took up the sport of golf. In 1946, he placed second in the National Blind Golf Championship. He later won the championship in Duluth, Minnesota in 1947. During the span of his blind golf career, Charley Boswell won 11 National championships and 11 International championships. The $17^{th}$ hole of Vestavia Country Club in Birmingham, Alabama, is named after Charley. One of his holes-in-one occurred there in 1970. The Vestavia club still continues to host the Boswell Cup in his honor. Charlie Boswell refused to live in the loser's bracket of life. It seems to me that those of us who are healthy of body and mind don't have any excuse for failure!

**Three Steps To Failure**

The first step to failure is to never try.
The next step is to be satisfied with the greatest enemy of excellence, mediocrity.
The final step is to let your dreams die,
while losing, you sit, and wonder why?

Author unknown.

# Chapter 9

After attending the College/NFL game on Friday night, our plans for the next few days were to visit the sites in Chicago. One of the first things we did was to take a cold plunge in Lake Michigan. We did not know how cold that water was until we had bolted from the bank and dived in. We spent days downtown and at the Museum of Natural Sciences. We had never seen as many roller coasters in one place. Raymond and I rode the rear car in every one of the six coasters we got on. We called it quits one evening while Raymond, Earl, and I were pitching baseballs to each other in front of our motel when one of us happened to let loose a wild pitch that knocked about a half dozen lights out on the motel sign. I have a faint recollection of who the guilty party was. We booked it back to the room before management found out about the lights.

Thursday finally rolled around. We were headed to Wrigley Field to see the Cubs play the Los Angeles Dodgers. It would be my first major league baseball game to attend. Wrigley, built in 1914, is the third oldest baseball stadium in the nation where annually, some form of baseball is played on a continuous basis. The second oldest is a park in Boston, that opened in 1912, named Fenway, home of the Red Sox. The oldest operating professional baseball stadium in the nation is Rickwood Field in Birmingham, Alabama. It was built in 1910. It was home to the Birmingham Barons. Ironically, according to Mickey Hiter, the field director, Nashville's Old Timers Field in

Shelby Park in Nashville, is the fourth oldest, also built in 1914 just after Wrigley. My unforgettable time at Shelby will come later.

To just be sitting at Wrigley Field, home of the Chicago Cubs was in itself enough to make my day. So many great games had been played there. All stars, hall of famers, both coaches and managers, had played here, some making game saving catches crashing into the ivy-covered outfield walls. Uncle Charlie for president! What a great venue to be attending, and the game hasn't started yet. I was blessed to see from the third base line where we were sitting, a bunch of future Hall of Famers. For the Dodgers in the starting lineup there was Gil Hodges, Maury Wills, Jim Gilliam, Wally Moon, Tommy Davis, Frank Howard, John Roseboro, Roger Craig, and Duke Snider. Sandy Kofax pitched the last inning of a 13-inning nail biter and got the win over the Cubs 4-3. The Cubs featured several stars as well, Frank Thomas, Don Zimmer, Ron Santo, Jerry Kindall, and Mr. Cub, "Let's play one more", Ernie Banks. They had recently acquired Richie Ashburn from the Phillies, whose autograph was on my birthday glove. During the game there were home runs by Ron Santo (2), Frank Thomas, and Wally Moon.

I sat next to Uncle Charlie during every pro ball game he took me to see. He was such an astute baseball fan. He would ask me what I would do in a particular situation during the game, "Would you bunt him down?" or "Think he will steal on the next pitch?" He was always in the game. He was my "road" dad, since Daddy had to work and take care of the milking chores. My daddy sacrificed a lot for me to go on those Bramwell vacations. I tried each day on the farm to do my best to make it up to him. August 18, 1960, was a day to remember!

On Friday night, the San Francisco Giants arrived for a series with the Cubs. The scheduling of Uncle Charlie was impeccable! Dodgers on Thursday, Giants on Friday. We always got to the park early to watch batting practice and infield. I was taking it all in. To sit back and get to see such stars as Mike McCormick, Joey Amalfitano, Don Blasingame, Orlando Cepeda, Filipe Alou, and of course one of my favorite center fielders, the "Say Hey Kid", Willie Mays. During

## The Loser's Ball

the bottom of one of the innings, a Cub hitter drove a fly ball that looked like it may go over Willie's head in center. He caught up to it and made his famous "basket" catch for the third out. The Cub fans got on their feet and applauded Willie as he ran in from centerfield. That was exactly what I came to see, legends at work! Unfortunately, the Cubs were victims of their second home loss in a row, this day to the Giants by a score of 2-1. The memories that were made with my cousins that week were priceless. I truly believe that times together like that were life altering moments for me.

Once we had returned to Tennessee to reality on the farm, I started my next level of preparation for the upcoming football season at MJHS. I got another job with our neighbor, Mr. Claude Harris, a beef cattle farmer, who needed some extra help cutting and getting up hay as well as cleaning out his cattle barns. His farm was a mile from the back side of our farm. I chose to run to work there and back. He offered me his truck several times, but understood that I was getting in shape for football.

It was somewhat of a shock to find out that we now had a new football coach. Coach Hibbitt had stepped down as head coach, but still remained as our science teacher. Coach Patton stayed on as our assistant coach, business education teacher, and head coach of the girls basketball team. Our new coach was John Lee Woodall from Lebanon. I knew things were looking up for the Bears when we defeated Lebanon in a pre-season scrimmage game. Many of my American Legion baseball team members played football for Lebanon. This was encouraging.

In another practice session, we had a visitor to show up in pads to help us out. He was Nealon Agee, a former Mt. Juliet football player that was graduating from Tennessee Tech. Unfortunately, in a pile up after a play from scrimmage, he suffered a broken leg. Everybody felt bad for him because he had gotten hurt. All of us apologized, hoping that he would realize it was not intentional. We never heard the last of that incident, however.

I was still looking for a car to buy with the money I was saving, so I had to borrow the family car to visit a couple of girlfriends down toward Mt. Juliet. Daddy had bought a 1958 solid blue four door car with no chrome, and with ugly tail lights. It had to be the plainest looking car that was ever made by Chevrolet. I tried to talk him into buying a 1957, which was a classic car model for Chevy, but he liked the cheaper deal better. If I wanted to drive anywhere, I had to travel around in "old blue" until I could get my own car later. I may have had a total of 5 dates with a couple of sophomore young ladies before Thanksgiving that fall. They were great girls, but the love bug just didn't bite. I have to admit that they were probably not too impressed anyway, and that the loss to them was most definitely not more than they could bear. Looks like that I am going to be able to go through another Christmas without having to buy a present for a girlfriend.

The 1960 football season ended with our team winning seven games and losing only three. It was Mt. Juliet's first winning season in nearly 20 years. This time we even beat Hendersonville instead of ending in another tie. There was enough motivation for each of us, especially the Glade boys, to work as hard as we could to make sure that we were ready for our final season.

During the Thanksgiving holidays, I finished stripping my tobacco and got it ready to take to the tobacco sales floor at Hartsville. When school had opened that year, we had a new guy from Donelson to transfer to Mt. Juliet. His name was Hatton Wright. He was a quarterback, but had to sit out a year to be eligible to play football for us next season. He was able to practice with us and became one of my best friends. It wasn't long before he was dating Hildred, one of the Davis twins. They were often seen together at school and at many other occasions. It was a real deal that they were getting serious about each other.

In the meantime, naturally, I am still the "Dutch" boy without hope, until my cousin, Carol, who was one of the girls basketball team managers, told me that her friend, Brenda Graves, confided in her, telling Carol that she "liked" me, and wish she could spend more time with me. Now wait! This is the same basketball girl that ran me off from the bleachers my freshman year. I guess I was happy that it just took two years for her to come to her senses! I thanked

Carol, but after having been scorned once, I was a little hesitant about touching the hot stove again.

Weeks later, Hatton told me on a Thursday morning at school, that he was taking Hildred to a school club meeting that night, and was going to pick up Brenda at her house to ride with them. He suggested, since I was going to the same meeting, that I drive my car and park in front of Brenda's house and all four ride together. Hildred also played basketball with Brenda. I should have known that there was a master plan in operation to put me and Brenda together in the back seat of Hatton's car that night. Further evidence of the apparent conspiracy was confirmed when Brenda got in the car and spoke to me showing no surprise at all that I was sitting in the back seat. She had to be in on it! Devious minds have no limit!

After the meeting the four of us drove west, down Highway 70, and sat at a table in Lee's Restaurant, a getaway for most of the kids back then. It had to be the best date that I could ever imagine. The four of us sat and drank water, never ordering anything to eat, and talked for over two hours. Brenda was low maintenance! My kind of girl. The funny thing about this was that the Fox had never devised a way to get into the hen house. He was lured into the hen house by a carefully conceived and successful trap. I was further convinced that Brenda was on a higher plane now than she was when I walked away from that Loser's Ball send-off two years ago that morning in the gym.

I had forgotten to mention to them that evening that I would not be in school the next day. I basically skipped school to take my tobacco crop to the sales floor in Hartsville to be sold, hanging around for my check to be printed, and didn't go back to school. On Monday, Hatton told me that Brenda was more than concerned about my absence. She asked him all day Friday, "Where is he? Is he mad at something I said?" or "Do you think I ran him off again?" Hatton said she quizzed him all day. When I found out about her concerns, I went straight to Brenda and apologized for not telling her that I would not be at school the next day. I could have told her that since I was a successful agricultural business man, I had to attend a financial meeting in Hartsville. But, I just told her that I skipped school to sell my tobacco crop! From that point on, we were hooked! It took 16 years, but I bought my first Christmas present for a girlfriend in December, 1960. I repeated it for the next 61 years!

# CHAPTER 10

*"Nothing in the world can take the place of persistence. Talent will not. Nothing is more common than unsuccessful men with talent. Genius will not. Unrewarded genius is almost a proverb. Education will not. The world is full of educated derelicts. Persistence, determination, and hard work make the difference."*
President Calvin Coolidge.

During the winning football season, I had badgered and shamed Coach Patton into giving up on his anti-social rule of his basketball girls not being permitted to talk to their boyfriends. I once said to him, "Coach Patton, I think your rule should apply to you not talking to your wife during basketball season. After all, you need to stay focused yourself." He evidently got the point. I would always meet the basketball bus at school on away games to take Brenda home. Her mother thought that was a great idea since Pap, Brenda's dad, who was a traveling salesman, was on the road during the week selling Stephens clothes, and Nannie appreciated not having to pick up Brenda at the school late at night.

Post 15 had a new manager in 1961, Mr. Edwin Grandstaff. I was excited to begin my final season of American Legion ball in Lebanon with Post 15. We did not expect it at the beginning of the season, but many baseball fans and sports writers would later comment at the end of our season that the 1960 and 61 teams were probably the best teams ever to play Legion ball in Lebanon. Our pitching/ catching staff was back, consisting of Mike Gannaway, Charles Dedman, Bob Jernigan, and Pat Martin as pitchers, and catchers, Charles Kolbe and Jimmy Jewell. Mike later got a baseball scholarship to pitch for Georgia Tech. Other players on our team played college ball at several other schools. Handbills were printed and hung in stores promoting our next games. I still have a copy of one for our home game with Shelbyville, on August 5, 1961.

The Lebanon Democrat sports staff followed us on away games and gave us a lot of coverage in the press. This was something that was new to me. After all of the hard work and effort put into my game, I felt that now I was as prepared as I could be, especially being a team member on this exciting team of outstanding baseball players. Last year we had won the Middle Tennessee Championship, and were now hoping again for a state title. This year I was our lead-off hitter, hitting two first-pitch home runs in the recent tournament against Clarksville and Springfield. Those wins put us in the tournament championship game against Columbia.

Columbia, along with my friends, Hal and Region, had beaten us earlier in the year. The rematch would be played on a Sunday afternoon in Columbia, and broadcasted over the Lebanon radio station, WCOR. It would be the station's first live broadcast of a baseball game. The Glade was playing a home game the same Sunday afternoon. Those who chose to not attend our game in Columbia, sat in the stands at the Glade game with their radios turned up full blast listening to the broadcast.

Ms. Ellen Schlink, who wrote articles for the Democrat several years later in her "My Hometown" column, told the story of her ride with Mrs. Edwin Grandstaff, our manager's wife, hurrying to arrive before the first pitch was thrown "to be sure not to miss Bobby Lannom's first pitch home run". She made it in time to see me hit a lead-off full-count fast ball over the right field fence to give us a 1-0 lead. The memory of that moment is really lost in the situation going on at the time. Region Peebles, my host at the Cardinal try-out camp earlier, was the starting Columbia pitcher. I can still see him following me around the bases staring at me with disdain again. Our eyes met after touching each base. As I approached third base, he finally yelled to me, "You did it again!" I just smiled as I touched third and headed home. What a moment!

Mike Gannaway went on to be the winning pitcher, in our victory to win the Mid-State Legion Championship on David Grandstaff's single to beat Columbia 2-1. I was told that the Glade fans attending the home game stood and applauded at the end of our game. After the game we shook hands with our buds at Columbia, a very talented team made up of super athletes. Region and I met near the mound. He said, "You had to do it to me again!" I replied, "And, you threw it down the middle again!" I never saw Region after that game, but learned of his going to Alabama to play football for Bear Bryant. Region never played there, choosing to return to Columbia. Ironically, my friend Tommy and Region became close friends later and played a lot of golf together. Hal went on to become a star Tennessee Volunteer quarterback. I had now played on two great teams with three baseball championships.

Our next games were to be played in Memphis in the state tournament on August, 29th, to determine the state championship. We lost two games to Chattanooga and Memphis Pepsi. I hit one home run there in our last loss to end my Legion career. Memphis Pepsi won the state championship. They had the same players as Christian Brothers High School's state championship team. Now I have the rest of the summer to play with the Glade and attend FFA Camp.

Our FFA chapter was winning most of the district contests. I was fortunate to be elected our chapter and District President, which meant a new FFA jacket. Mr. Coley was busier than ever before, preparing to take his first bunch of chapter officers to the 1961 reopening of Camp Clements, our state FFA leadership camp, near Sparta, Tennessee. It was now under the leadership of our new State FFA Advisor, Mr. Kenneth Mitchell from Dickson.

I know I say this often, and with grateful thanks, but my life has become intertwined with so many fantastic men, women, and friends who supported me and guided my journey throughout my entire life. It continues to happen today. Success in sports and throughout life is a group project. I hope all young athletes learn this principle early. Select the group leader first, whose address is; Only One Way, Heaven, Universe, with zip code, No. 1. Surround yourself with men and women who definitely know more than you do, listen intently to them, trust and obey your God, follow His precepts, become a Christian, and treat others like you would like to be treated. You will be qualified with confidence to proudly and humbly quote 2 Timothy 4:7-8. Kenneth Mitchell was to be no exception as another role model for me.

Four Glade boys, Tommy, Eddie, Butch, and I were four of the six Mt. Juliet chapter officers to attend Camp Clements FFA Leadership Camp that summer. I was fortunate to get elected camp Vice-President. A friend from Humboldt, Tennessee, Ralph Barnett, was also elected to the camp officer team. Our paths would cross several years later in a significant way. It never ends.

My final season of Legion ball and playing with the Glade went great. My batting average for the 1961 Legion season was .431. I pitched again for the Glade, getting a few wins. Tommy and I turned a few double plays and hit well for the Glade. Tuckers Cross Roads, consisting of many Legion players and former Lebanon Babe Ruth stars, won the Cumberland Valley League Championship over the Glade that year. I don't have room in this book to tell the many stories about playing with the Glade men's team. The stories of games at Carthage, Hartsville, and Sykes are priceless. Yes, we won a few fights as well!

However, I will tell about a championship game that happened while playing at Sykes that ended in a strange way. After running off the cows, the game began. It was being played in a cow pasture with a grass infield with bases staked down to keep them in place. Foul lines were so crooked that they appeared to be lined off by the town drunk. Strictly bush league if you will. It was in the bottom of the ninth with the Glade leading 6-5. Sykes had runners on second and third with two outs. A fly ball was hit to our left fielder, Robert

Milton Lane. All he had to do was to catch the third out, game over, the Glade wins the league championship. As he ran in to make the catch he stepped in a fresh juicy cow pile, slipped and went to the ground sitting in the middle of the cow pile as the ball landed behind him with both runs scoring. The Glade loses 7-6. That is my first and only cow pile Loser's Ball championship loss.

There are advantages and disadvantages of car ownership and having a driver's license. Brenda had a curfew and had to be home by 11:00 pm. Daddy didn't have but one time for me to be home, since I had to meet him at the milk barn each morning at 4:30 am. He suggested that I use good common sense and get home the same day I left! The catch was, even after I bought my own car, I had to park it beside our house and walk through a large field, a section of woods, and a barn lot in pitch darkness or moonlight to get to Mama Pearl's house. Bummer!

I have endured the following: outrun Bill Fennessey's bull, scared to death when I walked past the barn where I woke up our mule who let out a blood curdling loud snort and wheeze that rattled the rafters, stepped too close to one of my old sows asleep in the high grass next to the path to the lot gate, then hear her run and snort like Godzilla was after her. During another nightly walk, I wasn't aware that Daddy had backed ole Fergie, our old tractor, in an open shed. As I passed the barn, I looked back seeing old Fergie parked there with headlights glowing in the moonlight that looked like an armored monster ready to run after me. It was just all part of life on the farm. It humbles you and keeps you on your toes.

Uncle Charlie and the Bramwells were preparing to get on the road again, and as usual, I was invited be a part of their summer trip. This vacation trip would take us to Washington, DC. Again, we all crammed into the Bramwell family car loaded with six of us and plenty of roadside table meals in the trunk. We saw all the sights in Washington including the Lincoln and Jefferson Memorials, the Smithsonian, toured the capitol, and drove around the White House. We even climbed up the steps to the top of the Washington

Monument. I had taken a wad of money to buy souvenirs for the Lannom family. Uncle Charlie offered to keep my money and give it to me as I needed it, but I was "old enough" to take care of it. After visiting the Smithsonian and sliding down the handrails on the south entrance, we loaded up in the car and headed back to the motel. When we arrived, I discovered that my wallet was missing. I had evidently lost it sliding down the handrails earlier. Uncle Charlie just handed me some money and said when I need some more let him know. He never said anything negative to me about the incident.

Two weeks after we had gotten back to Tennessee, I received a package in the mail from the Smithsonian Institute in Washington, containing my wallet and all my personal items in it with the exception of my money. Lesson learned.

In Washington, Uncle Charlie as usual, had gotten tickets to see a major league baseball game, this time between the Washington Senators and the New York Yankees, on July 18, 1961. It was another dream come true. The Senators featured stars, Harmon Killebrew and Marv Throneberry. I watched the Yankees, with legendary players such as Tony Kubek, Clete Boyer, Bobby Richardson, Mickey Mantle, Roger Maris, Moose Skowron, Ellston Howard, Yogi Berra, and Whitey Ford. The Yankees won the game 5-3 on their way that year to winning back-to-back World Series in 1961 and 1962. That was the same year, 1961, that Roger Maris hit 61 home runs to break Babe Ruth's season record of hitting 60 on September 30, 1927. Again, I was afforded a great opportunity and so thankful to sit in the stands and witness that major league baseball game during the same year of the Mantle/Maris home run dual and the season's success of the Yankees. I did somewhat regret that I wasn't in the gang of youngsters seeking autographs that day, but I just chose to take it all in and record the memories.

In an interview with the great Branch Rickey, who was the part owner and general manager of the Brooklyn Dodgers from 1942-1950, and responsible for signing Jackie Robinson, the first black player in the majors, he was asked, "Mr. Rickey, can you name your

*Not a lot of nice glossy photos were taken during my early playing days. I apologize that this is the only photo I have of our back-to-back Mid-State Champions Post 15 Lebanon American Legion team of 1960 and 1961. My hope of playing for the Vols was based on just two years of Babe Ruth and two of Legion ball. I had to cram a lot of success in those two years, and still not know if I could realize my dream. I am on the first row, second from the right.*

*1961-62 Mt. Juliet FFA chapter officers at Camp Clements FFA Leadership Camp. Left to right: Tommy Knowles, Bob Lannom, Mike Hedgepath, Johnny (Butch) Lawson, Mackie McClusky, and Eddie Foster. Four of us were from the Glade. Mike and Mackie were from Mt. Juliet. All of us but Butch played football.*

Bellevue, or Antioch. We now had a good chance to become a strong contender, and to get an opportunity to play for a championship.

Some anonymous writer, when talking about teamwork, said, *"None of us are as strong as all of us."*

To emphasize the importance and significance of teamwork there was a story told of a mule pulling contest held at the 1897 Nevada State Fair. The first-place winning team pulled 14,000 lbs. The second-place team pulled 13,000 lbs. Someone had an idea to hook the two teams up to the sled and see how much they could pull together. Of course, the estimates of the combined team pull were around 27,000 lbs. Every observer was shocked when the dual team pulled 35,000 lbs. That was a 30 % increase over the total of the individual teams. That's the power of teamwork.

Coach Agee ran us till we dropped. His practices were designed to put us in the best physical shape we could be in to compete for a possible championship. After waiting for three years, those of us who had withstood the torture of countless Loser's Balls, felt that it was about time for redemption. Instead of our school colors that were black and gold, we felt they should have been changed to black and blue our first two years.

We were all about whipped near the close of one tough practice when Coach Agee yelled out, "Okay, after the next blood we will call it a day." My friend and fullback, Pat, had a nose that was susceptible to bleeding. He hid behind me while we were lined up for a one-on-one blocking drill and punched himself in the nose. He kept it hidden until he charged into Wayne Wright our left guard. Pat came up off of the ground with blood streaming from his nose. Coach Agee took a look and blew his whistle, "Good practice everybody! Get your shower, do it again tomorrow!" Pat was our sacrificial lamb that day.

Coach Agee was not as mean as you may think because of our practices. He was exactly what and who we needed. We had a lot of talent on that team. We just needed someone to take charge of raw talent and blend it into a team, a football team that had confidence and grit to outlast our opponents physically, and never give up regardless of the score. As the date for our first game drew near, I felt like it was going to be a much better finish for us.

The previous state ratings that came out at the beginning of the year already had shown the higher rankings we had attained since our 7-3 season last year. Instead of like our first two years going without a win and being ranked 212 out of 216 Tennessee high school football teams, we moved up at the end of last year to about mid-way in the rankings. I think that we were ranked around 125. Changes were made, and now that the NIL (Nashville Interscholastic League), was divided into classes based on enrollment numbers, we were now playing schools near our size in the Class A Division. We were all glad that the statewide ranking system was abandoned. We were not playing schools anymore like Father Ryan, Glencliff, Madison,

## The Loser's Ball

greatest moment in baseball?" He responded, "I don't think I have come to it yet."

That statement made by this great baseball executive resonates with me and my life. It reminds me of what Coach Lou Holtz said, *"If what you did yesterday looks big, you haven't done anything today."* Whether it is a devastating Loser's Ball or a monumental victory, as soon as they end, they become part of your past. The question is, what are you going to do today, tomorrow, and in the future ahead of you?

I learned to summarize this with this simple statement, "Bloom Where You Are Planted." If you come from the ghetto or a mansion, maybe, even from a small rocky dairy farm in a very rural setting, there is nothing to prevent you from blooming instead of going to weeds. My optimism for the rest of 1961, and on into 1962, may just include my next Branch Rickey moment.

A couple of weeks before practice started at Mt. Juliet in the fall, we were caught by surprise that we would start the season with a new head football coach. His name was Nealon Agee, the former Mt. Juliet star and Tennessee Tech graduate, whose leg we had broken in that pile up last year when he suited up to help us in practice. Pat Hackney warned us that it wasn't going to be a bed of practice roses any more. Coach Woodall's approach had been to not work us as hard as we had expected. We thought a lot of him much as a friend or buddy, but would soon find out that Coach Agee's approach was the complete opposite. I spent the next two weeks prior to the start of practice to be in the best physical shape I could achieve. I ran the cross roads mile runs every day, even after some tough days at work on the farm. I still ran back and forth to Mr. Harris's farm to work.

Daddy told me that even if everybody else was better than me, I could still be in better shape than them because I could control that part. I recently read a quote from Derek Jeter, the legendary shortstop for the Yankees. He said, *"There may be people that have more talent than you, but there's no excuse for anyone to work harder than you do."* Derek and Dad thought alike! Makes sense to me. So, when practice started, oh, was I thankful for that preparation!

# CHAPTER 11

*"Once you know what failure feels like, determination chases success."*
*Kobe Bryant*

We were finally adjusting to our rigid practice schedule. Hatton was doing a great job as our new quarterback. I was happy to see him doing so well since we had become great friends and did a lot of double-dating. Vesta church was only seeing me now on Sunday mornings. I was at Center Chapel church on several Sunday nights and most Wednesday nights with Brenda. I couldn't think of a better place to be. Pap and Nannie treated me just like one of their own. I even managed to go with Pap on a number of coon hunts. He had a pack of great coon hounds that were treated with the best of care. One Saturday night his dogs treed a big old sow coon, who escaped and led us on a chase until 3 am. The next day Brenda told her daddy that if he is going to keep me out that late, my coon hunting days would soon be over.

There were six children in the Graves family. Brenda's oldest sister, Donna, was married to Rusty Ferrell, a Glade boy like me. Rusty and I always reminded Pap that his girls had to go to the Glade to get the best. Her younger sister, Susan, was the same age as my little sister, Lugene. Gilbert was the oldest. He became a Wilson County commissioner serving for 42 years. Mahlon and Eddie were the other two boys who adopted me as their brother. I was in great company, all Christians, who honored their parents and loved their friends.

The next story is what I have chosen to title, "Shoeless Bob."

It was nice to have an increased number of observers gathered at our football practices each afternoon. This was something new that we had never seen happen. The fans, like us, were anxious to hopefully see a winning team. The community obviously sensed a big change in how our practices were going. Coach Agee, (called "Mush") by his friends, but not us, was in total control of putting this team together. He had quickly earned the respect of all of us in only a couple of weeks. Pat, our tough running fullback and I were elected team captains. Pat's brother, Bob, along with Leslie Earhart, were elected co-captains. Coach told me that I would be calling many plays in the huddle, but he would send in plays as well.

Our first game with Blanche, strangely, was on a Monday night at home. The Nashville Banner even went out on a weak limb to pick us to win the Class A championship with improving Hendersonville and Hume-Fogg Tech as contenders.

We won our first game, beating Blanche 13-0. I caught a 19-yard pass from my QB friend Hatton Wright for our first touchdown. I threw an 8-yard pass to my Glade buddy, Eddie Foster for our second TD as we won our opener. We traveled next to Spring Hill where we won, 20-6, our fourth game in a row. We had won our last two games last season, and now two more wins. I scored a couple of touchdown runs and Pat added the final TD on a 1-yard plunge. We needed one more win to tie the school record of five consecutive wins.

We played a tough Hume-Fogg Technical School and inched out a close one, 14-12 to tie the school record. I sustained a concussion late in the first half as we led 14-12. I remember seeing Brenda walking the chain linked fence keeping an eye on me as I tried to shake off my sting. I finally came around after sniffing my fourth ammonia capsule administered by Sonny Hardaway, my classmate and manager/trainer. Coach benched me for a good reason, but I still tried to get him to put me in the close game. Pat's year-older brother, Bob Hackney, sat me down and looked straight at me and

## The Loser's Ball

with a strong convincing confidence said, "Listen, little buddy, as long as I am out there, they ain't gonna score, so sit back and enjoy the game.!" I saw that 6'1 205 defensive end, completely shut down any effort by Hume-Fogg to score around his end. The game ended 14-12, just like Bob said it would.

We suffered our first lost in our next game to a powerful Greenbrier team who got their 14$^{th}$ consecutive win at Greenbrier by a one-sided blowout of 38-0. That was not just a Loser's Ball but a "bean ball". We were completely dominated in that game. They had a tremendous fullback of iconic proportions by the name of Ronnie Walton, who scored three touchdowns plowing behind a line led by guard, Terry Gann. Ironically, as it may seem, I would become close friends with these two guys later.

We traveled next to Westmoreland where Pat had one of his best running games, gaining 110 yards in 10 carries. Westmoreland was undefeated, but succumbed to the Bears that night 13-0. We were now 4-1 and off to one of the best starts in MJHS football history. The next week that followed was unbelievable.

On Monday, we found out that our game with Hendersonville was rescheduled to Thursday night instead of on Friday. It had boiled down to the game of the year between the two teams, the winner, who would more than likely win the Class A championship. At practice on Monday afternoon, sports writers from the Nashville Banner and Tennessean were there to do interviews and make pictures for their coverage that week.

The game was moved to Thursday, to allow other team coaches and players to attend our big game. Although the Banner had earlier picked us to win the title, Hendersonville was now undefeated at 3-0-1, and had been picked an 11-point favorite to beat us. Our loss to Greenbrier had been the difference in the ratings. I was in a dead heat with Hendersonville's running back, Milton Blackford for the league's scoring title. Headline articles, featuring our game, were showing up in the Nashville papers written by Edgar Allen of the Banner and Jimmy Davy in his "Prep Parade" column.

Mt. Juliet had never won a football championship, neither had

Hendersonville. It was just what you wanted in high school football. Everywhere we went that week, we were asked about that big game on Thursday. The Glade supporters got into it as well. After all, there were seven experienced players on our team from the Glade. At the same time, Lebanon was having one of its best years. Three players, former Legion baseball team members, were leading the way. David Grandstaff, who knocked in our winning run against Columbia, was Lebanon's quarterback. His picture along with his two star ends, Bruce Skeen and Henry Harding, both my former legion teammates, appeared in the paper that week.

We had a pep rally on Thursday morning of the game. Coach made sure that we were prepared to say the right things to avoid any negative comments from making Hendersonville bulletin board material. I was told that I would be asked to stand and make a few comments in the pep rally. Beforehand, we had likened ourselves to the coyote and the roadrunner cartoon characters, the wily coyote being the Hendersonville Commandos, and the Bears as the road runner.

After practice on Wednesday, following coach's words of caution, we rehearsed our "team speech." Our principal, Mr. Higgins, finally at the end of the pep rally, asked me to stand and make some remarks. I stood up and yelled out my part of the roadrunner's famous two words in the cartoon as he zipped out of the grasp of the coyote, "Beep Beep!" and the rest of the football team sitting around me stood up and yelled out, "Yeeeeaow!" The student body went nuts! That was the shortest, most motivational, most likely to never be printed or quoted, but long remembered speech I ever gave. Our team was ready to suit up that morning! Little did I know that that speech would be played out on the field Thursday night.

Hendersonville had a new coach, Roy Hall, as well. He was quoted that week saying how fired up his team was and ready to play, just making the game more dramatic for the fans. Coach Agee stayed calm and cool all week, just tending to business on the practice field and shielding us from catch phrase hungry sports writers.

After practice on Tuesday, I checked my football cleats and discovered that there were several loose cleats that I could not tighten up. Sonny tried to fix my shoes but the threads were just about all stripped out. He did the best he could to tighten them up hoping they would stay. During our shorts practice on Wednesday running through our plays, I finished them off. Both of my shoes were junk, torn up! I had maybe two cleats on the heel of one shoe and none on the other. My thought was, why of all times on the season's biggest game of our lives, I tear up my football shoes?

Nobody on the team wore a size 9. I had a small foot, probably about right for a 5'7 155-pound kid. I told coach about it. There were no shoes my size anywhere. Most baseball folks should remember a player of baseball fame, named Shoeless Joe Jackson, who was involved in the 1919 Black Sox Scandal, where he and members of the White Sox "allegedly" decided to throw the World Series against the Cincinnati Reds. Joe once had gone to bat in his sock feet because his shoes hurt his feet and gave him blisters. Thus, his nickname, "Shoeless Joe." It appeared that if I don't find any shoes by Thursday night, I will be "Shoeless Bob."

On Thursday morning with no success while talking to the folks at Jimmy Nokes Sporting Goods in Lebanon, Coach Agee was told by them to call Coach Clifton Tribble at Lebanon High School. The store manager told Coach Agee that the Lebanon coach had often bought several pairs of shoes at a time to keep in stock for his players. Obviously, they had a larger budget than MJHS. Coach Agee made the call. Coach Tribble agreed to take a look to see if he had some shoes that would fit me. I found out around lunch, the day of our game, that Coach Tribble had called Coach Agee back. He had found a new pair of shoes for me. He told Coach Agee that since he and some of his coaches were going to our game that night, he would arrive early enough to get me the shoes. I was literally prepared to be the first high school football player to play an entire game barefooted when we left on the bus for the game that afternoon.

When our team bus arrived at Hendersonville near the visitor dressing room, we were immediately unwelcomed by a crowd of Hendersonville students banging on the side of our bus. One of our team members who didn't play a lot, but was a die-hard Bears player, took over as he had done on a few other occasions not known by the coaches. His name was Johnny Page. Earlier in the school year while Johnny, Pat, and I sat at our assigned chemistry class lab table together, Johnny unwrapped some ingredients for us to experiment with when our chemistry teacher, Ms. Carter, wasn't looking. So Pat and I hooked up the Bunsen burner and Johnny stirred the mix, placing it on the burner to be heated. It wasn't long before the white vapors appeared and everybody in the chemistry lab had tears running down their faces, even Ms. Carter. We had officially and successfully manufactured "Tear Gas" in the lab which caused not only the chemistry class, but the entire Mt. Juliet High School to be evacuated! We were not caught even after displaying the evidence by having the reddest eyes.

Again, I hope the statute of limitations has expired. All I can say is, Johnny to the rescue against the bus bangers. He first rolled a window down and pulled out a can of lighter fluid. He squirted some in his mouth, lit a cigarette lighter in front of the open window and spewed the fluid into the flame and created a human blow torch. Those panic-stricken rowdies scrambled over each other to get away from our bus, never to come near the flame throwing dragon any more. I couldn't believe what had just happened. We were not nervous anymore about the game to be played. That distraction had just removed any game anxieties. In a recent visit to check on my former Coach Agee, I shared this story with him that he never knew had taken place.

I tried to stay focused and not get nervous about the game. I found out when I started out of the dressing room to head to the field, while thinking more about having no shoes than anything else, Pat stopped me and asked, "You gonna wear your jersey backwards?" Yep! Little number in the back, big number in the front. A big thanks to Pat for helping me turn my jersey around. At least my shoulder pads were not on backwards. I tell these stories now that were dark secrets to everyone except our team.

Just about 10 minutes before kick-off, Sonny, our manager, gets

## The Loser's Ball

my attention. It was, as you would say, the stories behind the story of the game itself on that Thursday night years ago.

I am warming up in my "flat" no cleat shoes. He is half way on the field, holding up a new shoe box, while motioning for me to come to the sideline. I quickly put on my new pair of Lebanon HS Blue Devil shoes that just fit, and returned to the field. Then, it finally hit me. Here I am, playing for a school I initially did not go to enroll at, wearing a pair of shoes from a school where I tried to enroll, but couldn't, and the football coach I would have been playing for sitting in the bleachers watching the game. I need help figuring this one out. I was ready for the game to begin, thankfully, so that I could then relax!

Hendersonville was stacked with some quality players that included: Quarterback, Roy (Buddy Davidson), their great running back, Milton Blackford, a tall and speedy receiver, Doyle (Shorty) Durham, center Jimmy Youngblood, and tackle, Chuck Hanebuth. Four of them would later make the Nashville Banner All Class A team at the end of the year. We countered with two great guards, Wayne Wright and Leslie Earhart, tackles, Billy Picket and Mike Hedgepath, with Mackie McCluskey playing a lot. Eddie Foster was our best end and an outstanding athlete. Other good ends included Paul Thomas and sophomore Paul Smith.

The heart of our line was my man, all 5'7, 135 pounds of him, my baseball buddy, Tommy Knowles at center. I considered him the best pound per pound blocker on our team. Tommy did not know what the word "quit" meant. On defense, Pat Hackney was a beast at linebacker. Hilton Hamblen, another Glade boy, was a solid linebacker and as tough as nails. Tommy played corner and I was at safety. We matched up with them very well.

Hendersonville scored first, but missed their extra point try, to lead us 6-0 after one quarter. With 3:12 left in the second quarter, I took a pitch from Hatton and headed around left end from the 12-yard line. All I had to do was follow "Raid", Doyle Sanders, our left halfback into the end zone to tie the game. Doyle was another Glade boy who actually scrape-blocked the defensive end and made a final block to free me to score. I remember holding on to Raid's jersey in front of me as I crossed the goal line. Pat bulled into the end zone to score the extra point. The Bears led 7-6 at the half.

Hendersonville took control throughout the second half and led in every statistical category. They actually ran 36 plays to our 19 in the second half. But...... the game is not about stats, it's about points! I was able to return a punt for 44 yards that set us up in good field position on the Hendersonville 26-yard line. About the only offense we generated in the second half was that short drive which resulted in Pat scoring our only touchdown in the third quarter to put us further ahead by a score of 13-6. Our extra point run failed. Hendersonville scored in the fourth quarter on a four-yard run with 6:32 left in the game to even the score at 13 with a tough extra point run by Blackford.

As we huddled with the receiving team after their score and before the kickoff, we called a straight up the middle run where everybody would block outside. As the kick returner, it was then up to me to find a route or head for the sideline to stop the clock if necessary. I received the kick-off on our 7-yard line and headed up the middle. So far it looked like we may get a good return by heading straight down the field. I then saw a defender coming from my left side that would have tackled me around the 35-yard line. Then out of nowhere I see a number "30" black jersey make a perfect legal block on the defender. It was Tommy. I hurdled over both of them and saw some open space as I cut toward the right sideline. With Milton Blackford chasing me, I managed to out run him as fast as my Blue Devil shoes would carry me to the end-zone for a 93-yard kick-off return, my one and only for the year! We made our extra point with always reliable Pat Hackney barreling through goal-line defenders for our extra point. During the writing of this book, we lost our great friend and teammate, Pat Hackney to Covid complications and pneumonia. After his funeral, I presented a framed picture of Pat to his wife, Carol, from a Nashville Banner photo of Pat lying a yard past the goal line cradling the ball for that big extra point. There was no better Christian man around than Pat Hackney.

## The Loser's Ball

We now led 20-13. Hendersonville's quarterback, Buddy Davidson led an 80-yard 16-play drive to score on a 33-yard pass to Shorty Durham. Pat and Hilton headed up a strong defense to stop Milton Blackford short of the goal line denying them the extra point to give the Bears a thrilling 20-19 victory. What a great win!

Many of the 2000 plus fans in attendance rushed the field after the game. Most of them were obviously happy MJHS fans. In an instant, Mike Hedgepath picked me up and put me on his shoulders. I felt very uncomfortable there and never really believed in any one individual getting credit for a team victory. Before I got him to put me down, Brenda ran over to us, and I bent down and kissed her. She went "Woooooh, what's that in your mouth?" I then realized that I had kissed her with my mouth piece still in.

Daddy told me that night at the house as we talked about the big win and about his attempt to pay for my shoes. He said that he had held out a $50 dollar bill to pay Coach Tribble for the shoes. Coach Tribble, a classy man and my favorite that night, just pushed Daddy's hand away and said, "Mr. Lannom, you don't owe me a thing. It was worth it just to watch Bobby tonight, running in those Lebanon Blue Devil shoes." What a great sport!

We closed out the season by winning our remaining four games which resulted in Mt. Juliet High School's first football championship, as the 1961 Nashville NIL Class A Champions. I almost ran Brenda off on Homecoming night when as captain, I crowned the Homecoming Queen at the half with a "too long of a kiss" which broke the unofficial MJHS time record, but that is another story, best forgotten! All was forgiven, but it took a lot of apologies and more expensive Christmas presents.

We were really banged up after our last game with Joelton. Pat didn't play that game because he had previously broken his leg and would not play anymore. I received three cracked ribs during the Joelton game. Other starters were suffering some non-playing injuries as well. I was proud of our Glade boys that night. Doyle, (Raid), and I were joined in the backfield by Ray Underwood, who later became a great back for Mt. Juliet. All three of us were from the Glade.

Actually, by officially having adopted Hatton as a Glade boy, our entire backfield was the Glade that night.

Coach Agee met with us on the following Monday afternoon before cleaning out our lockers. He congratulated all of us on our accomplishments, also informing us that Leslie, Bob, Pat, and I were selected to the Nashville Banner All Class A Team. He said that we were honored to have been selected to play in the Watertown Lions Bowl. He explained to us that he was going to leave the decision to play in that bowl up to a vote by the team. He realized that many of us would not be able to play. Coach made it clear that it was our decision. I remember the statement made by our (tongue in cheek), never say much tackle, Mike Hedgepath. Mike said that he felt that we had achieved our goal in winning the championship, and that he would like to go out a winner and be remembered for the hard work and never giving up on our goal the last four years. He said, "My vote is not to play in that bowl. If all of us can't play, then none of us should play." It was a unanimous vote!

I believe that vote was a strong sign of team commitment and evidence of the bond we had formed over the years. We had endured many Loser's Balls to get to this point. I can't give you many details about those 22 losses we suffered, but I can remember most details about those 9 wins in 1961. Both losses and wins were worth every moment.

Hendersonville was selected in our place and went on to win the Lion's Bowl game. Their banner now hangs on the wall of their football dressing room. I have seen it there many times. I still have the picture of Pat and me as captains, accepting our championship trophies on behalf of our great team, with the other three division winners at the 18th Annual Nashville Banner Banquet of Champions on December 14, 1961, at the Maxwell House Hotel in Nashville. The guest speaker, by the way, just happened to be Ted Williams, Boston Red Sox Hall of Famer. I still have his autographed picture. Just a little more icing on my cake! Four years and four championships! Life is good!

# The Loser's Ball

*"But those who wait on the Lord shall renew their strength; they shall mount up with wings like eagles, they shall run and not be weary; they shall walk and not faint."*

Isaiah 40:31

*"Today, I will do what others won't, so that tomorrow I will do what others can't."*

Jerry Rice

I really admired Helen Keller. This Alabama girl lost her sight and hearing after a bout of illness when she was only 19 months old. At age seven, Anne Sullivan taught her reading and writing. She became the first deaf-blind person in the United States to earn a Bachelor of Science degree. She was a strong and heroic activist for those with vision and hearing losses, a prolific author who wrote 14 books, and hundreds of speeches and essays. The story of her life was the basis for the movie by William Gibson, The Miracle Worker. Thank you, Wikipedia. What I remember most and must include in this book is one of her quotes which is one of my favorites:

*"I am only one; but still I am one.*
*I cannot do everything,*
*but I can do something.*
*I will not refuse to do*
*the something I can do."*

So many folks put their lives on hold, decimated by self-pity, and frozen in the time zone of watching others with less, accomplish much, much more than those who settle for the absences of either victory or defeat. The bottom of the ninth comes to all of us soon enough in our short lives on earth. Your victories or defeats don't come until the game is played. Go down swinging or round third coming home with a walk off homer. At least, do your "something!"

*This picture appeared in the Nashville Banner sports section prior to our big game with Hendersonville for the league championship. Coach Nealon Agee, his first year as MJHS head football coach, had us prepared. Left to right: Fullback, Doyle (Raid) Sanders, Hatton Wright our quarterback, me, tailback, Pat Hackney, linebacker and running back, Bob Hackney, defensive end.*

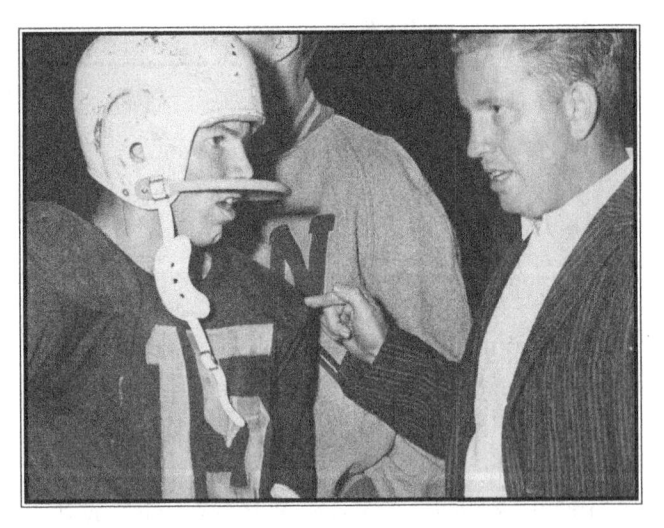

*After we scored the go-ahead touchdown, Coach Agee is telling me the play to call to score the extra point. Back then, most extra points were running plays. Kicking them was not in style yet. Pat Hackney bulled into the endzone for the game-winning extra point.*

Brenda was an outstanding basketball player. She played as a guard during the time when the girl's teams were made up of three forwards and three guards, better known as the days of girls "Three on Three". She was All-District and a member of the 1962 District Championship team. We even wore the same number 15 on our uniforms. We were fortunate to be selected as "Most Athletic" by our classmates.

All District guard for the Bears, Brenda Graves. Her coach, Mr. Patton, said that it took a very good forward to score on Brenda. Her quickness and agility were credible assets in crucial game situations. I loved to watch number 15 play her game.

# Chapter 12

*"It's not your aptitude, but your attitude, that determines your altitude."*
Former Tennessee State University
football coach, John Merritt.

    During the Christmas Holidays, all of the Lannom family drove to Nashville to enjoy the season break and share Christmas with the Bramwells. Naturally the subject came up about baseball and my options. I had been offered a scholarship to play baseball at Murray State University in Kentucky, as well as an opportunity to play football at Middle Tennessee State in Murfreesboro, just 15 miles from our house. Uncle Charlie and Daddy already knew the answer when they asked me which option I was going to choose? My answer was, "Neither, I want to play baseball at Tennessee."

    The discussion continued for a short time about the pros and cons, but mostly about me being sure of knowing that I was giving up a lot to take a big chance on playing at UT. Daddy had already told me that the decision was up to me and not to be worrying about the cost. He was happy about my decision. I felt better since I could contribute a chunk of my farm money to make it easier on him and Mama.

    Uncle Charlie stopped the conversation and said, "I believe the decision has been made. It's time for me to go to work on this." He

## The Loser's Ball

told me to get my American Legion baseball statistics together from last season and to let him know when I have them. It would include numbers like batting average, RBIs, home runs, runs scored, stolen bases, etc. He emphasized that I needed to call him immediately when I got the information. A couple of days after New Year's Day, I let him know that I gotten my stats from our manager, Mr. Grandstaff.

He called me back later that day and told me to be at his house the next morning. I arrived at the familiar Linden Avenue address and met with Uncle Charlie. He said, "Come on, let's go. We are going for a drive." The last time I did this we ended up at Coach Jim Turner's house looking at baseball memorabilia of the Yankees.

We arrived at the home of one of Uncle Charlie's friends by the name of Mr. Kirby O. Primm. Mr. Primm was on the Nashville city council with my uncle and was Vice President of Third National Bank. After all the greetings and introductions, we sat down as Uncle Charlie handed my sheet of paper with my baseball stats to Mr. Primm. I was thinking at the time that this man must be important enough as a council member and bank executive to be of help with my chances of going to Tennessee. After taking a few minutes to look over my stats, Mr. Primm was very complimentary and told me that he was glad that I had made the decision to attend Tennessee.

He told me that the Vols were getting a new baseball coach for next season, but he was not aware of who it was at the time. He seemed to know more about Tennessee than the average council member or banker in Nashville.

"I think I can be of some help, Bobby." he said. "Let me keep this copy of your stats so that I can include them with a letter to the university athletic department, asking them to take a look at you when you get on campus this fall."

He went on to add, "I don't know if Charlie told you or not, but I serve on the University of Tennessee Board of Trustees." I almost fell off the couch! Uncle Charlie knew how to pick the right one.

Mr. Primm sent Uncle Charlie a carbon copy of the letter that was sent to Tennessee, dated, January 5, 1962. My uncle later gave me that copy which has remained as one of my "prizes" for over 63 years! Brenda had placed it along with other letters and documents in marked envelopes and stored them securely for these many years, even with all of our moves over time. The copy of that letter appears in the picture section of this book.

I finally found a used car that I purchased for $300 from one of Daddy's friends. It was a slick looking two-door 1953 solid green Chevy with nice sounding glass packs exhaust system. It was loud enough for one of Brenda's neighbors to hear me coming down the road headed for Brenda's house. She would often call and tell her that Bobby was on his way.

By February, I had practiced my FFA speech so many times while milking that my cows knew it as well as I did. I won the FFA District public speaking contest and was on my way to compete in the regional, where the winner would later get to compete in the state finals at the state FFA convention. Our parliamentary procedure team had already won the district and regional contests, and was headed to the state convention in Knoxville, to compete for the state championship. I wish that I had taken some of my cows with me to the regional speaking contest. They would have come in handy when about two thirds through my speech, my mind went blank for about ten seconds when I couldn't remember the next lines. My chance to compete for the state FFA public speaking championship vanished that evening with my lost to the eventual state winner.

Mr. Coley had devoted a lot of time grooming me to run for a state FFA officer position. I spent a lot of hours in my preparation to get ready for the selection process prior to the 1962 State FFA Convention. I took a bus to Knoxville a couple of days early to go through the interview process of becoming one of eight fortunate young men out of over 20 applicants to be selected for the Tennessee Association 1962-63 state officer team. We would not know the results until they were announced the last hour of the convention on Wednesday, before it adjourned.

My first task was to serve as our chapter president and compete to win the State Parliamentary Procedure contest against the winners of East and West Tennessee. My cousin, Johnny Lawson, from

Vesta, served as our Parli-Pro team Vice-President. I was so proud of "Butch". He had a hard life growing up and to see him perform on stage in front of 2,000 FFA members at the state contest just gave me chill bumps. He never missed a beat in the competition. Buddy Henry, "Nick", couldn't have done better as Secretary. Mike Hedgepath, our "meek, ha!" tackle, spoke his part as our Sentinel with perfection. Eddie Foster and Mackie McCluskey were perfect in their roles as Treasurer, and Reporter. I was so proud to have been a part of that Parliamentary Procedure team, especially with three boys from the Glade, as we stood on stage receiving our State Champions plaque for Mt. Juliet High School FFA.

We neared the always dramatic end of the last session of the state convention on Wednesday, when the new state officer team would be announced. It still remains one of the most thrilling moments at the convention. To see so many talented young people holding their breaths for their name to be called is exciting. The new state officer names were called out with all of the candidates standing together in the rear of the convention auditorium.

One by one each office and new officer names were called out. First the Sentinel, Larry Bates, Springfield, then the Treasurer, Jimmy Rogers, Benton, followed by the Reporter, Dick Sims, Sparta. The name, Alfred Davis from Loudon, was announced as Secretary. As each name was called, the new officers, upon hearing their names, literally ran to the stage to join their team members. The list was getting shorter. There were only four more names to be called. At least 15 of us were still waiting.

East Tennessee Vice-President was next. My friend, Bill Melton ran to the stage when his name was called. The new West Tennessee Vice-President's name was called. Edgar Lee Paschal took off flying to join the others on stage. I am still standing and waiting. The suspense was incredible. With only two names left to call, I heard the name of the new Middle Tennessee Vice President called; Bobby Lannom, from the Mt. Juliet chapter. I broke the convention land speed record to join my new team on stage. The last name to be called was our President, Ronnie Fielder, from the Dickson chapter.

My last goal in the FFA had been achieved. Out of 14,000 Tennessee FFA members, I was one of eight state FFA officers selected for 1962-63. This time, however, my new jacket was bought by the Tennessee Association FFA. What a way to end the school year and to await our graduation day. Mr. Coley was all smiles on the way home. I paused to think while returning back to the Glade about those nights at my first Creed contest, the State FFA convention in Memphis, when Mr. Coley and I had sat up late planning my future in the FFA. I was on a journey with a foundation of knowledge that in order to be successful in life, sports, or business, winning is accomplished when you surround yourself with remarkably talented and supportive team members. I would not be at this point in my life today were it not for the support of my family and men and women like Bill Coley, Charlie Bramwell, Kirby Primm, Billy Thornton, Van Dobson, Jim Lancaster, Nealon Agee, Kathryn McCrary, Camelia Sanders, Charles Davis, Nell Vaughter, Nell Gann, Claude Harris, Brenda Lannom, my parents, grandparents, family, ministers, friends, teammates, the list goes on and on.

Before I started writing this book, I took the time to sit down and compiled a list of names who played large rolls in my life. It was not a list of acquaintances, but of real people who were involved in supporting me and encouraging me to be the best I could be. I still have that list. There are nearly 400 names on it. By the way, I keep adding names to that list. It is unbelievable when you stop and identify names of your "Big Team" who made a difference in your life. I challenge you to do the same. They were truly the folks that the late and great Zig Ziglar spoke of when he said in his book, *See You At The Top*, "You can get anything you want out of life, if you help enough other people get what they want." So many have helped me get what I wanted out of life. I have tried to live that out in my life by helping others to get what they want.

I can never out give God, nor those who have contributed to my ability to deal with Loser's Balls and to enjoy blessed success. If I have learned anything about the privilege of being on championship teams thus far, it is the importance of teams in your drive for success. John

Maxwell, leadership author, speaker, and founder of his nationally known, John Maxwell Team, said, "TeamWork makes the Dream Work."

Prior to graduation, Mr. Coley had gotten in touch with our local Farm Bureau office in Lebanon, about a potential agriculture scholarship for me. I completed an application to be mailed to the University of Tennessee. I contacted Mr. Jim Lancaster, our family friend and insurance agent and asked him if I needed to do anything more. On March 27, 1962, Mr. Lancaster wrote a letter on my behalf to Webster Pendergrass, the Dean of the UT College of Agriculture. I received a $500 Jesse Jones Agriculture scholarship as a result of another supporter who took the time to help me.

I had also received a response from the new head baseball coach at Tennessee, Coach Bill Wright. He acknowledged the letter forwarded to him from Mr. Primm and told me to meet with him as soon as I arrived on campus prior to the start of classes in the fall. I wrote him back thanking him and looked forward to meeting with him.

There were just two things to work on now, graduation, and the "Deal" Brenda wants to make with me before graduation. There was no doubt that we were truly in love with each other. Everything seems to be headed in the right direction. I have received two confirmations, Brenda and I will get married, sometime, and I have been accepted by the University of Tennessee to attend there in the fall. I was indeed blessed to have Brenda by my side. In spite of our youth and deep love for each other, we thought things out in a mature way. We both knew that marriage would be sometime in the near future.

I wanted Brenda to attend David Lipscomb University as she had planned, but that discussion ended when she told me she had a "deal" to make with me. She said the deal was that she did not want to attend college, but, go to work, save her money, get married, and put me through college. Then she added, "If you agree to take care of me the rest of my life." Before we graduated from high school, we had it all worked out. Who was I to refuse a deal like that?

After graduation, Brenda went to work for the Donelson Clinic in Donelson, Tennessee, just a few miles from her home. She was a fantastic business honor student in school and perfect for her new job in accounting, payroll, and general business operations at the medical clinic. I worked for Mr. Harris, on our farm tending to my cow herd and raising my tobacco crop plus Sunday baseball with the Glade. Each of us saved every penny we made for our big day in the future.

I had to leave my little car at home since freshmen were not permitted to have cars on the UT campus back then. I didn't like the rule, but I had to conform. Daddy drove me to Knoxville to help find me a place to stay. We decided that the dorms were too expensive, so we found this little old house with an upstairs apartment to rent. It was located on campus near where the Haslam School of Business is located today. When I got moved in and said my good bye to Daddy, he later remarked that he had a hard time dropping me off, leaving me waving at him as he left.

The next day I visited Coach Wright, the new baseball coach, at his office under Section X of Neyland stadium. He and I hit it off that morning. He also served as an academic counselor for the football team, so he was very helpful in getting me registered for classes as was my ag advisor. He told me that he did not have a scholarship for me since the ones he had when he arrived as the new coach were already filled. He seemed excited to have me and immediately made me a member of the freshman team. Back then, freshmen did not play on the varsity team. We would have another coach helping him and play our own schedule of games. He did say that he could cover the cost of my books for my freshman year. He issued me my practice gear and said to be ready for indoor workouts after classes were underway.

I left a little disappointed but understood the situation I was in. No experience playing high school baseball was now looming as a major bummer in my efforts to earn a scholarship. I was basically a walk-on from nowhere land with no records except a couple of years of Legion ball trying to make the line up for a major Southeastern Conference university baseball team. I had my work cut out for me. Really, this was nothing new. I was experienced in Loser's Balls having many thrown at me since I was 12.

# The Loser's Ball

I had read about a person in some leadership capacity who talked about the ten most powerful two-letter words in the world; "If it is to be, it is up to me!" I cannot fail. I must not fail. Too many people have embraced my dreams and given of themselves to get me here at this point in my life. Okay, Bob, it is now in your hands. Failure is no option! Basically, it means to work your butt off to make your dreams come true.

Serving as a state officer and performing my duties made my first quarter's stay more bearable. Between my FFA duties and baseball, I had to do triple duty, however, in studying to make good grades. My decision to rent that apartment was a big mistake. I had to share a bathroom with two other guys. They were good guys, but their interests were much different from mine. I was being re-educated for sure. I was in love and lonely. Being without Brenda was tough. Every radio station seemed to play "lonely" songs. They were very popular songs like Bobby Vinton singing, "Lonely, I'm Mr. Lonely, ain't got nobody to call my own." Brenda Lee's song just hit the hardest. "All Alone Am I, Ever Since Your Goodbye."

I wrote Brenda a letter every night. She sent me letters daily as well. It was just wearing on both of us. I would hitch-hike home often on weekends and ride a Trailways bus that on the way back stopped at every dinkie bus stop from Lebanon to Knoxville. I would then take a cab to my old house often arriving at two or three in the morning. I managed to stick it out.

I went home one weekend and Daddy helped me load up my tobacco crop and rode with me to Hartsville to sell it. Brenda and I had talked about possibly getting married next year after my first year at school. I later used that tobacco money to buy her engagement and wedding rings. In December, after completing my first quarter at UT, I talked to Pap and Nannie and received their blessings to marry their daughter. Brenda and I got engaged on a cold and snowy Christmas Day. We were both just 18 years old.

After informing Daddy and Mama of my desire to move into the college dorm the next quarter, they both understood and would make it happen. I sat aside some of my savings to help defray the extra cost of living in the dorm verses the ole house. Daddy did advise me that our decision to get married soon was a very serious one. His words to me that I have treasured all my life were, "You can't live on love." I just told him to stay relaxed and watch it happen! I didn't mention it to him that he married my mother when she was 18!

Both of our parents were super. I know as a parent now, that they must have thought that the two of us were not thinking ahead. I believed, however, that they also knew of our maturity and determination to never let anything get in our way of fulfilling our dreams together. If I didn't get Brenda, I think my little brother, Larry, would have. He adored her and sat right beside her while we were going to games and other places. Brenda would put her arms around him and tell me to look at her new boyfriend. He had a mile wide smile.

In January of 1963, I moved into the men's dorm at 1720 Melrose Avenue. I was assigned a room on the seventh floor of Melrose. I roomed with a great guy from Columbia, Tennessee, Jimmy Sack. Two doors down the hall were two guys from Greenbrier, Tennessee. Their names were Ronnie Walton and Terry Gann. These were the two members of that Greenbrier football team that beat us up in our only loss. Ronnie and Terry became two of my best friends at school for the next two quarters while I lived in the dorm. They came to several of my baseball games that spring. We had a mutual friend from Pennsylvania by the name of Paul Regan, who gave me the nickname of "Mick" after Mickey Mantle. We called him "Yank". All three of us shared in common the missed love of our girlfriends back home.

My music changed. Instead of listening to "lonely" songs, Terry, who was a great guitar player, and I would sit in the middle of the large shower room where the acoustics were good and sing Kingston Trio songs, like "Michael Rowed The Boat Ashore", "Chilly Winds", "Hang Down Your Head, Tom Dooley" and our favorite fun song, "Tattooed Lady". We would often sit together in our little study hall area and write our love letters to Brenda, Terry to Linda, Yank to his girl, Paula. We often read our Bibles together and talked about what great blessings we each shared through our Lord. I really believe that my stay and making friends with Jimmy, Paul, Ronnie and Terry was my salvation the rest of my freshman year. Again, friends to my rescue!

We were introduced to our freshman coach, Don Lumley, a former minor leaguer player with the Knoxville Smokies, a minor league team of the Detroit Tigers. He was also a former US Marine. He and his wife, Carolee, had a son named Rick. Coach Lumley was a left-handed batter like me and was an outstanding hitter and former first baseman for the Knoxville Smokies. He would be my mentor as well as coach. On our team was Bill Ferrell, an outstanding right-handed pitcher from Rule High School in Knoxville. Tom Pritchard and Darryl Lowe were on some scholarship help as well. I played shortstop that year, Pritch played second and Darryl was our third baseman. Our first baseman was John Burpo, who was always keeping the dugout alive and well. Before we played our first game, we had our pictures made wearing our Tennessee baseball jerseys. I was so proud when I found out that the photos were sent by the athletic department to each of our individual hometown newspapers.

Besides my daddy, Mama Pearl, and the rest of my family, there were others who were happy to see that photo, especially, Uncle Charlie and Mr. Kirby Primm. I shall always be thankful to our friend back then, Bud Ford, who was a grad assistant working for the University of Tennessee Sports Information Office. The first step of my fabulous dream was complete. Bud did a fantastic job of covering and reporting our games to be printed in the News Sentinel or Knoxville Journal sports pages.

Our first game against Hiwassee College, was played at Lower Hudson Field, the name of our home field, now renamed Lindsey Nelson Stadium. It had only three sets of bleachers, one behind home plate, and one down each base line. A four-foot-high chain link fence stretched around the outfield. Our seating capacity may have been around two to three hundred at the most. This was in 1963, when Tennessee had not had spectacular baseball records in the past. There certainly were no traffic jams near Lower Hudson on game days. Bill shut out Hiwassee for four innings without giving up a hit. The game was tied at one apiece in the fifth when we scored two runs, the first being my inside-the-park home run to put us ahead. We went on to win the game 3-1.

My first Tennessee Vols win and a home run in my first game. I appreciated Bud's write up for the paper which featured the caption, "Ferrell and Lannom Pace UT Frosh Win." What a way to start my career! I was just glad that Coach Wright was watching.

We finished our freshman season in a winning fashion. Coach Lumley was my first real baseball coach that taught me so much that season about things that I had missed growing up with little baseball experience. I soaked up every word he spoke and paid attention to his suggestions, especially as a left-handed batter, how to hit left-handed pitching. It was a double blessing to play with great young players and to be coached by a veteran baseball player like him.

Next on my agenda came the time for me to retire as a state FFA officer. That would happen at the War Memorial Auditorium in Nashville, in April. I had gotten to travel across the state of Tennessee, meeting many FFA members and advisors, while giving countless speeches at FFA chapter banquets and FFA events. Brenda attended the session where I gave my retiring address at the convention. It would be my last time to wear my FFA jacket. I am convinced that the FFA has made a major difference in my life. The motto of this great organization is: Learning to Do, Doing to Learn, Earning to Live, and Living to Serve. Coupled with its mission statement that the the FFA provides: Premier Leadership, Personal Growth, and Career Success, what more can explain it better? Without it and the dedication of our great teacher and advisor, Bill Coley, the paths of the many lives he touched would have been entirely different.

Through the FFA, I gained confidence, leadership, and personal relationship skills that are applicable in coaching, teaching, or running a successful business. Even in the FFA, you don't always win. You learn to accept defeat, but not to like it. You discover your weaknesses and change them into strengths by practice, determination, perseverance, and teamwork. This Glade young 'un was immensely blessed and thankful. I have one year now behind me. It's time to get busy and plan on the consummation of my "deal" with Brenda.

January 5, 1962


Mr. John Bailey, Assistant Coach
University of Tennessee Athletic Department
Knoxville, Tennessee


Dear John:

    Bobby Lannom came by here to see me several days ago and told me of his keen interest in securing a baseball scholarship at the University of Tennessee. I realize that you do not have anything to do with baseball, but I am asking that you bring this matter to the attention of the person who does, with the request that acknowledgement be made of receipt of the attached information which I am furnishing you concerning Bobby.

    I do hope that Roger Bird and David Wells can be sold on the idea of coming to the University.

    With every good wish for the New Year, I am

                  Sincerely yours,


                  K. O. Primm
                  Vice President

*As a result of Uncle Charlie's visit, this letter was written by Mr. Kirby Primm, a Nashville banker and member of the University Board of Trustees, to the Tennessee Athletic department. A letter I have treasured for these many years. It was the introduction that got me started as a future Volunteer.*

March 27, 1962

Dean Webster Pendergrass
University of Tennessee
Knoxville, Tennessee

                Re: Bobby Lannom
                     Mt. Juliet, Tenn.

Dear Dean Pendergrass:

    I would like to recommend to you for consideration for a scholarship in one of the agriculture departments at U.T. the above referred to individual.

    The accomplishments of this young man are remarkable. Even though Mt. Juliet High School is small, Bobby was 4th in a class of 52 with a 94.5 scholastic average. He was also given the following honors: (1) Most Popular Boy, (2) Best Boy Athlete, (3) Most Versatile, (4) Capt of Football Team, (5) Best Personality, (6) Local President of F.F.A., and (7) District President of F.F.A.

Post 15 Am. Legion

    In Babe Ruth Baseball League playing for Lebanon against very formidable competition, Bobby hit 431 last season. I believe he has been contacted by your baseball coach.

    Dean, I have known this boy and his family well for the past 10 years. They have been very good friends and clients of mine since I came to Wilson County and a good Farm Bureau family. The Lannom family lives about 10 miles South of Lebanon near Gladeville Community. This family is by no means wealthy but neither are they destitute. Mr. Lannom owns the farm where they live. In my personal opinion this is the type youngster we should try to give help to make sure he goes to college.

    If I could be of help in anyway in securing more information for you or your staff in regard to this boy, I would appreciate the opportunity to do so.

    Hope things are going well with you. Stop by Lebanon to see us sometime.

                            Yours very truly,

                            Jim K. Lancaster

JKL/gv

*I owe the academic scholarship I received to my Ag Teacher, Bill Coley and our Farm Bureau Insurance agent, Jim Lancaster for this letter sent to the UT Dean of College of Agriculture. There are so many supportive members needed in making your dreams come true. I had the best. My apologies for the poor quality.*

*My first photo wearing a Tennessee Volunteer baseball uniform. Each new player's photo and write-up was sent to his hometown newspaper, mine to the Lebanon Democrat. The feeling was hard to describe! So much hard work, supportive friends, and enduring Loser's Balls, but it was now up to me to determine my future.*

## Chapter 13

*"One half of knowing what you want, is knowing what you must give up before you get it."*
Sidney Howard.

*"You were born to win, but to be a winner, you must plan to win, prepare to win, and expect to win."*
Zig Ziglar

Robert Wallace Lannom and Brenda Jeanne Graves were united in holy matrimony on June 7, 1963 at the Center Chapel Church of Christ. We were "tied" to start the top of the first of our many innings together. I finally had to sell my little green Chevy after running over an apparent hunk of snow in the middle of Central Pike after our engagement, driving down to pick up Brenda to go out. The hunk turned out to be a concrete footer that had fallen off a truck hauling construction junk, I assume???? It literally tore the bottom of my little car up. I had to ram it against a power pole in front of Brenda's house to stop it. That shook the electric lines so hard Nannie, Pap, and Brenda, ran out to see what was happening. Nannie yelled out, "Look! Bobby has crashed into the light pole!" If I had not hit that pole, I would have still been driving that car with no breaks today.

I found a nice 1956 blue and white Chevy four-door sedan at Ed

Martin's used car lot in Lebanon. It had a few miles on it, just 88,000. I know, but that was all I could afford to pay, even knowing full well that you get what you pay for. It cost me $500 of hard-earned milk money. It was all that we needed, ran well, good tires, with a nice clean look. It would be our "get-away" car after the wedding.

Daddy was my best man, Donna, Brenda's sister, was her maiden of honor, and our little sisters, Lugene and Susan, were our six-year-old flower girls. It was Darrell Davis's first wedding. He was Brenda's family preacher, who was over married to his beautiful wife, Lavergne. We always kidded Darrell about our marriage lasting since it was his first. After the reception, Darrell and Lavergne drove us all over the place to escape Brenda's brothers, who said that they knew where I had hidden the get-away car. We found it unmarked and climbed in heading for the famous Rowell Motel near Crossville, Tennessee, at the edge of the Cumberland Mountains. We drove to Gatlinburg the next day.

After our honeymoon stay in Gatlinburg, we headed home to stay at Donna and Rusty's store house that they had generously fixed up for our cottage before heading to Knoxville in the fall. With the help of my cousin, Ira Lannom, who worked for O E Willie Construction, I started the summer working construction for them building the city of Gallatin's water treatment plant on the Cumberland River just across the bridge in Sumner County. It was a terrific transition for both or us. We took a lot of kidding from her brothers and cousins, but they were fantastic. Brenda's brother, Eddie, would tell everybody at our horse shoe games on Friday night just across from our cottage, "Yall hurry up, don't make Bobby late for his curfew!" It was great.

Pap and Nannie wanted to go with us to Knoxville to help us search out a place to call home for the next three years. Nannie stayed with some kinfolks in Knoxville, while Pap rode around with us in our search. While driving down Gay Street in Knoxville one morning, Pap asked me to pull over. He had spotted a cigar stand and needed some cigars. Pap was more of a chewer than a smoker. I noticed that on our coon hunts together. We parked and got out. Pap was a traveling salesman and if you know anything about his breed, he was not reluctant to talk to anybody about anything. He asked the older gentleman who owned the cigar stand if he knew of any rental houses or apartments anywhere. The gentleman replied that he and his wife had an upstairs apartment that they wanted to rent.

Brenda and I spent the next two years on Luttrell Avenue in the home of two of the sweetest people on earth, Mr. and Mrs. Haynes. We paid $35 a month rent. It was furnished, but Brenda wanted to use her new formica top kitchen table and chairs. Now, we could concentrate on finding a job for Brenda. We looked on Alcoa Highway, North Knoxville, and other places where Brenda filled out numerous applications to no avail.

We finally spotted a job posting on the UT campus with an opening at a place called Pilot Oil Corporation. Would you believe it? The address was on the second floor of a rental building on Gay Street about a block from the Haynes cigar stand. I dropped Brenda off for her appointment and parked the car sitting there until she came out. We had one car, no cell phones, and made it three years in Knoxville with nobody getting hurt or bent out of shape. Don't tell me that it can't be done!

I became concerned about the time it had taken for the interview. I found out why when Brenda came almost floating to the car. I had to calm her down to get the scoop. Her interview went great. Mrs. Thompson, the office manager interviewed her along with her boss, Mr. Jim Haslam, the President of Pilot Oil. Brenda hugged me and told me that she had gotten the job. Brenda also said that in addition to her accounting duties, Mr. Haslam wanted her to be his secretary in preparing all of his correspondence to the large number of members of the Orange Tie Club. Mr. Haslam was president of the club that year.

She also found out when telling them in her interview that I played on the Tennessee baseball team, that Jim Haslam was the captain of the 1951 National Champions Vols football team. It was like nothing the both of us could have ever imagined. First Pap buys cigars, next we move in. Then down the street Brenda gets a job with one of the nicest and highly respected business men in

Knoxville. Brenda and I said a big prayer to God, thanking Him for his providential care of these two young kids beginning their lives together.

After Brenda went to work, they hired another girl, Vivian Lowery, who became one of our best friends in Knoxville for the next three years. Mr. Haslam was always complimentary of Brenda and respected her work ethic and ability to do the jobs right, never missing a cent in her accounting and payroll duties. Brenda started with Pilot Oil with just four people in the office; Mr. Haslam, Mrs. Thompson, Brenda, and Vivian. There were only 11 Pilot gas stations then in 1963. On game days he would tell Brenda to "get out of here and go watch that boy play baseball." and never reduced her pay. We were just convinced that God put Jim Haslam and the Haynes in our pathways.

Everybody that lived during that time remembers where they were on November 22, 1963. I was crossing the street in front of the old Ellis and Earnest Drug store when someone shouted out, "President Kennedy has been assassinated!" I watched the coverage sitting in the barber chair getting my hair cut. It was a sad day for our nation to close out that year leading up through Christmas.

Brenda and I felt confident that we were now going to make it. We didn't eat out of tin cans but were very frugal with our spending. I would always have a calf to sell to buy a much-needed tire or battery for our '56 classic little car. It just seemed like that when we needed something really bad, God took care of us.

Daddy had pulled the plug on the dairy business when I graduated from high school and went off to UT. He, all of a sudden, thought that the beef cattle business was better for him especially when his milker left town. I asked him one weekend when Brenda and I came home to visit, I said, "Daddy, why didn't you think about going into the beef cattle business about six years ago?" His answer was, "I had good cheap labor then, no need to."

When they would come to Knoxville to visit, their little white Chevy II was always loaded with frozen beans, corn, beef, tomato juice, and other goodies. We had refused to accept any money from them as part of our independent commitment, but, they could get away with food. Nannie would still make Brenda tops, a dress or two and have them ready to give her when we went home on weekends. They were the best parents.

When spring came, I was now a member of the Vols varsity baseball team. After a good start as a freshman, I was provided a little more financial assistance, but still not a full scholarship. I could eat all of my meals at Gibbs Hall, the residence of the athletes, by just showing up at mealtime. Our baseball locker room was located in the basement of the Stokely Athletic Center. We had just a short walk across the street to the baseball field. We were now under the leadership of Coach Bill Wright in his second year.

I now had the greatest competition that I had ever faced going up against juniors and seniors on the team. I did not get to start that year at the beginning of the season. I was not a happy bench warmer, period!! I resorted to doing the things that got me here, and that was to spend as much time as I could in the batting cage, running, and finding someone else to work out with me. John Burpo loved the game. He was the one who probably spent more time with me working out when we had extra time. John has remained one of my good Texas friends today. He and his wife came two years ago to my annual big game Buck Breakfast in Gallatin.

As the season got started, I became a little depressed, to say the least. I had made my commitment with Brenda and wanted to contribute more financially to make it easier for her. I saw baseball as my work! It started weighing on me that spring. Making the varsity team was okay, but I lived to play the game, not watching it while sitting on a plank! For all young athletes who have and may now have this feeling, just take my advice since I have been there and experienced it. While you are enjoying your "Loser's Ball", learn what it means to pay your dues. Learn the definition of patience under control. You don't have to be happy, sitting on the bench, but you can get prepared to be ready when the roll is called and it's your time at the plate. You may just be the one called on to drive in a winning run or end a game with a highlight catch.

## The Loser's Ball

I spent my first two years in high school not winning one football game, playing when nobody else wanted to be in the arena. I tried tackling guys weighing more than a hundred pounds my size. If you are willing to pay those dues when conflict goes against you and the chances of victory seem to evaporate before your eyes, remember winners prevail because they outlast defeat. You can suffer defeat without being defeated. Defeat is no match for perseverance, determination, hard work, courage, and a never give up attitude. In spite of all the good things Brenda and I were enjoying, I found myself feeling my worst, involved in the game I loved the most. Hey, Bob, it's too early for you to dwell in the loser's bracket. It is time to give it all you've got and put it in fast forward. When my time comes, I will be prepared to perform. There is no other choice. That's all I've got to say about that!

My good friend, Coy Meadows, and I were battling it out for a starting position in the outfield. I had been moved to the outfield when a much better shortstop moved into my old position. That was good for the team. I had no problem with that. About half way in the season, Coy sustained an injury and Coach Wright put me in center field. When Coy healed up, coach made Coy one of our pitchers. Coy was a good hitter as well. In a game against Vanderbilt, I saw him hit a ball on the roof of the gymnasium in left field at Vandy. Once I got extended play in center, I played that position for the rest of the season and the next two years. Patience-Persistence-Practice-Performance all lead to success. Remember sometimes your "Loser's Ball" will become your "Opportunity Ball." Put it in your pocket and move on! I probably would never have worked so hard if I started without a challenge. A loss just may be what you need sometimes to awaken the spark within you to be your best. If you think about it, in the dictionary, failure comes before first!

During our freshman year in 1963, the varsity posted an 11-15 record while going 8-10 in the SEC. As sophomores we liked to think that we made a difference in 1964, by going 17-14 overall and 8-9 in the SEC. It was good to at least have a winning season. The Vols had only achieved three winning seasons since the 1951

SEC Championship team, who had 20 wins and only 3 losses. We won games playing Clemson, Jacksonville State, Cornell, Vanderbilt, Kentucky, Florida, Georgia Tech, LMU, and Milligan.

We played Georgia Tech in Atlanta, where I got to visit with my former Post 15 American Legion teammate from Lebanon, Mike Gannaway. I was glad that Mike didn't pitch against us in that series where we split two games. A great thing about my first varsity year was the opportunity to travel and play at other ball parks. Even back then, many of them were much better than Lower Hudson back home. We didn't get to visit the Glade or Central Pike during the summers since I was playing summer ball in Knoxville as was most all of my teammates. I needed the experience and enjoyed the competition. I could also pick up a summer class or two in the mornings to stay on schedule to graduate on time. Brenda had settled into her work at Pilot Oil and stayed busy with Mr. Haslam's assignments, involving UT sports as well as the service station business.

Coach Wright let me know that three of my Vol teammates and I had been selected to play for a new Knoxville Recreation Baseball League team called the Knoxville Prospectors, managed by Captain Earl Cronan, of the Knoxville Police Department. A meeting was set up at Chilhowie Park for everybody to meet and get to know each other and hand out uniforms. My baseball life and career was about to make a giant leap in 1964, that defies description for a little farm boy from the Glade. A summer that I will forever cherish.

The following statement was given to me from a salesman from Wilson Sporting Goods. I think that it bears the attention of all young striving athletes who want to be at their best in their sport. It is entitled, The Will To Win.

"The arena may just be a back yard. Up for grabs is not the world's championship. Just bragging rights to who's best on the block. It's not a venue worthy of legendary prose. But it's a place where legends often begin. Because from such beginnings, the taste of victory is first savored. That insatiable taste that instills the desire to be the best.

It's more than all of those sports page clichés of extra effort and 110%. The will to win is a work ethic. A dedication. A commitment to never giving up. Find these traits in an athlete, and you'll find an athlete who is the first one at practice and the last one to leave. An athlete who toils away from the spotlight, perfecting those little nuances that can later make all the difference.

Though the odds are long of ever achieving fame and glory, this serves as little deterrent to this athlete. Because even when he or she faces others with more natural talent, they don't let it affect their style of play. They persist when others quit. And that makes every victory, no matter how small, sweet. Sweet payment beyond measure for every drop of sweat spent.

And long after one's athletic skills are eroded by time, the commitment stays within to face life's professional and personal challenges. These are the ultimate games. So, to every athlete with the will to win, comes a renewed commitment from Wilson: Your best effort demands that we give you nothing less than our best."

(Thank you Wilson and no charge for the commercial message!)

## CHAPTER 14

*"It's hard to beat a person who never quits."*
Babe Ruth

*"Courage is being scared to death but saddling up anyway."*
John Wayne

### New Team-New Beginning

A few days before our scheduled game at Chilhowie Park in Knoxville, the Prospectors assembled for our first time as a new team. I knew that in addition to me, three more Vols players would join the team. David Tiller had proven himself to be an outstanding pitcher as a freshman. He showed a lot more maturity and command of his pitching performance than most freshmen. Larry (Choo) Tipton, also a freshman, was excellent behind the plate, and had a great arm. He was our catcher. He was a tough out at the plate and hit well his first year with the team. Then, there was Bill Ferrell, our terrific right-handed pitcher, who was already being touted as a possible early draft signee. I joined as the team's center fielder. In spite of my slow start as a sophomore, I managed to hammer out a decent batting average just under .300 by the end of the season and scored several runs. I made a few "catches" in center, playing good defense. Two

## The Loser's Ball

other Vol teammates played with another Knoxville team to start the summer season.

Our manager, Knoxville city police Captain, Earl Cronan, welcomed everybody, said some encouraging words, and turned the meeting over to our head coach, Sid Hatfield. Coach Hatfield was the head baseball coach at Tennessee Tech University in Cookeville. We lost a 15-5 game to them this past season in Knoxville. We found out that he was a pitcher and third baseman for the 1951 Tennessee Vols, who won the Southeastern Conference Championship, and played in the College World Series in Omaha, losing to Oklahoma 3-2 in the finals. He was, in spite of the Vol loss, voted the MVP of the 1951 College World Series. He had played minor league ball with the Cleveland Indians.

I was impressed to say the least. Coach introduced the other players, some who had been involved in collecting money to start up the Prospectors team to play in the Knoxville City League. Ron Cronan, would be our shortstop. He was the son of Captain Cronan, and had been a minor league player with the Dodgers organization. We later heard some good stories of him being in the same spring training camp with the record base stealer, Maury Wills. Ron would be one of our playing coaches. Wayne Cronan, another of the Captain's sons, would back up Choo as catcher, and would be a utility fielder where needed. Coach Hatfield's traveling buddy to Knoxville games was our elder statesman and fantastic second baseman, Martin (Pete) Peters. Pete, at the time, was the Dean of the Tennessee Tech University Graduate School. He was an outstanding switch hitter, having played his college ball at Lincoln Memorial University (LMU). Pete had been inducted into about every Hall of Fame awarded at LMU, having coached basketball and baseball for many years. He was 41 years old, and had played with several teams in previous national tournaments. He was another member of the brain trust coaching us. Pete didn't speak up much, but like EF Hutton, when Pete spoke everybody listened.

The final infield spot was filled by our freshman coach, the former Knoxville Smokey, Detroit Tigers affiliated first baseman,

Don Lumley. Coach Lumley, which the Vols boys all concluded, was probably the main reason that the four of us were selected to be a part of the Knoxville Prospectors. He knew us pretty well, having coached us all as freshmen. There was no doubt that the four of our infielders were highly qualified to be player coaches. We now know why Captain Cronan spoke softly and briefly! I could see that by the end of the summer I would be earning a Master's Degree in baseball.

Veteran amateur players like the wily Earl Lawson, whose control was so good, he could throw his nasty slider in the mouth of a quart fruit jar. J B Stephens was an experienced pitcher. Jim Loveday, a former LMU standout outfielder, who was hard to retire at the plate, was a good stick. Jerry Bishop, was a smooth and talented left-handed pitcher. Other quality utility players included: Bill Boatman, Wayne Coleman, Tom Bass, and Charles Murphy.

We would begin the season with 15 active players and 15 uniforms! We remained without a sponsor the entire season, so money for additional uniforms and gear was not available. We would be playing five or six other teams for the city league championship. I admired Pete and Sid for driving from Cookeville to Knoxville twice a week for our games. Sid Hatfield put this team together and headed up the funding efforts to get this new team going. He said that is the reason he had named our team the Prospectors, was because they had prospected for funds to start the team. How could you not play your tail off to support these great men? It was like being in a room full of geniuses. The depth and scope of my baseball knowledge gained that summer was incredible beyond measure.

I don't remember a great many details about that season's regular city league games. We played so many. The first one, of course, is one of the most memorable. We played that first game at Chilhowie Park in Knoxville, not far from where the Knoxville Zoo is located today. Again, I guess I always liked beginnings such as the home run I hit in my first game as a Vol. About half way through our first game with the Prospectors, I hit a line shot between the center fielder and right fielder, for my first home run with my new team. Brenda

## The Loser's Ball

was there cheering me on. We won that game and finished the city league season as league champs with a record of 28-1.

I took advantage of every dugout moment to sit next to Coach Lumley. He had a habit of talking to himself every time he made an out and sat down on the bench. When he sat, I learned Lumley Baseball 1 0 1. I asked him to say out loud what he was thinking, what he was telling himself about the outs he had made. I filed those comments away and found myself improving my hitting so much by his comments. He eventually, would tell me about when to look for certain pitches in the count, how to spot the rotation of the ball leaving the pitcher's hands, how the pitchers would often give away their pitches by the way they held their glove, gripped the ball, or the change in angles of delivery. Priceless information. Plus, for a young left-handed hitter like me, how to be more successful against left-handed pitchers. He would jokingly say, "Awwwh! Just take two and hit to left." In one game, I saw him hit a long fly ball over the center fielder's head for a triple. When he came up to bat again the next time, the center fielder played back against the scoreboard, which was 410 feet from home plate, Coach Lumley hit the ball about ten feet up off of the scoreboard for another triple. Coach was amazing! I had the honor of him being my teammate that summer.

At the conclusion of the regular season, Sid let us know that the State Tournament would start in a couple of days. We now had the opportunity to add three more players from the city league to our roster. Sid, I am sure, with collaboration from Ron, Pete, and Don, picked all three of these players from the second-place team. The Vol boys were glad to see the addition of two more Volunteer players, Tommy Pritchard, our second baseman and utility player, and Jim Axon, a hard-throwing right-handed pitcher. Pritch was an excellent hitter and glove, and talented enough to play any position in infield and in the outfield. When Jim was on with his control, he was tough to hit.

Our third addition from the second place Knoxville team was an older experienced veteran, Art Oody. Art could hit often and for power. He would play most of the time in the outfield. Being without a sponsor, and no more uniforms to share, our three new teammates wore their own Knoxville uniforms. Here we are, a team with no sponsor entering the AABC (American Amateur Baseball Congress) Tennessee state tournament in 15 uniforms of one style, and 3 others that don't match. Luckily, Knoxville was the host city that year, making it much easier on us not having to travel across the state.

The championship finals were played in the Knoxville Smokey's Bill Myer Stadium and in a near-by city park. The Prospectors would play the team from Nashville, sponsored by Ray Batts Furniture Company. Like the Prospectors, Ray Batts was loaded with former pros, outstanding college and city league players from Nashville. Some of their players were, Jerry Vradenburg playing first base, a Belmont graduate, who was a star there in both baseball and basketball. Ronnie Bargatze, who played shortstop, was a fantastic infielder and great hitter. Donnie Fortner, a former Vanderbilt pitcher, would lead the pitching staff along with a recently released pitcher from the New York Yankees, Tom Shafer. They were backed by other experienced players that were no strangers to amateur baseball. While on first base after a hit or walk, I engaged in conversation with Jerry Vradenburg. I could tell that he was a classy guy. He was always complimentary throughout our games against them. He had the enviable qualities of what coaches should embrace, respect for your opponent, and a good sport to boot. Jerry, Ronnie, and Donnie would be a part of my baseball career in another chapter to follow.

We were fortunate to defeat Ray Batts of Nashville, and win the State AABC Championship. 1964 is turning into a pretty good year so far. Our next step would be to play for the Southern Regional Championship. Again, as the host team, we never left Knoxville. Home again! Ray Batts also qualified to play in the Regional as well as us. After suffering only our second loss of the season, we managed to make it to the finals and met Ray Batts again. In a hard-fought battle, the Prospectors were victorious and won the 1964 Southern Regionals, our third baseball championship in two weeks. I hit a home run in that tournament that would come up in a conversation with a new friend years later. I now have had the honor of playing on seven championships on great teams with a chance to win one more this year. Now, it was off to the National AABC Stan Musial World Series championship tournament in Battle Creek, Michigan.

I have not taken a lot of space in this book to write about so many things that happened in our games that summer. The magnitude of the emotions were just overwhelming to me. I can best describe it as phenomenal. The details of the games are really insignificant when placed in perspective of the whole turn of events. It seems that the Loser's Balls have gone on retirement for a while as we achieved the high level of play in these tournaments. They always find you, so I must be prepared to deal with them, knowing that they will occur. I was not prepared to getting accustomed to winning at this level before, especially headed for a World Series. It was just hard to believe that the first year of this year's existence as a team with no sponsor, that we could manage to be in this position. I considered myself to be a blessed individual playing for this team.

Our friends from Nashville received a blessing as well. Ray Batts got the word from AABC directors, that another regional team had been disqualified, and under the rules that region forfeited its right to play in the national tournament. Since it was the Southeast Region's time, they were permitted to take a second team to the tournament. Ray Batts Furniture out of Nashville would be joining us in Battle Creek to compete as the 8$^{th}$ and final team to play in the Stan Musial World Series. We were headed to the "cornflake capital."

Brenda stayed home to work and had asked Vivian, her co-worker to stay with her in our apartment while I would be gone for a week or more. Mr. and Mrs. Haynes were excited about my baseball trip as well as Mr. Haslam and Mrs. Thompson. They assured me that Brenda would be in good hands while I was away. I felt good about leaving Brenda with so many fantastic folks.

Daddy said the whole town of the Glade knew about our going to Battle Creek and wished us well. Mama Pearl, in her candid manner, simply told everybody, "I told Bobby that he would one day play in a World Series." I recalled her making that statement, but thought little of it until it sank in when we arrived in Michigan. We packed and loaded up in six or seven cars belonging to my teammates, with clothes, unmatched uniforms, balls, gloves, bats, and all the gear we could cram in car trunks and headed off to actually play our first away games! We got separated shortly after we left Knoxville, because two or three cars had flat tires, one a blow-out, and many stops to get gas, eat, etc. There was no Bramwell fried chicken or roadside table dinners, however, on this trip! We were strictly on our own with expenses except that I had heard that the Knoxville Recreation Department helped with gas expenses.

By the time the first car reached our hotel in Battle Creek, it was a wait and see who would arrive next. I had arrived in about the third car and was waiting on the rest of our team to show up when we saw this huge beautiful orange and blue chartered bus swing into the hotel parking lot and pull up under the overhang at the front door. You could hear the air shut off when the bus driver stopped to let the occupants off. We sat on benches outside the hotel front door and watched the exodus. Painted on the side of the bus were the words, J. Schrader Company, Sponsor of Lakewood Ohio Baseball 1964 Northeast AABC Champions.

When the doors opened, each player got off the bus, wearing orange blazers and dark navy-blue pants, carrying matching personal bat and equipment bags. They were followed by their Head coach, assistant coaches, trainers, team physician, and equipment managers. They had every need covered except for a manicurist. The equipment managers were carrying two sets of uniforms covered in plastic like you would see coming from the cleaners. It looked like a major league team who arrived in the wrong city to the bunch of us who didn't know if we were going to have enough players to play tomorrow. Finally, everybody arrived.

Earl Lawson got there in time to see some of those in the lobby that we had named, the "Baltimore Orioles". Earl just walked by us on the way to his room, leaned over to us and said, "The bigger they are, the harder they fall!", and kept walking. We looked at each other and shook our heads, each probably silently hoping that we will not be playing the "Orioles" in the tournament.

As I thought about what had just transpired, our team's travel troubles compared to their first-class arrival, I recalled a familiar Bible story about the young shepherd boy, David. The Philistines had a military giant, named Goliath, who belittled and mocked King Saul's Hebrew army. He terrified them daily as he came out and challenged them to send out a fighter to meet him in battle. Little David recognized the need and volunteered his services to King Saul to confront Goliath, with no armor except a sling and five smooth stones. With God as David's supporter, he fired one stone with his sling and killed the giant, Goliath. We all felt like we would be the David if we ever had to face the Ohio team in battle, but would need some hot bats instead of a pouch of rocks.

Once we got settled in our rooms, I went to the hotel lobby and asked the guy behind the front desk if there were any sights near the hotel to visit. The desk clerk suggested that since I was here for the games, to walk about two blocks down the street to a bank window where all of the tournament trophies and awards were displayed. I don't remember just how long I stood in front of that bank window staring at all of the prizes to be handed out to the championship team. In front of me was the giant Quaker Oats Championship trophy, the AABC National Championship banner stretched on display on the back wall, the individual winner trophies, and the black bats that would be engraved with the player names of the champions and shipped to each player after the tournament.

For a little farm kid from the Glade, who had to be creative and work with limited playing experience and resources, and suffering Loser's Balls at every corner, there was no rush to leave the view that I was enjoying right now. So many people had worked and supported me to make it possible for me to be standing in this spot. I finally walked slowly away, stopping to turn and look back briefly, then returned to the hotel with the picture of that bank window display in my mind. Tomorrow, it begins!

# Chapter 15

*"The quality of our expectations determines
the quality of our actions."*
Andre Goodin

### Birth of the Loser's Ball and Life in the Loser's Bracket

I must confess that my next two years as a Volunteer baseball player were put on a temporary shelf in anticipation of what was now before me. I had two more years to play as a Vol, but right now, I am consumed with the greatest opportunity that I have ever had. To play for a national championship doesn't happen too often for most athletes. I was as prepared as I thought I could be. It reminds me of a quote from our former great president, Abraham Lincoln who said, "If I had nine hours to cut down a big tree, I would spend the first six sharpening my axe." I just hope that my axe is sharp enough. It's for sure that I have worn out a bunch of axe handles hitting rocks.

We were scheduled to play our first game with E.B. Smith Chevrolet from Portland, Oregon, on Thursday, September 17, at 5:30 pm. Portland had previously won back-to-back national World Series Championships as the Pacific Northwest Regional Champions in 1961 and 1962.

Our game was to be played at Bailey Park in Battle Creek. The weather was not cooperating with the tournament's schedule at all.

There had been a misty drizzle most of the day. The field was damp but playable, not what any team hoped for to start a big tournament like this. The outfield grass was like a dew had covered it. The balls would have to be replaced more often than with a normally dry field of play.

Our ace, Earl Lawson, pitched that night for us. Portland got off to a good start, leading us 3-0 after five innings. Later in the game we took the lead 4-3 and headed into the bottom of the ninth with Portland getting their last chance at bat. I was feeling pretty confident at this point. We just need three outs to win our first game. I was in center, Pritch in left, and Oody in right field. Portland started the inning with a single by their second baseman. He tagged up and went to second on a deep fly ball to Oody. With one out and the tying run on second, Ron DePlanche, their nineteen-year-old shortstop doubles to tie the game at 4. A pop-up results in out number two.

Portland's next hitter, Jim Satlich, their best hitter came to bat. Satlich was the main reason Portland had won their championship in 1962. They had their best man right where they needed him. We had a lot of decisions to make in the outfield. Do we play in close enough to be able to make a play at the plate, but not too much that would allow a routine fly ball to go over our heads? The grass is so wet the ball is bound to be slowed down. Lots of decisions. We cheated in as much as we could. Pritch moved in as well as Art in right. I came in as far as I dared with such a good hitter batting for Portland.

The birth of the original and most significant Loser's Ball was about to happen. Satlich hit a sharp ground ball to the left of the pitcher's mound that eluded the diving Ron Cronan at shortstop into center field. DePlanche at second with two outs, took off at the crack of the bat headed to third and home. I charged in and picked up the wet ball that was kicking up a rooster tail of watery mist as it rolled toward me through the wet grass. I bare handed it and stepped quickly to make a throw at the plate. Realizing that DePlanche was nearly home with no chance to get him, I just held that ball in my hand and walked toward our third base dugout. Portland 5 Prospectors 4, game over!

The last time I had taken a baseball without permission was that game at the Glade when Daddy turned the truck around and I had to return that Loser's Ball to Van Dobson, our manager. I decided to get permission this time as I walked past the third base umpire, I asked him "Can I keep this ball?" He replied as he walked away, "I don't care, it ain't mine!" I stuck it in my back pocket and joined up with the guys after congratulating Portland on their victory. It was only our third loss of the season, but our worst one to accept. At least I would have one trophy from this tournament to take back home.

We found out later that Nashville Ray Batts had defeated Gleem Painters of Waterbury, Connecticut, by a score of 8-6. My buddy, Jerry Vradenburg hit a booming home run with his teammate Corky Hartman on in the 14$^{th}$ inning for the win. Jerry went 4 for 4 in his first game. When we got back to the hotel, I took the Loser's Ball and wrapped it in what I thought was a very appropriate covering. I rolled it up in toilet paper to help to dry it out and put it in my suitcase never to be touched again until we returned to Knoxville. We had a choice, to "give up", or to "give out" giving everything we had to climb out of the loser's bracket. One more loss and we are done. There would be no police escorts or ticker tape parades for a loser when we got back to Knoxville.

We were scheduled to play Wynnwood State Bank from Dallas, Texas, the next day on Friday afternoon. It was easy to spot from walking by the hotel on which floor the Tennessee boys were staying. After washing out our uniforms in our bathtubs and showers, we just opened up the windows and hung our laundry there to let the Battle Creek air dry them for the next game. We were truly hillbillies to say the least. To me that was like old times on the farm. I had no problem exposing my duds to the city. I did wonder though, how it was over at the "Orioles" camp with them wearing their second uniform while the managers were at the laundromat or cleaners readying their dirty ones.

After breakfast, I made my way down the street to visit the bank window again. The display took on a different feeling than on my first visit there. The trophies, banner, and bats seemed to have been moved farther away from the front of the window for some reason. They hadn't been moved. It was just because of our first loss that they seemed that way. Maybe, I saw them as a little harder to reach, or that they were gradually slipping from our grasp. It was just different. But, they were still there and had remained unclaimed up to now. We were still in the hunt with some long corn rows to hoe for victory. That, too, I had done before.

Sometimes the apparent losses we suffer are really appearing as opportunities for better things to come. I had learned already in my short life to expect brief interruptions in my journey to the winner's circle. At least I was playing in good baseball shoes. Again, I walked away from the bank window and as I did the day before, stopped and glanced back at those trophies, just to make sure that they were still there.

Later in the day we learned that our game had been rained out and was rescheduled for Saturday. Instead of getting to play, we had a very good team meeting. It was the first time that we had gotten together as a team to discuss our loss the night before. Sid opened the meeting in a positive manner. I smiled when Pete made the statement, "We just have to put last night's loss in our pockets and move on". I am with you, Pete. That's literally what I did! Earl had pitched a complete game but took the loss to Portland because we didn't hit the ball well enough to give him enough runs against a very talented team. Ron commented that we just need to shake it off and get with it at the plate. Coach Lumley put the whole loss in perspective by saying, "We are not finished yet, we just need to do what we came here to do and that was to win this thing." Sid closed out the meeting and told all of us to get a good night's sleep and be ready to go tomorrow.

J B Stephens was on the mound for us against Dallas on Saturday at Post Park. We named it "Post Toasties Park." Coach Lumley had the hot bat getting three hits, two RBIs, and scored a run. He killed the ball. I hit the ball better in that game after going 0 for 4 against the Portland team, but it seemed that my line drives were right at first or second for easy outs. I went 0 for 4 again. J B went 6 1/3 innings before Bill Ferrell relieved him and pitched shut-out ball the next 2 2/3 innings to close it out for a 3-1 win. It felt good to come off of our loss and get a win that afternoon. In the meantime, Lakewood (Orioles) had beaten Dyersville, Iowa 7-1 to go up 2-0 in the winner's bracket. Ray Batts won their second game by beating Portland, Oregon 5-0. It was now looking like our friends from Nashville were the ones to match up with the tournament favorite Lakewood.

The fields continued to be blanketed with a cool misty rainfall just about every day. The ground crews at both parks did an exceptional job to keep the fields in playable condition considering the wet weather. Our next game was set up to be played on Saturday night, but it was rescheduled to be the first game of our double header on Sunday. Bill Ferrell was on fire for our first game against Waterbury. I had seen that look in Bill's eyes several times while pitching at Lower Hudson Field in Knoxville for the Vols. He struck out 6 and gave up only 5 hits pitching a complete game to give us our second win 5-1. Coach went 2 for 4. Unbelievable! I got my first tournament hit going 1 for 4, and scoring a run. Nashville Ray Batts suffered their first lost to Dyersville, Iowa by a score of 5-1. We had now tied Nashville with 2 wins and 1 loss. Lakewood continued on their winning track by winning their third game 3-0.

Jerry Bishop, our smooth lefty, started our second game on Sunday against Dyersville. He went 7 1/3 innings against them giving up only 2 runs to get the win by a score of 7-3, eliminating them from the tournament. Coach went 2 for 5, but Art Oody our pick-up right fielder went 3 for 4, scoring a run and knocking in another. We now had three wins and one loss, which now put us in the finals against either Lakewood or Nashville. Unfortunately, Lakewood beat our buddies from Nashville and eliminated them from the tournament by a slim margin of 3-2. Lakewood's big reliever, O Donnell, came in and shut down the Ray Batts team to propel Lakewood to a 4-0 record to play in the championship game on Monday against us.

## The Loser's Ball

There were always good crowds at the tournament in spite of the bad weather, but we saw a shift in the crowd's preference to cheer for by the end of those double header wins on Sunday. It became embarrassingly obvious, even when we would come up to bat. We would hear our names called and cheers started emerging in different parts of the bleachers calling out, "Come on you hillbillies, bow your necks." The crowd evidently picked up our tenacity or grit to fight out of the loser's bracket to earn our spot to be in the finals. The underdog was excited knowing that we had the locals pulling for us. What a roller coaster ride so far, rain outs, double-header wins, and reaching the finals.

On Sunday evening following dinner, I made what would be my final walk the two blocks down the street from the hotel to my bank window. It was funny as I stood there glaring again at trophies, the banner, the big trophy, and bats. They seemed to have been moved closer to the front again for some reason. The vision I had of my visit after our loss was now in the past. The awards seemed to be brighter, shined and polished, more within reach than before. Of course, I know they had never been touched for a week, but in my mind, I was convinced that they were ready to be hauled off to Knoxville in cars, not in an orange and blue chartered bus. The only problem was that we had to win two games, while Lakewood had to only win one to snatch the spoils. I turned and walked away toward the hotel, pausing again to turn around and take just one more look. My last thought as I walked away was, It's David against Goliath. This is it, Brenda, dad, mom, Mama Pearl, Uncle Charlie, Coach Wright, Van Dobson, Mr. Grandstaff, Coach Robinson, Coach Barrett, Mr. Primm, and many more waiting to hear the news by tomorrow night.

I do not ever pray to God for a win. I'm afraid He may be for the other side! Seriously, that night before I went to sleep, I simply thanked Him for allowing me to be here in this moment and to help me just to do my best tomorrow night, as well as the rest of my teammates. I am already blessed.

The championship game(s) was scheduled for Monday night, September 21, 1964, at Bailey Park Stadium. The first game would begin at 6 pm with the second game, if necessary, to begin 30 minutes after the end of the first game. It had boiled down to David, the sling-throwing shepherd boy, going up against the giant, Goliath. The comparison is just that, and certainly no disrespect to the great Lakewood J Schrader sponsored team. They had it all, and we were basically a bunch of new comers, a first-year team, no sponsor, arrived at the battle field in cars with flats and blow-outs vs. their shiny and beautiful chartered bus. Our uniforms did not match and were air-dried by the city of Battle Creek in our hotel windows. We had an advantage that they did not have. We were the crowd favorites, while they, by their record of having won nine straight games, five in their region to go undefeated, and four games in this tournament, the obvious statistical favorites to win it all.

The crowd on that damp, wet night was estimated to be about 1,200 in attendance. Not bad, considering the bad weather. In attendance was Mr. C O Brown, the director of the parks at Bailey Park. We had the privilege of meeting Mr. Brown at dinner one night when he met with us to wish us well. I know that he had to be a neutral observer, but all of us came to the same conclusion that he had a soft spot for the Tennessee boys. Maybe he just pulled for the underdogs sometimes. A betting man would, however, have put his money on Lakewood to win the championship.

The first game started promptly at 6 pm. We were the visitor and would get to bat first. After going scoreless in the top of the first, Lakewood got two runs off of our starter and veteran, Earl Lawson, in the bottom of the first. You could feel that many of the fans were already convinced that it would be only one game played tonight.

I remembered what Earl had said about that big bus and the intimidating entrance that the "Orioles" made last Thursday, "The bigger they are, the harder they fall." Earl Lawson regained his remarkable slider, and with fruit jar accuracy, went on to pitch eight scoreless innings, scattering eight hits and striking out 9 batters, while we scored 5 runs to win the first game 5-2. I went 1 for three, scored a run, and had a stolen base. Ron, our shortstop went 3 for 4 while Jim Loveday got 2 hits. We got 11 hits in that game to boost

## The Loser's Ball

our confidence and to rekindle the crowd's support as well. I could feel the breeze blowing our way now. Both teams in the finals are now tied 4-1. The championship game begins in 30 minutes or as soon as the ground crew has the field ready.

In the first game, Lakewood's ace reliever, O Donnell, who had been receiving great press all week, continued to do well. During that game he only pitched one inning giving up one hit but striking out two batters. We assumed that he was being held for the next game if needed to finish us off and stop the madness. He was a big guy and could throw a baseball. After our win, the crowd was "engaged" to be humble about my description. There was no question who they were pulling for now.

The championship game began after about a 35-minute delay to get the field ready. The Prospectors were the home team for the final game. Our young shepherd boy, David Tiller, our freshman Vol pitcher, started on the mound, holding Lakewood scoreless for the first three innings. Our bats came alive in the bottom of the third, scoring 6 runs and taking a big lead. Choo Tipton, our Vol catcher, smashed a double in the frame to knock in two runs. The fans were loud enough to even distract us from the game. It was awesome. Dave had his sling going. He gave up a couple of runs in the bottom of the fourth to make it a 6-2 Prospectors lead. He only gave up six hits and 2 runs to the powerful Lakewood hitters in his four innings of pitching.

Ron Cronan, our shortstop, who had relieved several times during the year, came in to relieve Tiller, but gave up three runs and three hits. We added another run in the fifth to lead 7 to 5. In the top of the sixth with two outs, Bill Ferrell, another Vol pitcher who was great all tournament, came in to close out the inning. The bottom of the sixth inning proved to be what we needed with just a two-run lead. O Donnell, Lakewood's ace reliever entered the game to try and put out the fire. He only pitched 1 1/3 inning before we got four hits and scored four runs to knock him out of the game. We now led 11-5.

In the bottom of the seventh, Coach Lumley singled home his fourth run of the game and went to third on Ron Cronan's double.

We now led 12-5. With two out in the bottom of the seventh, Ron's brother, Wayne, came to the plate with Lumley on third. Wayne hit a sharp grounder to the left of the second baseman for an apparent easy play to throw to first. He misplayed the ball, Wayne reached safely at first and Coach scored our 13$^{th}$ run. Interestingly, I was the on-deck hitter to hit after Wayne and was standing next to the home plate umpire ready to step in the batter's box when all of a sudden, the umpire removed his mask and stepped out in front of the plate, waving it in the air, yelling out, "Ball game!"

I was in shock! I was not aware that there was a tournament rule which stated that when a team has an eight-run lead after seven innings the game is over! We had just won Knoxville, Tennessee's first Stan Musial World Series AABC National Championship by a "mercy" rule score of 13-5! We didn't do the pitcher's mound pile-up for fear of hurting too many old men during the celebration, but we did a lot of hugging, hand shaking, and back slapping. It was hard to tell who was the happiest, the crowd or us.

We capped off one of the most spectacular seasons in my baseball career to this point. I had my best game of the tournament going 2 for 4, scoring a run, and knocking in another. I was pleased to have hit .428 in the two title match ups that night. We finished the 1964 season with 39 wins and only 3 losses. We lost three games that year by scores of 1-0, 5-4 and 5-4, only three runs. The bank window was now bare. The trophies were at Bailey Park being handed out to a bunch of college kids and veteran baseball players, who refused to let a Loser's Ball ruin their dreams of winning a national championship.

I learned so much that summer, some things related not necessarily to baseball in a direct way. I learned that sometimes our objectives and goals may be interrupted in many ways giving us the impression that since we failed to achieve our dreams, we were ourselves failures. By turning Loser's Balls into opportunities, we often achieve unbelievable outcomes that we had never even set our goals to achieve. This was demonstrated when I signed up at the beginning of the year to simply stay in baseball shape and get better during the summer for my third year at UT. It had never crossed my

## The Loser's Ball

mind that I would end the summer playing with such a talented and fantastic group of guys, as a National Champion.

That is what comes to those who reach for the moon, but end up with a star instead. The next morning, we watched as a beautiful orange and blue chartered bus left the hotel headed to Ohio as we loaded the hardware in the cars and headed home to Knoxville. The return trip was made without even one low tire. After getting home and spending time with Brenda telling her about my week, I went to my suitcase and picked up the Loser's Ball, unwrapped the toilet paper from around it, sat down on the couch and just sat there staring at it. Brenda sat down beside me as I told her the story. I made her promise to never let this ball leave our possession or get lost in any future moves we make. It still remains in my trophy case. I do plan to go back to Battle Creek one day to visit Bailey Park and roll that ball in the grass in center field one more time. This makes 8 championships. Will there be more? Or will I be hit by another Loser's Ball? If so, bring it on!

I wish to thank the sports staff at the Battle Creek Enquirer, Bill Broderick and Stephanie Angel for permitting me to copy several box scores and write ups from their archives featuring the AABC World Series games. Thanks guys.

*The Knoxville Prospectors, 1964 Stan Musial World Series Amateur Baseball National Champions, was made up of former minor league pros, six Tennessee Vols, and a bunch of talented baseball veterans who overcame a major Loser's Ball to win it all. Number 14 is all smiles. Mama Pearl's words to me later, "I told you that you would play in a world series."*

# CHAPTER 16

*"I learned that something constructive comes from every defeat."*
Tom Landry (Former Dallas Cowboys Coach)

*"You're never a loser until you quit trying."*
Mike Ditka (Chicago Bears)

I returned to classes after enjoying a week or so of transition from summer baseball to starting up the fall quarter at school. Coach Wright was very pleased about the playing time our players got during the summer. Everybody played somewhere, but a few of us had bragging rights for sure. My Prospectors summer assured me of a starting position in center field for the Vols for next spring. I was also informed that I would be on a 90% scholarship which would cover my tuition as well as continuation of books, and meals at the training table in Gibbs Hall. I was on my way to doing my part of covering the family expenses. All that was missing was our housing allowance to come next. Brenda and I were doing great just paying $35 a month staying at the Haynes home. Looks like our plans are going well.

Once I attended classes for a couple of weeks, we decided to take a weekend and go home to see our parents and in-laws. We would always stay at Brenda's but I would end up at the farm all day on Saturday helping Daddy with jobs to do on the farm. I was happy to do that, especially since there were no cows to milk. There was always a long breakfast with lots of catching up during each of my visits. Nannie would always fix a huge Sunday dinner for the Graves clan. It was a special household. The men would eat first, and the girls would wait on us till we had moved outside in the shade or ventured off to the barn to look at the latest tractor her brother, Gilbert, had bought. The girls did this so that they could simply take all the time they wanted to eat and talk for a couple of hours in the kitchen. That was the tradition for years.

Brenda and I packed up on Sunday afternoon and headed back to Knoxville, talking about how good it was to see everybody and talk with them about my baseball championship. Sometimes when things are going so well, the unexpected Loser's Ball is thrown at you without warning. Just before we got to Lebanon, Brenda bent over and cradled her stomach and cried out that something was wrong. She said that the pain in her lower abdomen was hurting. "Bob!" she said, "I need to go to the emergency room, I am hurting so bad." We were fortunate that we were still close to home. I pulled into the parking lot of the emergency room at McFarland Hospital in Lebanon, and helped her inside. Our family physician, happened to be making his rounds, and was notified to meet with us in the ER. After examining Brenda, he recommended that she spend the night in the hospital and undergo some testing the next morning.

We let our parents know that we had to change plans and wait to see what was going on. After returning from her tests, Doc informed Brenda that she had a bad looking ovarian cyst that had to come out. He had already scheduled surgery for that Monday afternoon. In the meantime, I managed to call my advisor at UT who agreed to notify my professors about missing class probably all week at least. I let Mr. and Mrs. Haynes know as well. Brenda talked to Mrs. Thompson at Pilot Oil, who told her to do what she had to do and not worry that she and Vivian would take care of Brenda's duties.

Brenda's surgery went well. During the post-surgery consultation, Doc said that she could go back to work in a week. I asked him if there were any complications or chances of this occurring again. He

## The Loser's Ball

told us that the surgery was successful and there shouldn't be any problems. Then the "bean ball" hit us! A knock-down pitch.

Doc told us to be prepared that Brenda may not be able to have any children. I cannot describe our reaction. I was numb, so was Brenda. We never expected to hear this report from our doctor. Brenda was so torn up and crying her eyes out. I realized that my thoughts needed to be with taking care of her and not let this news destroy us. I held Brenda and let her know that the main thing is that she is okay. We will worry about other things later. It was just the two of us hanging on to each other and trying to cope with the hardest thrown Loser's Ball in our short marriage. We sat there and prayed to God together, asking Him to help us to get through this and give us the strength we needed.

We had a week to rest up and were encouraged by both of our families before heading back east again the following Sunday. Mrs. Thompson and Vivian were Brenda's salvation. Our friends at our church in Knoxville were super. They basically made us their project in checking in on us, with visits, taking us out to dinner, and things that loving Christians do for each other.

We made it through that bean ball. Brenda and I brushed it off by telling each other that with two more years of college, we didn't need to have kids right now anyway. Really, we simply stuck this news in our back pockets and moved on with our lives. Brenda remained so strong. There were times that we talked about the adoption process and even asked some of our friends who had adopted children what they did in going through the steps. That was as far as we went, however. We just stayed busy, prayed a lot, and continued our plans to graduate in 1966. We made it by the power of our faith, family, and friends. You can't go wrong with these three key ingredients dealing with Loser's Balls.

After enjoying the Christmas holidays, it was time for Bob to get cranked up and ready for the 1965 Volunteer baseball season. Coach Lumley was no longer coaching the freshman team. He had been called back into the Marine Corps, and was sent back to Vietnam to fight in that horrible war. We started off the season by losing our first four games to Georgia Southern, Florida, and Auburn. We won the next 7 out of 8 games. We finished the season with a winning record of 14-10 while going 8-5 in the SEC. It was not a grand and glorious year at all. I was ready to get with my Prospectors for another exciting summer.

Bill Ferrell had signed with the Minnesota Twins and would not be with us. Pritch and Jim Axon had returned to their old Knoxville team. Choo decided to play summer ball in Virginia in the Shenandoah League. We had some vacancies to fill for the 1965 edition of the Prospectors. Sid, Ron, Wayne, Pete, Earl and the rest of our team were back with the exception of a couple of guys. Vol left fielder and pre-season junior All SEC performer, Jack Ervin, was a welcomed addition. Jack was a fantastic left-handed batter who had a great arm and was blessed with speed. Sid brought a few of his Tennessee Tech players with him and Pete this year. Herbie Muniz would play shortstop. Ron Cronan would move to first base to replace Coach Lumley. David Pratt, a gifted lefty, would be our replacement for newly acquired Minnesota Twins pitcher, Bill Ferrell. All we needed was a catcher to replace Choo to get us back at full strength.

Little did I know that I was about to personally meet the Nashville Vols player that I had watched from the bleachers at Sulfur Dell in 1959 as a bug-eyed 15-year old. His name was Buddy Gilbert. Sid had known about Buddy and his early history as a catcher. Buddy was called up to Cincinnati for the 1960 season. He only had 20 at bats as a major league player, but had shown the world his arm strength when he and Roberto Clemente were talked into a throwing duel. Buddy actually won the event against Clemente by beating him with center field throws to second, third, and home. I remembered his arm strength the day my Babe Ruth team watched him in warm-ups.

Buddy went three for twenty in the majors. Two of his three hits were home runs. He left the majors because of a salary dispute and moved back to his home town in Knoxville. Sid talked to Buddy, who agreed that he would catch for the Prospectors in 1965. I had come full circle. Now my 29-year-old youth idol is my teammate. How often does this kind of stuff happen?

## The Loser's Ball

Once the season started, we added another pitcher, Mike Levi to our team. The '65 season flew by with the Prospectors dominating the Knoxville City League again. We ended the season as city champions again and started making plans for the state tournament. I had played my last Prospector's game in Knoxville. The state tournament was held in Chattanooga, on the field where the Chattanooga Look Outs played. Dad and Mom drove down to watch us play a couple of games. We faced a Memphis team in the title game and won our second straight Tennessee AABC State Championship. The next step was to play in the Southern Regional tournament in Orlando, Florida.

Throughout the year Earl Lawson, Dave Tiller, Dave Pratt, and Mike Levi, combined for outstanding wins on the mound for us. We couldn't have asked for better performances. I remember leading off our first inning and the first pitch of the championship game in Orlando. I was hit in the middle of my back by a wild left-hander unleashing a rocket fast ball. I couldn't get out of the way. It hurt big time, but I made it to first base. Earl Lawson, our 1964 championship pitching hero, felt my pain and who would not be pitching anymore, went back to the motel for his "Lawson Linament". When he returned with it, he pulled up my shirt and rubbed that brew of fire on my back. My pain instantly disappeared, but I was afraid that my skin had dissolved. Earl just said, "Give it some time, you'll see." Sure enough, the tonic worked just as it had done on his veteran pitching arm many times. I now understood how he pitched so many complete games. That game went 15 innings. If it were not for Earl's brew, I would not have made it.

Another unusual moment occurred during the game when I was playing in center field around the 8th inning with the game tied. Hurricane warnings had been issued for high winds in the Orlando area, which started to arrive as we got deeper into the game. With two outs and a runner on first, the hitter smacked a long high fly ball that was headed for the center field fence. There was no doubt that it was going to get over me. I had no choice but to turn and run as fast as I could toward the fence, hoping to pick up the ball and try to prevent the runner on first from scoring.

The strong winds were blowing in toward home plate from center field. Just as I approached the warning track, I looked up and the ball seemed to have stopped dead in the air. A gust of wind had held that ball up as it seemed to fall out of the sky as I made the catch with my back toward home plate, facing the center field fence for the third out. Hey! Another example to never give up. You just may have the gold drop in your hands if you keep digging! Dave Pratt pitched a complete extra inning game.

We left Orlando with our second straight Southern Regional AABC Championship. Vivian had told Brenda that she just may as well move in with us since she was getting plenty of time on Luttrell Avenue. We are headed back to Battle Creek to defend our 1964 National Championship. Vivian had already packed her bags without being asked this time. I was now looking for team championship number 12.

I found this poem written by Walter D. Wintle that has meant a lot to Brenda and me in overcoming adversity and battling through many Loser's Balls, and even some "Beaners".

Thinking: The Man Who Thinks He Can

If you think you are beaten, you are;
if you think you dare not, you don't;
if you like to win but think you can't
it's almost a cinch you won't.

If you think you'll lose, you're lost,
for out in the world we find
success begins with a fellow's will
it's all in the state of mind.

## The Loser's Ball

> If you think you are out-classed, you are,
> you've got to think high to rise;
> you've got to be sure of yourself before
> you can ever win a prize.
>
> Life's battles don't always go
> to the stronger or the faster man;
> but sooner or later the man who wins
> is the man who thinks he can.

We are headed back to Battle Creek for our second year in a row. Again, we had no sponsor and had to drive in cars again, crammed full of players and our gear. This trip was made without any calamities or tire problems. We didn't see any huge intimidating buses arriving at the hotel this time either, but I paid my visit to the same bank window as quickly as I could. There is not one superstitious bone in my body, just all of them! There were 8 teams again, playing for the 1965 Stan Musial AABC National Championship.

In addition to the Prospectors, the following teams made it to the tournament: Wynnewood State Bank, Dallas, TX, Gleam Painters, Waterbury, Conn., Dr. Barnard Molars, Portland, Oregon, Max Larsen, Battle Creek, Michigan, Blues, Beloit, Wis., Sutton's Market, Waterloo, Ind., and A.C., Riverton, Ill.

The first-round winners were: Waterbury 5 Dallas 4, Battle Creek 9 Beloit 8, Waterloo 9 Riverton 0 and the Prospectors getting revenge on Portland, Oregon, who made the Loser's Ball famous in our first game with them last year, by a score of 9-3.

Again, my most memorable moments in the '65 tournament were this game against Portland. The Prospectors hammered out 16 hits in the opening game in defending our title. Jack Ervin, my Vol teammate, knocked in 5 runs, including a three-run home run. In doing my research on that game, thanks to the sports staff and others at the Battle Creek Enquirer, I was able to get copies of the game's box score. I was fortunate to be the lead-off hitter for our team that year. It didn't take long for me to realize that Coach Hatfield had put me there to get on base for the long-knockers behind me to score more runs. Jack batted in the second spot in the line-up. Buddy Gilbert hit in the clean-up spot, fourth in the line-up.

When I got a copy of the box score for the Portland game, it was just one of my proudest moments. In addition to getting a stolen base, I went 3 for 5 at the plate, scoring two runs and driving in a run. Buddy Gilbert, my youth idol, now my teammate, went 3 for 5 as well. Together, we accounted for 6 of our 16 hits. I just had to make a picture of that box score and put it in the picture section of this book. The Enquirer actually had a short article about the game and mentioned my name along with Buddy in the article. Things like this happen when you aim at reaching your initial goals, but blessings beyond your wildest dreams often reward you in so many unexpected ways. I would have lost the farm if I had bet this would never have happened. Amazing! I can't describe it. And my deepest appreciation to the sports staff at the Battle Creek Enquirer for copies of the write ups and box scores.

We ended up finishing tied for third place in the tournament. We came so close to playing in the championship game if we had beaten the eventual tournament champion, Waterloo, Ind. We lost to them 12-10 in a slugfest. We actually hit 5 home runs in the semi-final game. Martin (Pete) Peters, switch hitter, hit two home runs, one left-handed and one right-handed at the age of 42. Waterloo sailed through the tournament undefeated. I had a good last year playing for the Prospectors. I finished the '65 season batting .361 with 18 stolen bases.

I came to Tennessee with a dream of playing for the Vols. My dream never included the bonus attraction of playing with a number of my teammates, former minor leaguers, veterans, and being coached by a fantastic man and former champion Tennessee Vol, Sid Hatfield. Playing together with former minor league players such as Ron Cronan and Don Lumley, plus legendary players like Martin Peters, Earl Lawson, Art Oody, and of course my now beloved friend Buddy Gilbert, were unexpected bonuses in my baseball career. I also met many great players from towns that were unfamiliar to a country boy.

In 1964, we beat a team from Debuque County, Iowa, in the fourth round. They were the Blackhawks from a very familiar town thanks to one of my favorite baseball movies starring Kevin Costner, James Earl Jones, Ray Liotta, Amy Madigan, and Burt Lancaster in his final film role, "Field of Dreams". The town, Dyersville, Iowa, which if I don't run out of innings, I plan to visit one day, and maybe watch a MLB game.

Brenda told me when we got back to Knoxville, that Coach Wright had called and asked for Jack and me to meet him the next afternoon, before we started our fall practice schedule, outside of his office at the south end of Neyland Stadium. A UT sports photographer, and reporters from the News Sentinel and Knoxville Journal in Knoxville was there to take photos. That's when Coach Wright congratulated us on being selected as Co-Captains of the 1966 Vol baseball team.

Jack and I were not expecting this honor to lead our team next season. It was a humbling experience to say the least. A copy of our picture and accompanying article was sent to our hometown newspapers. When the Lebanon Democrat ran the article and Daddy saw it, he called me and said that he was more prouder of that honor than any batting average or wins that I had ever gotten. Everything seemed to be heading in the right direction. I just hope the Loser's Balls stay out of our lives for one more year at least. What will the future hold? Just get ready and prepare yourself for your last year as a Vol. Make every day count. You are about to head into the ninth inning of your dream playing for the Tennessee Vols.

```
PORTLAND, ORE.        KNOXVILLE,
Dr. Bernard Molars    TENN.
                      Prospectors
            ab r h bi              ab r h bi
Jones ss      4 0 0 0  Lannon cf    5 2 3 1
Te. Burke 2b  3 1 1 0  Ervin lf     3 1 2 5
Baldridge cf  4 1 2 1  Cronan 1b    4 1 1 1
Heniges lf    4 0 1 1  Gilbert c    5 0 3 0
Marshall 1b   4 0 0 0  Peters 2b    4 1 2 0
Stamsos c     4 0 2 1  Muniz ss     5 0 1 0
Hanson 3b     4 0 1 0  Hatfield 3b  4 0 1 1
Tom Bur'e rf  1 0 0 0  Loveday rf   4 2 2 1
Hump'eys rf   2 1 0 0  Levi p       2 2 1 0
Duerr p       1 0 1 0  Tiller p     1 0 0 0
Becic p       3 0 0 0

Totals        34 3 8 3  Totals      37 9 16 8
Portland               100 010 010—3
Knoxville              004 040 10x—9
E—Stamsos. DP—Portland 1, Knox-
ville 1. LOB—Portland 7, Knoxville 10.
2B—Te. Burke, Duerr, Gilbert. HR—
Ervin. SB—Heniges, Lannon, Cronan.
         Pitching Summary
           IP   H  R ER BB SO
Duerr (L)  2⅓  6  4  4  1  0
Becic      5⅔  10 5  5  5  5
Levi       5   5  2  1  3  0
Tiller     4   3  1  1  0  1
  WP—Duerr. T— 2:34. U — Hjortaas,
Grygiel.
```

*How often does a young kid get to play on the same team as his boyhood idol? Buddy Gilbert and I played for the 1965 version of the Knoxville Prospectors, defending our '64 championship, in the Stan Musial World Series. I received permission from the Battle Creek Enquirer to reproduce this box score. I was the lead-off hitter that year and Buddy batted fourth in the clean-up position. Each of us went 3 for 5, getting 6 of our team's 16 hits to win our opening game in the tournament. This remains as one of my prized possessions even though my name was misspelled.*

# Chapter 17

*"The gem cannot be polished without friction,
nor man perfected without trials."*

Chinese Proverb

*"Show me someone who has done something worthwhile,
and I'll show you someone who has overcome adversity."*

Lou Holtz

Before school started, we received some good news from the athletic department. With the completion of the new Golf Range Married Apartments now available for rent, we received an application to apply for married housing. The other great news we received was that my baseball scholarship now was 100% complete. I was on full scholarship. The new apartments, located in west Knoxville, near West Hills on Sutherland Avenue, would cost $90 per month, but, our married housing scholarship allowance was $110 per month. Brenda and I said goodbye with sadness, love, and appreciation to Mr. and Mrs. Haynes and moved to our new two-bedroom apartment, and had an extra $20 per month for groceries.

During the summer, Mr. Haslam had completed construction on the new Pilot Oil Corporate offices in West Hills, less than a couple of miles from our apartment. He even hired me to help out in finishing up the painting details and clean up prior to the move from downtown. A new station was added with the corporate offices behind it. Pilot was taking off and growing in leaps and bounds. More office staff was now added at the new headquarters.

The irony of the deal with me working for Pilot Oil for four or five weeks, was that I had to turn in my time to Brenda! She didn't cut me any slack either. My time cards had to be exact with no "fuzzy" extra time. Brenda's motto had to have been taken from a quote from Quincy Jones: *"Once a task has just begun, never leave it till it's done. Be the labor great or small, do it well or not at all."* That was her code of ethics for her work wherever she went and performed her financial responsibilities to near perfection.

The timing was great. I could now drop Brenda off at Pilot and drive to school for my classes and practices. Our apartment was on Vivian's way home, convenient for a ride for Brenda without me having to pick her up in the afternoons. I will always remember the great times when we lived there with one of my teammates, Terry Smith, and his wife Kathy, living across from us. We had some knock down and drag out Canasta card games you wouldn't believe. Terry and Kathy were from Covington, Georgia, and such great friends our last year in Knoxville.

Later during the season, we had a road trip to Athens to play Georgia. Mr. Haslam told Brenda to pack her bags and go cheer for the Vols. Terry and I rode the team bus. Brenda and Kathy drove to Athens and stayed with Dr. Peaches Smith, Terry's dad and mom's house in Covington. Brenda was paid while at our games. Mr. Haslam said it was in the best interest of the Vols to have her there supporting us against our rival Bulldogs. Jim Haslam is just simply a one-of-a-kind human being and friend. We won both games, by the way!

Sometime in November we made two big decisions. The first one was to think about starting a family. The second one was really a no-brainer. Our 1956 blue and white Chevy started "clacking", bad evidence of a big need for new piston rings and a major, far too expensive engine overhaul. We decided to take up Uncle Coochie's offer of helping us locate a new car. He was named officially at

## The Loser's Ball

birth, Clifford Donald Graves, Pap's brother. Uncle Coochie was a salesman at Jim Reed Chevrolet in Nashville. I sold several of my calves, cows, and tobacco allotment to help in financing the purchase. We went home for Christmas in a brand new 1966 Chevy Chevelle. Here we are, we told ourselves; too young to marry, too broke to eat out, saving every nickel and dime to get by, and going out and buying a new car. Although God didn't make any payments for us, He got us through once again.

I did everything that I could in preparation for the upcoming baseball season. All of our players did the same thing. I could sense a big difference once our bunch became seniors. There were some good younger players now as freshmen and sophomores. Larry Fielder and Tommy Giles were outstanding players. I had witnessed the great progress of our juniors, like Choo Tipton, Jim McBride, Dave Tiller, and others improving every year. Workouts were more focused. Players were working more on strength building and paying attention to overcome any deficiencies in their game. The batting cage was always busy during the fall and early winter months.

Once we got underway in early spring, we got the sad news, a big Loser's Ball. Coach Don Lumley was killed in Viet Nam and would leave a wife and son on their own. How I loved that man! It was a tough loss to have been so close to him and now, not able to talk with him or ask advice from him again.

As a team, we dedicated the 1966 season to him, honoring him for his impact on those whose lives he had touched. I think of a song that the late John Denver recorded, Some Days Are Diamonds. The chorus goes like this: *"Some days are diamonds, some days are stone. Sometimes the hard times won't leave me alone. Sometimes the cold winds blow a chill in my bones. Some days are diamonds, some days are stone."* I still think of him so often.

Our lives are filled with some days being great emotional highs, diamonds, if you call them that. Other parts of our lives seem to be nothing but stone, Loser's Ball, sliders, curves, sinkers, high fast balls, and even bean balls. We don't have a choice but to respond in a positive manner or live our lives in the loser's bracket all the time.

When we get in a big hole, the best exercise is to dig out. There is no solace, no reward, no wins, no peace, and no happiness if we make the decision to wallow in self-pity and join the POMS club. (Poor Old Me Syndrome). I love the words of Paul in Galatians 6:9; *"Let us not grow weary in doing good, for at the proper time we will reap a harvest if we do not give up."*

After having two winning seasons in a row, we were ready to graduate as seniors with the first Tennessee baseball team to hopefully have three consecutive baseball winning seasons. We were confident that we would succeed in meeting that goal. Our other goals were to win the Southeastern Conference and go to the College World Series in Omaha, Nebraska. Only one other team had done that, and that was Sid Hatfield's 1951 Vols, who did both.

Our first 10 games resulted in a record of 6-4, not quite up to our hopes. During the next 15 games, we rallied to a record of 13-2, including a nine-game winning streak. We beat teams like Notre Dame, Kentucky, Georgia, Auburn, Maryville, Tennessee Tech, and LMU. Closing out our last four season games we went 3-1, including two big wins over Vanderbilt. During our three years of playing Vandy, our record was 12 wins 1 loss. Vandy was not very good back then, but that would change later.

Following is a story of our last Vandy win in Nashville, the last regular season game for me as a Tennessee Vol. Earlier as a freshman during my first game as a Vol, I hit a home run against Hiawassee. We were leading Vandy by a big score in our last game before the SEC championship series. My entire family was there in the bleachers at the Nashville game, including Uncle Charlie, cousins, and even some Glade friends.

It was the top of the eighth inning, the score was 18-1 in our favor. It was to be my last at bat. I had a count on me of three balls and no strikes. I have no idea why I did this even today, but I backed out of the batter's box and told the catcher, "Look here, I've got my family in the bleachers, and they aren't here to see me walk. Tell that pitcher to throw me something I can hit." The catcher calmly stood up and simply replied, "You got it, fastball down the middle."

Obviously, they were already living in the loser's bracket, because, here it came, a beautiful fast ball right down the heart of the plate.

My last swing in a regular Tennessee season baseball game resulted in a home run hit over the right field fence with the ball sticking up like a snow cone on the top of a construction dirt pile. It was retrieved by my fast fleeted little brother, Larry. I never looked at Coach Wright when I rounded third base. I just stuck out my hand with my head down to avoid eye contact. I nodded and kindly thanked the catcher as I crossed home plate. What a memory! That one was for all the family and friends there who had supported me over the years beyond measure.

Coach Wright handed out copies to all of us of the latest edition of the college baseball newspaper, "Collegiate Baseball News". The front cover of the newspaper had a picture of our starting line-up, each of us holding our bats in front of us. The article included the rankings for the teams at the end of the season. USC was number 1, followed by Florida State at 2, Michigan at 3, Washington State at 4, and Tennessee at 5. We ended our regular season with 22 wins and 7 losses, the most games ever won by a Tennessee baseball team in school history.

We lost 2 games to Mississippi State in the SEC championship series. Ken Tatum, an All-SEC pitcher, ended up pitching and getting the win in both games due to a three-day rain delay after our first lost in Knoxville. Tatum went on to pitch in the majors for the California Angels. Our final record was 22-9. I had a good SEC tournament going 4 for 7 (.571) against Tatum, but it was not our best two games. I finished the '66 season in the SEC hitting .331. I was also fortunate to end my tenure at UT by breaking the single season individual scoring record. I scored 32 runs in our 31 games. I didn't even know about the record until Bobby Tucker broke it in 1970, when they played more games and a friend told me about it. There were no awards, rings, ceremonies, or team banquets where trophies were handed out. That's okay. I never played for trophies anyway. As a team, we also did something no other Tennessee team had previously done. We had three consecutive winning seasons!

Personally, there was something else to be more excited about at our house.

Right after Christmas, before our season got cranked up, Brenda told me that she thought that she was pregnant. Her visit to see her doctor she worked for at the Donelson Clinic, Dr. Anderson, confirmed her excitement. What a wonderful gift from God! We were the happiest two people in the US of A. We had kept our faith and hopes up silently, without talking about our doubts, but now, Wow! All of that was lifted from us.

Needless to say, my last season was played with a different mindset than the previous two years. It was my best year in baseball to be a part of Tennessee's first ever SEC Eastern Division Championship. That now makes 12 championships. Will there be more? Brenda has just about fulfilled her part of the sweet "deal" we made as seniors in high school. Now, Bob, it is time to get a job and continue keeping your end of the deal.

I had kept an eye on the vocational agriculture teaching status at Gallatin High School in Sumner County, just across the river from our Wilson County homes. The teacher there had just retired and a vacancy would be announced shortly, I assumed too much. To get my foot in the door, I wrote a letter to Principal, Dan Herron, to let him know that I was interested and would like to schedule an interview. A few days later I got a letter from Mr. Herron, stating that he was not interviewing anyone because he had decided to permanently close the agriculture program at GHS. I couldn't believe it. Another Loser's Ball! That was the job I wanted since it was only 25 miles from home, and had unlimited potential to be one of the best FFA programs in the state.

I had another opportunity, but it was too far away. Dr. Sam Reed, a former ag teacher and now the Superintendent of Dyersburg City Schools, had written me a letter and offered me the ag job there. I knew him well and had been to his county while I was serving as a state FFA officer. I knew Brenda would not want to live that far away from her big family so I had to come up with plan C. The "C" stood for Bill Coley.

## The Loser's Ball

I notified my former ag teacher at Mt. Juliet, who was now an FFA/Ag supervisor for the state. He told me that he would get back to me in a few days. Fortunately, Mr. Coley was from Sumner County, and knew just about all of the agriculture movers and shakers there. He told me to meet him on a certain day to drive over together to talk with Mr. Herron, who had agreed to meet with us at 2:00 pm. In the meantime, our day began around 9 am. We had meetings with the chairman of the Sumner County School Board, Mr. Billy Dick Brown, who was not aware of the decision to drop ag at GHS. We met with the President of the Sumner County Farm Bureau and three other ag leaders/parents in the county. We even met with Mr. Dick Reese, owner of Reese Mule Co., who was one of the largest mule suppliers in America. He wanted his two boys, Dickie and Rufus to be able to take agriculture classes. The Reese Mule Company was also known for the mules they supplied for the Grand Canyon tours in Arizona. Rufus now cures country hams and sausage for sale at his farm. All of these men, women, and parents, like the Carters and McKees, were supportive and gave permission for us to drop their names in our meeting with Mr. Herron.

I believe Mr. Coley and I did our best sales job on Mr. Herron. I had the job two hours after our conversation began. Dan Herron and I worked together for over twenty five years in education in Sumner County. He became a dear friend of mine and I loved him up to the day he passed away.

My work wasn't complete just yet. When school ended it was time for us to pack up and head back to Wilson County. I remember when we left and started our lives together in Knoxville, Brenda cried because she was going to miss her family and friends. The week we left Knoxville, she cried for the same reason. We had spent three years there and had so many friends we loved like brothers and sisters.

Other than friends and teammates that we had left behind, we left an old bookcase in the median of I40, somewhere between Rockwood and Crossville. Brenda had a nice little tummy now, but I still had to return to summer school to take two classes that I could not schedule because of spring baseball conflicts. Coincidently, the two classes were Dairy and Ag Mechanics. Dr. Miles, my dairy instructor said that I could probably teach the class myself, but he got paid to do it! He was a super nice guy to me all summer. I had to make farm gates and cattle handling equipment in the Ag Mech class, things that I had done in my high school agriculture shop, but I did learn some new valuable welding techniques that would come in handy in my shop instruction.

Both instructors were told about the impending arrival of our new family member. They were gracious and understanding. I was scheduled to graduate on Friday, August 25, 1966. While I was away Brenda had moved in with her mother, Nannie, from our little rental house from cousins Oko and Betty Hamblen just down the road. Coach Wright had gotten me a room in my old dorm at Melrose, rooming with a football player, Bill Baker, a great roommate who was attending summer school like me. I would always leave on Fridays to go home every weekend to check on Brenda.

During the first weekend in August, Brenda let me know about 5:30 am that it was time to head to the hospital. We arrived at the Baptist Hospital in Nashville around 6 am. My mother showed up to be of more comfort to me than Brenda, I think. Brenda was pretty cool about the whole deal. She wasn't there over an hour before she was transported to the delivery room. Lucy, Brenda's sister-in-law arrived just after Brenda had left. The three of us did not have to wait long before Dr. Anderson came in and congratulated me on the birth of our new daughter, Julie Gayle Lannom, born at 8:00 am on August 5, 1966. Mom and Julie were doing fine and I could go back in a few minutes. I will never forget what Lucy told Brenda when she saw her holding Julie, "Girl, you didn't waste any time. Next time you have a baby, all you will need is a BAND-AID and a bucket!" That was Lucy.

After all the families came in, the reality finally sank in. I am now a daddy and have just inherited a major responsibility. I really need to start my new job and career. Leaving Brenda and Julie and going back to summer classes was tough. I started out at UT as "Mr.

Lonely", and here I am again. But, this time there is now a brighter light at the end of the college tunnel.

Nannie and Brenda's sister Donna (Dee), kept Julie, while Brenda, Daddy, Mama, and I attended my graduation in Knoxville on August 25, 1966 as scheduled. I saw people getting all kinds of degrees, Magna cum laude, Summa cum laude, etc. I was glad to get my degree……….. "Laude How Come!" We drove immediately back home following graduation because I had to be in the classroom Monday morning, August 28, at Gallatin High School to begin a new phase of our lives as a family and now an educator. Okay Bob, you have the weekend to rest, then, it's time to go to work and live up to your part of the "deal". Brenda has succeeded in fulfilling her contract. Go to work!

*The official baseball newspaper in 1966 was Collegiate Baseball News. After winning the Southeastern Conference Eastern Division Championship and being ranked 5$^{th}$ in the nation, they took this picture of our starting lineup. It appeared as the front-page cover photo of their newspaper at the end of our season in 1966. Left to right: Tom Pritchard, Bob Lannom, John Burpo, Jack Ervin, Darrell Lowe, Larry Tipton, Tommy Giles, and Danny Neff. Our guys finished with a .316 team batting average.*

*Our 1966 team was excited to see all of the Lindsey Nelson Stadium improvements. Among them was the addition of the Volunteer Division Titles to the left center field wall. It didn't take long for me and my former teammates, Coy Meadows, and Larry Fielder, to point out that we were the first Vol team to win a Division title back in 1966. We also set a school record for most single season wins that year.*

*My cousin, Kay Smith, and I make many trips together to Knoxville to watch some exciting football and baseball games. Kay was an outstanding coach and school administrator. We still laugh about her uncle calling us the meanest two kids in Vesta.*

*My '66 Vol teammate, Coy Meadows, left, and I spent the week in Hoover Met Stadium in Hoover, Alabama, to watch our Number One ranked Vols win the 2024 SEC Baseball Tournament.*

# Chapter 18

Years ago, William Danforth, wrote in his book entitled, I Dare You, "95% of all individuals lack the determination to call on their untapped potential". He stated, "The overwhelming majority quickly settle on being just status quo, feeling sorry for themselves and their misfortune, while the remaining 5 % of the successful minority, continue up their ladder of success".

Dan Herron was beginning his third year as Principal of Gallatin High School. I had gotten to know a lot about him when I would come home during summer school and spend time at the school getting things ready to begin my new job as FFA advisor and teacher there. He had taken over a very relaxed and somewhat disruptive situation at GHS that needed some discipline and leadership to right the Green Wave ship.

I had to convert a paint finishing room, which was located in the Gallatin Junior HS shop, into a classroom. The high school did not have a shop or available classroom since the earlier decision was made to shut down the ag program. I preferred to have had my classroom in the shop area anyway.

When I arrived for opening day, only teachers showed up to get things ready for students the following day. I was pleasantly surprised to see my baseball friend from Ray Batts Nashville, Jerry Vradenburg present. Jerry had been hired by Mr. Herron away from White House High School as the new Green Wave girls and boys basketball coach. Jerry and I renewed our previous times together on the baseball field. Jim Baron, a former Mississippi State tackle, joined our staff as our new head football coach. He gave me a hard time about our loss to State in the SEC championship. These two men would become legends at Gallatin High School. Jerry's boys' basketball team would soon win the Tennessee High School state championship in 1973. Jim Baron along with his coaching staff, would rebuild the football program to greatness in three short years and set the stage to eventually win the Tennessee TSSAA Football championship in 1978, serving as an assistant coach under a new head coach, Calvin Short.

I arrived at Gallatin just in time to join the parade of championships, by working with parents and some fantastic young students, in helping to rebuild the vocational agriculture program into perennial winners in our district and regional FFA competitions. Mr. Herron was the power behind the changes without a doubt. He coined the phrase, "Green Wave Pride", but always gave credit to his coaches and faculty members as a winning team effort. I was blessed again to be working in an environment where the emphasis was on the team, not the individual. Coaches, Vradenburg, Baron, and Short made sure that wins came to those who believed in team achievement instead of individual and egotistical performances.

We found a rental house for us to move into just before Christmas. It was a nice home with some of the best neighbors in the world living behind us. Jimmy and Sarah England, along with their kids, Al, Mike, and Teresa, became our extended family. Teresa was a terrific baby sitter for Julie. She would become a vital part of our kid's lives throughout the years to come.

When spring came, I talked to Brenda about playing baseball with Jerry and Pat Webb in the Nashville Tri-State League. Pat became my best partner when I settled in my classroom. He would take the less than motivated ninth graders and put them in his shop class and recommend the kids most likely to fit my program. Pat coached basketball and football at the junior high school. He also became my best quail and deer hunting buddy as well. Jerry and Pat had played for Nashville baseball teams for several years.

I joined the team of Nashville Sporting Goods, owned by Walter Nipper in downtown Nashville. We were coached by the legendary W.P. (Perk) Williams. Perk put me in center field at my regular position. When I was taking a three-week educational seminar, he paid to fly me on a Southern Airways DC 9 from McGee-Tyson airport in Knoxville, to Nashville to play in a big tournament. That was the most memorable and only flight I ever took to play baseball. When they started up the engines, with black smoke belching from them, there stood two airport fire fighters holding fire extinguishers, I felt less than safe. I just hoped those guys would be riding along with me on the flight.

While playing with Sporting Goods, I met another guy who would be a life-long friend of our family, Boots Kirby. Boots and Jerry would one day be inducted into Shelby Park's Old Timers Field Hall of Fame. Jerry and Boots attended Belmont University together. I have a copy of a line-up sheet with the four of us leading the batting order of Sporting Goods. Boots led off, I hit second, Pat hit third, and Jerry hitting clean-up. Priceless! Pat retired from baseball and Jerry went on to play for Coursey's Bar-B-Que. Boots and I remained on the NSG team. We didn't win the league championship, but with Brenda watching me, with Julie in the playpen, we enjoyed some great times at the ball park together.

I got to play with some other old timers during my games in Nashville my two years with Sporting Goods. It was a very relaxed transition from the highly competitive games as a Vol, especially trying to earn my scholarship. There were no heated rivalries, brawls, or even ill-tempered words between players. It was during those years that I got to see my little brother, Larry, excel as a pitcher for Mt. Juliet HS. Yes, they finally got a baseball team just after Larry started there. During Larry's senior year at MJHS, he pitched 59 innings as a starter and struck out 82 batters. He had one of the nastiest curve balls around. I am glad that I was sitting in dad and mom's living room when Lipscomb University Head Coach, Ken Dugan, signed Larry to a baseball scholarship that night in 1968. In Coach Dugan's book, "Coaching Winning Baseball", Larry is pictured several times,

## The Loser's Ball

demonstrating the pitching techniques he used to star for Lipscomb the two years he played there.

Boots Kirby became one of my closest friends and teammates. I played center field and he played left field for Nashville Sporting Goods. He was a very talented player, good hitter, strong arm, and fast on the base paths. He was also a "character". There are just some people you love to hang around with. He possessed the gift of gab that would bring tears to your eyes from laughing so much. Needless to say more, Boots enjoyed the game of baseball.

We were playing a game at Shelby Park on the famous Old Timers Field. When our side was retired, we ran out on the field during a brief shower of rain to take our positions. I looked over at Boots as he pulled out one of those fold-up umbrellas and holds it over his head. The infield umpire saw it as well and stopped the game. He walked out to Boots and asked him, "What do you think you are doing?" Boots replied, "I'm playing left field." The umpire responded, "Why do you have an umbrella out here then?" Boots calmly said, "Because it's raining." He was told by the umpire that if he wanted to continue playing, and since the umbrella was not part of his uniform, he could either get rid of it or leave the field. Boots handed the ump the umbrella and told him that he could borrow it if he wanted to. That was not funny to the ump!

I do not recall during my years of playing or watching thousands of baseball games that I ever saw the following occur on the field. I must confess that Boots Kirby and Bob Lannom are the only ones, to my knowledge during modern times, to have committed this stunt in baseball. It happened during my second year playing for Sporting Goods. We were playing the game at the Old Timers Field at Shelby Park and were well ahead in the late innings when it happened.

Boots had just singled and was on first. Batting next, with one out, I drew a walk to move Boots down to second base. We had played together in many games and had our own signals about stealing bases or getting into run-downs, etc. Boots gave me the signal for us to do a double steal on the next pitch. The batter took a ball low in the dirt as Boots slid safely into third and I made it to second without a throw. The opposing team manager came out of the dugout and calls time out to talk to his pitcher. Boots and I got together between second and third and watched the conversation.

Neither of us could think of a reason for the conference except for the manager to probably be telling the pitcher not to worry about those sorry guys stealing bases with a big lead this late in the game. Perhaps we both got the message at the same time. To this day, I don't recall, either because of a poor memory, or an unwillingness to accept the responsibility of the next action to occur, we agreed to perform our plan to perfection. After the conference on the mound, we returned to our bases and the ump motioned to put the ball in play.

Our next batter steps into the box in hopes of picking up a couple of runs batted in. As the pitcher gets his sign, Boots leads off of third on the second base side while I am leading off of second toward first base. When he goes into his wind up to throw home, Boots breaks for second and slides in safely as I bolt for first and slide in without a throw. We simply "un stole" first and second and went back to correct our un-sportsmanlike double steal.

The catcher is standing there still holding the baseball, not knowing what to do next. He hadn't been coached to know how to deal with this situation. The pitcher is staring at the sky with his jaw dropped, and shaking his head in disbelief. Our guys in the dugout are on their knees gasping with laughter and hysterically pounding the dirt.

The home plate ump quickly pulls off his mask, clutching it in his right hand and jettisons in front of the plate, waving his arms back and forth, nearly knocking over the catcher still hanging on to the ball not knowing to throw it to third, second, or first. He can't throw it back to the pitcher. He's still watching clouds and wouldn't see it coming. The two umps come together for about five seconds. Short discussion.

The home plate ump charges toward second, points at Boots, and yells, "You're out!" Then he points to me and does the same. Both of us, holding our arms out to our sides, reply, "Nobody touched us

## The Loser's Ball

with the ball. We were just amending our ways and returning to our original bases in good sportsmanship." The ump was sharp and knew the rules. He just put it plainly. "You are making a travesty of the game. You are both out by the rules. Now get off the field you clowns!" I felt bad, but it's always good to do a little rule testing, occasionally, just to make sure the umpiring staff is on their toes. They were on top of it.

Here's a little history provided by Chris Landers, on that MLB rule instituted in 1920. Herman "Germany" Schaefer's Washington Senators, were playing the Chicago White Sox. Clyde Milan was on third as the winning run. Schaefer stood on first base with just one out, the perfect opportunity to attempt a steal to draw a throw from the catcher that would allow Milan to score from third and win the game. On the next pitch, Schaefer takes off to second but the catcher holds the throw. It didn't work this time, so on the next pitch Schaefer goes back to first to try it again. That started a big rhubarb between the managers and umpires, but there was nothing they could do about it. When Schaefer tried it again, they caught him in a run-down and Milan broke for home only to get thrown out by the second baseman. MLB added the following rule in 1920: Rule number 5.09 (b) (10). "After a runner has acquired legal possession of a base, he runs the bases in reverse order for the purpose of confusing the defense or making a travesty of the game. The umpire shall immediately call "Time" and declare the runner out." As Forrest Gump said many times, "That's all I got to say about that!" Boots and I still laugh today.

Special thanks to Chris Landers of CUT4 on his article on "7 Strangely Specific MLB Rules." August 23, 2017, specifically, his story about Herman Germany Schaefer.

We couldn't have picked a more historic park to pull that stunt. I arranged a visit to amend my indiscretion. I met with Mickey Hiter, Director of the Sandlot Baseball organization, who personally does the maintenance on the two Shelby Park fields including the Old Timers Field. Mickey was the Lipscomb catcher, who caught my brother, Larry, during their days playing together for Coach Dugan.

He commented on Larry's style of pitching. He said that he was an "in your face "pitcher, and wasn't afraid to pitch inside to hitters. He said his curve ball was almost unhittable. He told me that when he and Larry were playing summer ball for Nautaline, Larry pitched two no-hitters in a ten-day period. I was there with Daddy to see one of those games.

Mickey informed me that the Old Timers Field is the fourth oldest baseball field in the nation, just behind Wrigley Field, Fenway Park, and Rickwood Field in Birmingham, Alabama. He had heard about the re-stolen bases incident, but now he got it from one of the culprits first-hand. Mickey also maintains the Old Timers Hall of Fame in the museum/press box building behind home plate. I recognized a number of my Nashville teammates and opponent's pictures on the walls, including Jerry and Boots, Ron Bargatze, Farrell Owens, and many others.

Before ending my visit with Mickey, I presented him a nice check for him to use for any expenses at Shelby and asked for forgiveness for making my one and only travesty of the game I loved. He said, "All is forgiven, I will use this money for seed and fertilizer." Summer baseball is still being played at Old Timers since 1914, on two excellent fields with many memories of stories of past performances by legends of Nashville baseball, and in its history, where a travesty of the game was committed!

*By being convicted and called out for making a travesty of the game I loved, I felt compelled to write a check to my friend Mickey Hiter, Director of the Shelby Park Old Timer's Field to compensate for my indiscretion. The money went for grass seed and fertilizer.*

*My brother, Larry, pitched for Lipscomb University in Nashville for two years. This photo appeared in legendary Lipscomb Coach, Ken Dugan's book, "How To Coach Winning Baseball."*

# Chapter 19

*"When I was a young man, I observed that 9 out of 10 things I did were wrong. I didn't want to be a failure so I did 10 times more work."*
George Bernard Shaw

Instead of expecting great things to come to you, you must prepare yourself to reach for great things in your future. Someone said that," The interstate to success is dotted with many tempting rest stops." You must capitalize on your strengths no matter how small. Winners find a way. Most people are much too inclined to do as little as possible because it is easier to be a result of the past rather than preparing themselves to be a cause of the future. If you prefer to hang out with large crowds, then settle with mediocrity. The least crowded place of all is among those who are at the top. Most are not willing to pay the price of admission to being the best in their field of endeavor.

The 1969 Nashville Tri-State League was to begin their summer schedule. I had been contacted by another team to play for them during the fall. Ezell Dickerson was building a team to match up with, and be able to win against the team coached by Larry Schmittou, Tennessee Pride Eggs, that was running away with the city championship each year. Larry had a great team consisting of Farrell Owens, Ted Jamison, Danny Burns, and Steve Garner. Simon Dickerson, the coach of Ezell Dickerson had put together a good line up of good ball players.

The new team members included; W.A. Wright, Ronnie Norton, Lee Crouch, Watson Brown, Mack Brown, Elliott Jones, Gary McDonald, myself, and others. I was fortunate to play center field with Mack Brown, Watson's younger brother, in left field that first season with Ezell. Mack, at the time was enrolled at Vanderbilt, where his brother, Watson, was the quarterback at Vandy. Of course, Mack became and still is a coaching legend, having won a national championship at Texas as their head football coach. He is now the head coach of North Carolina, where he began his early coaching career. Mack left Vanderbilt and transferred to Florida State, where he graduated as a running back for the Seminoles. Watson would lead Vandy to one of their best records while there at quarterback, including getting a big win over Alabama by a score of 14-10, their first win against Bama in 13 seasons. Watson had been drafted by the Pittsburg Pirates as a shortstop. We played together for two years while I was with Ezell. We came close to the Tri-State championship during the '69 season but came up short. It was great to have these guys as teammates that year.

Back in Gallatin, the FFA program was really growing. So was our daughter, Julie. During my first two years there with our great start and winning a number of FFA competitive events, I thought it was the best time to talk about getting a new truck donated to the FFA from one of the local auto dealers in Gallatin. I was told that it would be impossible to get a new truck that way. I was advised to see if the board of education would buy us one. I dismissed that idea as quickly as I heard it.

Since we were renting our house from the financial manager at the Ford Dealership, Wade Motor Company, I presented my landlord, W.A. Douglas, with the idea of Wade donating the use of a new truck to the FFA chapter. I explained that the students and I would build a camper top for the truck with advertisement of the dealer's sponsorship written on it. It wasn't long after our sign painter in town, Haynes Sloan finished the lettering that Bob was driving a new Wade Motor Company Ford truck to school every day. We put a number of miles on that truck hauling students on judging field trips, competitive events, camp, convention, and other FFA activities. Vic Jenkins Chevrolet started providing the truck for us a few years later. Mr. Vic and his son Scott Jenkins, became avid followers and supporters of our FFA program.

Gallatin was a community where excellence was of prime importance to its citizens, whether it was sports or an ag program. I was definitely at the right spot. Sometimes, all you have to do is ask and make sure to recognize the great dealerships, banks, businesses, and organizations who support your program. I think that the truck deal became the catalyst to encourage more supporters. Soon, the banks went in together and paid for our annual FFA banquet and awards. Our annual calendar was funded by small businesses that covered the cost of printing. Farm Bureau and Farm Credit picked up the tab to take our students to state conventions. Businesses like Brown Milling Company, Hudgens Equipment, and the Farmers COOP, were super and all in. We now had enough demand by students wanting to take our agriculture/FFA program that Mr. Herron, our principal, asked and got permission for us to hire a second teacher.

Girls were now allowed to enroll and be members of the FFA. I was glad to see that happen, because I had met so many girls at school who wanted to go to college and major in ag business or marketing, but could not get the training and leadership skills provided through the FFA, because of the restrictions. Of all people, I was certainly aware of those type of rules and policies since they were similar to my earlier baseball restrictions.

We hired a graduate from UT Martin, Larry (Pete) Carpenter. Pete and I hit it off from the onset. Brenda and I became close friends with Pete and Pat, his wife, and young family. Pete became a part of the team that was missing in our program. We even shared the same birthday in July. It was just meant to be.

Together, we made plans to sometime in the future build a greenhouse for our department to teach floriculture, horticulture, landscaping, and plant science. It was also be a great way to raise money from plant sales to pay for the expansion of all of our award programs, camp, and convention trips. Our students would actually be the workers to lay the blocks, cut the rafters, and cover the greenhouse with plastic for the roof and walls. We made the program so inviting with the buy-in from a bunch of fantastic students and parents, it was hard to enroll every student who wanted to be in the program. Basically, we had a waiting list even now with two teachers.

I must tell the story of how we got the finances to build our greenhouse. Like the truck deal, I was told that I would never get the board of education to fund the project. I admit that I had my doubts, but with our truck deals now a reality, I became a little more optimistic about the school board's involvement since it was directly tied to instruction. I don't like to be told that I could never do anything! Never is just not a good word for me. I had already learned that "N-O" is just the first two letters of NOT NOW!

There was a lady who served as the "money" person who controlled the Superintendent's purse strings, named Mrs. Kelley. She was a gentile, southern lady, who was careful with the board's money. Tight would be a better description. As a matter of fact, she had all of the board office secretaries to not tear off their adding machine tape, but let it fall off on the floor, rewind it, and use the back side to save money. That's tight! When I first told my friends of my plan, they discouragingly remarked, "Good luck Bob, but just remember, we told you so!" Like I preached to my kids, my students, and friends, "Go find a way! Don't give up! Do not be afraid to ask or try a different approach to reach your goals."

A gentleman in the area, by the name of Mr. Hix, had a little greenhouse on his property near his home. He had been nice to help us with some ideas about greenhouse construction and operation. He raised beautiful orchids in his greenhouse and sold them to florists in town, including a shop called, Lady Belle's Flowers.

When I stopped by one day to visit with Mr. Hix, he told me that he was going to shut down his greenhouse and get rid of his orchids. I suggested that he sell or donate them to our ag department. He agreed to donate them along with some good advice on how to raise them in the windows of our ag shop. Fortunately, we had these high windows on the south side of our shop the full length of the wall. The students were helpful in building the benches on the wall below these windows for the new arrival of many pots of orchids in our first "greenhouse".

I had never raised orchids. I bought a couple on two occasions for Brenda to wear to our proms. That's was at the time the extent of my knowledge about orchids. I also knew that they made girls happy when they got one.

Mr. Hix taught me all I needed to know. That first year we sold a lot of beautiful orchids to Mr. Hix's previous clients, and made money for the FFA. That's when the greenhouse construction idea really began to "bloom." I selected one of our most beautiful orchids, took it over to Lady Belle Braley's flower shop, and got her to make a beautiful corsage and place it in one of those white boxes as if I was going to give it to the prettiest girl in school to take to the prom. When I told her my mission and who I was taking it too, she didn't charge me a penny. She, aware of my challenge, just wanted me to let know how that adventure turned out.

I made an appointment with Mrs. Kelley at the school board for that afternoon. She was so polite to me whenever I had met with her on earlier occasions, truly an asset to the school system. I took my box with me and walked into her office not allowing her to see what I had in my hand. I sat down and we chatted for a while about school and our FFA program's success, and about girls now being permitted in the program. I then presented her my box and slid it across her desk and said that it was a gift from our agriculture department. She carefully opened the box, and asked with a glow of excitement, "Oh!, Mr. Lannom, is this for me?" I said, "It sure is Mrs. Kelley. We are having to grow these orchids in the windows of our old shop, because we do not have a greenhouse to raise them properly."

I went on to tell her that if we had a greenhouse, we wouldn't have to just teach; cows, sows, and plows anymore. We could get our girls interested in classes like floriculture and horticulture as well as the boys in learning greenhouse management and landscaping. There was a heavy dose of salesmanship floating all around that room to say the least, but I believed in what I was selling, which I knew was one of the first rules in sales. I believe that the sale was closed when I asked her, "Do you mind if I pin this corsage on you, Mrs. Kelley?" Her response was dollar signs in my eyes and ears, "Mr. Lannom, I think that this is a marvelous idea. How much money do you think it will take to build your greenhouse?" I quickly said, "Our students can build it for $1,500 plus an additional $500 for start-up supplies. We will have a built-in fund raiser and never have to ask the board for instructional supplies in the future." (Basically, all that we were getting from the board then was $100 per year). We had nearly 200 students in our program. That calculated to 50 cents per student! Too some people, though, $100 sounded like a lot of money. The pitch worked.

For a short dude I felt like I was 6'4 as i walked like a giant out of Mrs. Kelley's office that afternoon with a check for $2,000! I could not have felt any better if I had just hit a walk-off grand slam in the bottom of the ninth to win the SEC Championship. What is the old Chinese proverb? *"Man who say it cannot be done, need to get out of way of man doing it!"*

It may take you a lot of rock hitting to get to this point in your life. If you are defeated, let it be caused by those who are smarter, bigger, or work harder than you, but never go down by self-defeat. That is the worst way to lose. Unfortunately, the world is full of these types of losers. Most folks just give up and crawl back to the house and are not determined enough to keep trying and work hard enough to win the prize.

The Gallatin High School FFA built the first school greenhouse in the Sumner County school system in 1969. Today, at every new agriculture/FFA program built in Tennessee, and at most high schools across the country, you will find a greenhouse as part of the learning facilities. Mrs. Kelley is to be thanked for making it happen at GHS as well as Mr. Hix, Lady Belle, a small box containing an orchid corsage, and a dream.

That greenhouse generated a lot of interest with another family across the river in Wilson County that proved to become a full-time business for Wallace and Louise Lannom, my parents. At the end of our first year, after eclipsing sales of over $5,000, our students helped to load up the left-over plants we had in stock into the back of our FFA truck. Cleaning out the greenhouse for the summer before school was out was now completed.

On Saturday, the next day, I drove over to the Glade to the home of my parents and after breakfast, Daddy and I drove the truck filled with plants to the Glade to set up our little sales center in front of the Baptist Church in the "square." During the next two and a half hours, we sold over $300 worth of plants to drive-by shoppers. We left the Glade with an empty truck and joined Mom back at the house for lunch. My daddy was impressed, so much that he asked me, "Do you think if a man had a greenhouse, he could sell lots of plants here?" Smiling at him I said, "Daddy, you just did it this morning. It's time to build you and Mama a greenhouse."

The Lannom Plant Farm in Gladeville, Tennessee, operated for the next 16 years expanding to the point that there were three greenhouses with annual sales of over $16,000 a year. Daddy finally retired from building airplanes to mixing soil and carrying on lengthy world-saving conversations with the regular customers that they had acquired over the years. They even added a new brick den to their existing old frame farm house. Maybe, just maybe, because of one orchid! You just never know what impact good ideas or deeds done, has in the future. Fun when it happens! Having the faith of a mustard seed or maybe an orchid bloom, is sometimes all that it takes to make bigger things happen.

When January, of 1970 began, I had no idea of the changes that were about to occur in our lives on Duncan Street in Gallatin, Tennessee. We learned that Brenda and I were going to be parents for the second time sometime in September. I anticipated that with two children, it would be difficult for me to play a lot more baseball without placing a big hardship on Brenda. We talked about the season in front of us and decided to finish out the year, and decide what to do after the summer. I knew at 26, I still had some more good years left to play my game, but first things had to come first on my priority list as well. We just filed the decision away and went on about finishing out the school year then wait to see what happens next.

The 1970 edition of the Ezell Dickerson team was complete with a lot of returnees including; Watson, W.A., Ronnie, Lee, Ray Carter, Elliott, Paul Wells, Russ Wingo, Lloyd Eskew, Morris Erby, Larry Graddy, Gary, me and a new pitcher from the Prospectors fame, Dave Pratt. It was one of my best seasons ever. I played relaxed and had a blast playing what I thought would probably be my last season to wear a baseball uniform in competition.

We finally accomplished our goal of winning the 1970 Nashville Tri-State League Championship. We had to play a team from Memphis for the Tennessee AABC State Championship of amateur baseball in Tullahoma, Tennessee, around the first week in September. We had found out that our new arrival would come during that week.

My Brenda was so uncomfortable, but she managed to sit in the bleachers and endured an exciting extra inning game against a good Memphis team for the state championship. My mom sat next to her keeping her refreshed and made sure to keep soft blankets available for padded seats. Brenda was insistent on staying and not going to the car and miss the conclusion of that game. I led off the bottom of the 12$^{th}$ inning with a triple. My ball hit the inside of the top rail of the center field fence and fell inside the park. Two more inches would have meant a walk off homer and win. My thoughts were finally, if we score, Brenda would be most grateful. Unfortunately, I was stranded on third and the game lasted two more innings before we finally won the 1970 Tennessee AABC Amateur State Championship in the bottom of the 14$^{th}$ inning. My third State Championship in amateur baseball.

We were scheduled to go to Atlanta, to play in the Southern Regional Tournament the middle of the week, but massive changes occurred, because of not only my decision not to go and leave Brenda, and miss the birth of our new daughter, but others had issues as well. Watson Brown could not go. He had to show up for football practice at Vanderbilt as their quarterback. Lee Crouch had to report to his school as one of its teachers. Dave Pratt also had to report to school duties as well. Ray Carter was another teacher who had to return to an out of state school to start his year. That meant that four of us; Watson, Lee, Dave, and I, each were hitting over .400, would not be a part of the team. Ray was hitting close to .300.

Ezell got to the semi-finals in the regional tournament in Atlanta before losing to Virginia. All of us felt so bad not to have been there. It could have been an opportunity for Ezell to play in the Stan Musial tournament in Battle Creek. That would have been another opportunity to win another AABC Stan Musial World Series Championship, but I still have no regrets. It was the thing to do. I would have never missed seeing our daughter, Amy Leanne Lannom born on September, 9, 1970.

Simon Dickerson, our manager was interviewed upon his return from the loss in the regional. He commented that if his team had been at full strength, there was no doubt that a trip to Battle Creek would have happened. I was then, and still am content, even though that was my very last baseball game. To end my sports career with one football championship and 13 baseball championships in 13 years from 1958-1970, was good enough for me.

It was a very wise choice to hang up my spikes. On August 23, 1971, the following year, eleven and a half months after Amy's birth, Robert Lee Lannom was born and made his way into the Lannom household. We decided that three was company and four would be a crowd, so Brenda and I settled for an outfield instead of four infielders. Those were the most wonderful and thankful times for us. We were so blessed and thankful to God to have three beautiful healthy children. I not only had my obligation to the deal that I made with Brenda, but now, there were three other reasons to retire from baseball and get involved in raising a family.

Great things were about to happen and what fun we would have seeing our kids excel in sports, in school, and their church activities. Oh, there is going to be some Loser's Balls to come our way, but our faith and confidence to beat them, remains strong. The groundwork has been laid.

# Chapter 20

Extra Innings
(The Game of Life)

In spite of championships
that have come your way,
the big game is tied,
that you yet must play.

Come fame or fortune,
or will it be a loss?
You can be assured
that there is a cost.

The lessons you've learned
on journeys before,
become your foundation
as you endeavor to score.

Move steadily forward
with the victories in sight.
They are yours for the taking.
Never give up the fight!

Bob Lannom

Now, it is time to sit back and take a break. Extra innings are about ready to begin. I debated on stopping my book here and writing a second one at this point, but decided that the preparations, the experiences, the determination, and commitment to success don't need to stop here. I must now transfer all that I have learned and experienced into the beginning of a much more important part of my game....the game of life. The transition from baseball to raising children, making a living for our young family, and continuing my "deal" with Brenda is now my top priority.

New adventures are to begin. My job is to teach and hopefully transfer what I have learned to the young and enthusiastic minds of our kids. To try and live my life through our kids would be a tragic mistake. They must make their own decisions and prepare their futures with the zeal and hard work necessary for success in their sports and finally one day, their game of life. Brenda and I must be the coaches, the supporters, cheerleaders, counselors, and assist them to reach their own goals and championships.

I see far too many parents trying to get their kids to be what they couldn't be, to frustrate them with their own objectives, rather than reinforcing them with the skills and opportunities for them to either win or fail on their own. Yes, kids need to learn what it feels like to lose. It remains our job as parents to not let their losses, however, make them losers. You can be beat, but not beaten. They need to know more of what it takes to be a winner, not only in the short time they play their sports, but in the long most important game of living their lives to the fullest. As parents, we must be visionary, able to not only see who our kids are in their youth, but what they can become as adults in the future. In business, that's what is meant by "supervision", seeing beyond the rock hitting to the great opportunities ahead i.e., "extraordinary vision".

During the Extra Innings, I hope to lead your thinking through some of the challenges and obstacles to reaching your goals. There are so many examples that I look forward to sharing with you. Some may refer to successes as good fortune or luck. I prefer to call them "great blessings", rather than luck. The late Bear Bryant, Alabama's legendary football coach, defined luck as *"When preparation meets opportunity."*

Hopefully, you will also find many valuable concepts to apply in your life's preparations to guide you in meeting your own personal and professional business goals. The lessons learned during my 13 years of successful sports competitions have certainly been appreciated, but the real test of applying and transferring these concepts comes during what I call the "Extra Innings or Game of life." Remember, you will not play sports forever. Hopefully, you will spend more years living your life beyond your physical sports competitions than you will actually live playing the games. That is why it is so important to prepare for that phase of your life. The real test of endurance, courage, will, and challenges are yet to come with family, employment, service to your community, and your relationship with God as you grow spiritually.

I hope that you will stick around. Right now, the outcome of the big game is undecided. Extra Innings are about to begin. Big challenges lie ahead. There are still some more stunts to be pulled to reach my goals. How has your preparation been going? Think you have hit enough rocks? Are you confident and skilled to meet the challenges?

Remember, there are no participation trophies in life! Get your team ready. Take them with you. You can't beat faith, family, and friends, especially having God as the captain of your team to help you overcome the many Loser's Balls that are coming your way.

With our kids, there are now three more reasons for me to lead our home team forward to success, I must not only be dedicated, but now "Dadicated" in leading and guiding them to their successes………..
Batter up!……… Play ball!

# Chapter 21

There are two great statements made by the former President of the United States, Teddy Roosevelt, that have stuck with me over the years since I left baseball and started my professional education and business career. On April 23, 1910, President Roosevelt gave one of the most motivating and impressive speeches ever remembered. It was entitled, "Citizenship In A Republic". A notable passage from that speech is better known as "The Man In The Arena." It was delivered at the Sorbonne in Paris, France.

The quote below is only a part of the oratory given on that day, but is the most recognized and repeated segment of his speech. He gets right to the heart of the worldly critics who were never engaged in the battles at the time. It has often been quoted by athletic coaches to their players to encourage them in spite of the jeers or boos they may hear from the bleachers, to press on for they are the true warriors in the battle, not the bleacher creatures.

### The Man In The Arena

*"It is not the critic who counts; not the man who points out how the strong man stumbles, or where the doer of deeds could have done them better. The credit belongs to the man who is actually in the arena, whose face is marred by dust and sweat and blood; who strives valiantly; who errs, who comes short again and again, because there is no effort without error and*

## The Loser's Ball

*shortcoming; but who does actually strive to do the deeds; who knows great enthusiasms, the great devotions; who spends himself in a worthy cause; who at the best knows in the end the triumph of high achievement, and who at the worst, if he fails while daring greatly, so that his place shall never be with those cold and timid souls who neither know victory nor defeat."*

Teddy Roosevelt

I have a copy of this quote hanging on one of my kitchen cabinets and see it every time I enter and exit my back door. Parents are sometimes the worst to yell out to their children's coaches critical comments and embarrassing statements. As a former coach, school administrator, and parent of young aspiring athletes, I appreciate exactly what "The Man In The Arena" is saying. While supervising high school football games, I regret to say that I have heard bleacher creatures crucifying their coaches, and at times even some of the players. Needless to say, I admit to a shortage of patience with this conduct, coming from many of whom have never suited up in competitive sports.

While I speak of Teddy Roosevelt, permit me to share another statement that he made from his speech, "The Strenuous Life", delivered in 1899. I like this one because I see it applying directly to me growing up and entering my new career in education and business. The message is pretty clear to those who think victories can come from "couching" it, instead of taking chances and having a good work ethic. Here is that powerful quote from his speech:

*"I wish to preach, not the doctrine of ignoble ease, but the doctrine of the strenuous life, the life of toil and effort, of labor and strife; to preach that highest form of success which comes, not to the man who desires mere easy peace, but to the man who does not shrink from danger, from hardship, or from bitter toil, and who out of these, wins the splendid ultimate triumph."*

Recently, I was watching a broadcast on a sports channel featuring comments made by the great Dallas Cowboy wide receiver, Michael Irvin, as he spoke to the Colorado football team after one of their practices under their new head coach, Coach Prime, Deion Sanders. He emphasized, *"The thing that gave me an edge was my work ethic. I was one of those guys who felt that the more you worked, the better you got. It was a confidence thing. I enjoy working."*

He went on to explain how important it is to have the "Will" to win, to push yourself toward developing your best "Skills" in order that you can enter every game, whatever it is, prepared physically and mentally to the best you can be.

I thought about what he said and felt that he was right on target, but that I needed to add a third aspect to what he was saying, especially having worked with many young athletes and students in their growth processes.

The first step to have the "Will" is vital. The second important step is definitely for young athletes to develop their "Skill" at their position. The third component is the "Thrill" or reward for exercising excellence in accomplishing the first two steps. However, I have seen that far too many young athletes want the "Thrill" before paying the price by neglecting the first two steps. They want to stand on stage without engaging in the preparation and work ethic in dedicating themselves to paying the price for success. Success does not come to those who choose to bypass the necessary will and skill development in any endeavor, be it sports or business. To rely on luck or the misfortune of others to be the factors to enable you to win the prizes are foolish mistakes. Winners don't await their fate.... They create their fate in this order: WILL…SKILL…THRILL.

I also love the last statement made by Michael in his NFL Hall of Fame induction speech. He said, *"You tell everyone or anyone that has ever doubted, thought that they did not measure up, or wanted to quit, you tell them to Look Up, Get Up, and Don't Ever Give Up!"*

I was fortunate to be in the teaching profession, but sadly to say, for only six years. The rest of my 24 years in education were spent in administration and supervision in our high school, county, and state department career education programs. Our oldest daughter, Julie, when she was six years old, would often go with me to my ag shop and classroom after school or on weekends to check the greenhouse

## The Loser's Ball

and pretend that she was me teaching my students. I even took the time to teach her about fertilizers and how they affected plant growth. I should have known then that she was destined to become a great teacher in our school system years later.

I was spending my last few weeks cleaning up my shop and classroom at the end of the school year in the spring of 1972. A frequent visitor showed up one afternoon, and stopped by to visit. We sat down at our usual table and began our conversation. Normally our Superintendent would talk about a number of things going on in his busy schedule and would often bounce things off of me to get my perspective, which I appreciated. I thought the world of Mr. Gene Brown and his no-nonsense management style and appreciated his visits to our ag program. He was a woodworker and frequently brought a board that needed smoothing or cut to size for a project that he was working on at the time. This visit seemed different from his normal mission. He was strictly business. I could tell something was on his mind. I wasn't worried about my job. Our FFA program was winning all sorts of awards and our shop had the closest wood planer available to him in the county!

He asked, "Have you heard about these new Vocational Director positions the state is putting in every county school system?" I answered that I had heard about the positions at some of our meetings. In his non bush–beating manner, he asked me, "Would you be interested in changing jobs to come over to the central office and be Sumner County's Vocational Education Director?" Actually, Brenda and I had talked about this possibility and had decided that if I ever got the offer, I would accept it. The first thing I did was to thank him for the offer and proceeded to tell him that I would take the job if he wanted me on his team. Again, in Gene Brown style, just like that he said, "Good! You start July $1^{st}$".

That was the interview, the offer, the acceptance, the whole deal done in five minutes sitting at my shop table that afternoon. That was the way things were done back then, but now, that would be an impossibility. I had some news for Brenda when I got home that day. I told her that I had no idea what the job entailed and that I would be known by one of two performance ratings. I would either be the best Vocational Director Sumner County ever had, or I would be the worst. Since I would be the first one, I qualified for either. With three kids now, we get a raise, plus more time to spend with the family since I wouldn't have to travel to FFA camp, Forestry camp, state and national conventions, etc. I looked forward to the challenges ahead. I did lose the use of my FFA truck, but that would be nice for the new incoming ag teacher taking my place. I believe that I had taken the right steps in becoming an educator which seemed to open a few more doors for transition into more leadership positions.

    I had learned playing baseball and football that it is perfectly all right and respectful to admit that you do not know it all. I also had learned that it is advantageous to find out who knows more about a subject than you do and include them in your visitation agenda to pick their brains. During the short time that I had before July 1, 1972, I made a number of phone calls to some of my contacts in the state department of education to find out exactly what the goals and objectives of the newly appointed Directors of Vocational/Career education were all about.

    Metro Nashville already had a local Director by the name of Dan Covington. Dan became a great friend and shared with me his role and duties as their Vocational Director. Dan and his wife Nancy, to this day remain among some of my closest friends. In a lot of new jobs, one has to first just be a sponge and soak up all the available information concerning any new job or opportunity. Many organizations just show you to your office and say, "Welcome, and Sic em!" It was really up to me to write my own job description that first year as I paddled through a crooked learning curve.

    I learned early that there was now someone for teachers to go to or to blame for their problems. I enjoy challenges and change, especially if the skills and preparations to meet and engage them are part of your character. Being the first in any job can be harrowing or enjoyable, depending upon how much you have accepted and put into practice the key guidelines leading to success. It generally requires a lot of "rock hitting".

Since I am and have been so team-oriented, the first thing that I did was to select and organize a Vocational/Career Education Advisory Committee from business leaders across each area of our county. The more credible input you have available, the easier it is to make the right decisions on any matter that comes before you. Each committee member was asked to go back to his/her community and select three or four advisors of their own to get even more feedback to be discussed at our meetings. I cheated a little on the teacher input by asking each of my ag teacher buddies to personally keep me posted on any events that needed to be addressed county wide involving all of our vocational teachers. Usually, the ag teachers are most reliable and informed of any major development that needs to be addressed, because they are probably the closest of most teachers to the businesses and parents because of their local community involvement. I included the principals and other teachers to serve as consultants and to meet with me as I visited their schools on a regular basis.

Again, I have never claimed in all of my life that I have all the answers. Thankfully, I learned that early in life. There is always a lot of people who know more about a subject than you. Whenever a new challenge came my way, I decided early before I stuck my nose into it that I would call on someone who knew more for help. My new job was just one example. I owe my thanks to so many skilled and helpful folks that freely helped me on many occasions.

For instance, when I needed to learn more about building cabinets for my new house, I took two weeks of summer vacation and worked with no pay for my friend, Jerry Ford, owner of Hartsville Cabinet Co. I clocked in like everybody else and learned their quality system of building cabinets. Jerry exposed me to so much.

I later wanted to build a walnut cannonball bed for our son, Lee. No better place to learn and get experience than to contact Mr. WT Barton and Son in Bethpage, Tennessee. I was told that Mr. Barton was hard to talk to and would never let anyone work in his shop where they specialized in building and reproducing beautiful antique furniture. His work was the best around. I spent two cold Thursday nights going to his shop, basically standing around a warm stove and just talking about what I wanted to do. The third time I went back, Mr. Barton said to me, "You are serious about this, aren't you?" I spent two weeks working with his son, Tommy. Tommy worked at night, so I was there as late as several midnights during those two weeks. I learned how to cut out Queen Ann legs, assemble furniture and again, worked for free. Mr. Barton told me my last night there as he led me to a back storage room in his shop that I could borrow his cannonball bed leg to use as a pattern to make my bed. Awesome, who would have believed this? I used his pattern leg to make Lee's bed posts as I spent one day per leg on my wood lathe in my shop. Returning his pattern when I finished and showing him one of my legs that I had made was another home run for Bob.

I spent another two weeks working free for Mr. Bob Ramsey of Ramcraft Clock Co. in Gallatin, who was kind enough to let me work there to pick up more skills. The bottom line is for all of us to be creative and humble enough to seek out the pros and simply ask them to show you the way. At no cost, except your time. You will be surprised how many folks that are out there who are willing to help you. It works.

There is no substitute for face-to-face contact. The same applies to coaches and their relationships with athletes. A lot of information is missed by forsaking those close-up personal conversations with teachers, students, or athletes. Learning that fact was one of my most valuable tools for encouraging students, teachers, and plant associates to get involved in the decision-making process. It is a leadership trait that must be generated by the person in charge such as an administrator, head coach, or plant supervisor. Rarely does the best information make its way from associate to employer unless there is a planned method for communication to happen.

With 125 vocational/career education teachers in my county, I had to install a large board in my office with the names and schools of every vocational teacher listed with space to write actual dates when I had individual conversations with each teacher and principal. I recorded every contact and visit no matter how short or trivial. I even had a color code that indicated the length of time and topic

# The Loser's Ball

we discussed on my visit with them. I started doing this when I discovered that earlier I was going to my "favorite" subject teachers more, while neglecting the others. I didn't know that they were actually keeping up with how many times I visited their room or lab during the year. That board saved my neck!

The whole idea is to create the opportunity for feedback and listen to what folks are saying. In dealing with teachers, students, athletes, even principals, understand that you have one mouth and two ears for a reason. Listening is the pathway to successful relationships with anybody. It works with everyone, especially, with husbands and wives. Too many bosses want to prove how smart they are by talking too much, when in reality, professionals tell us that a person who is a good listener actually appears to be more intellectual. Daddy told me that his daddy, who was always a quiet grandfather to me, made a statement to him one day. My grandfather said, "It is better to keep your mouth shut, and appear to be a fool, than to open it and remove all doubt!" You can't stick your foot in your mouth if it is closed!

Pat Summit, former UT women's basketball coach, in her book, <u>Reach For The Summit</u>, pointed out that she required every one of her players to look her directly in the eye during her conversations with them. If one of her girls "rolled" their eyes while she was talking to them, they were not in good graces with the coach for some time. That is one skill that Pete, JJ, and I taught every one of our FFA students. They spent a lot of time during our leadership classes learning to give firm handshakes and look each other in the eyes while practicing how to meet and greet people. Every student we had could walk up to any bank president in Gallatin and impress them with their introductory greeting. Jobs are won or lost by just being able to make the best and only first impression. Unfortunately, our young kids today are better at "thumb talking" on their phones than meeting people face to face. Sad!

Julie had started school with Amy and Lee waiting in the wings to follow in a few years. Brenda and I bought our first house on a dead-end street in Gallatin where we would be for a number of years. I bought and tore down an old log corn crib in the Glade and converted it into a log cabin play house for the kids. I built it in the back yard and nailed up our first basketball goal on the back wall. It was a cardboard egg crate that served the purpose until the "team" started growing.

Before long there was a demand for a basketball goal to be built, so I found an old basketball goal with attached posts ready to set in the ground, and poured a large concrete court in front of the cabin. Julie was the one chosen to make the first goals. With some lifting, Amy tossed in a few to get her started. Lee, unfortunately less than two, was too busy washing gravel in his mouth around the fish pond I had built. We had to stay alert to keep up with them. A wooden fence around the back yard was soon to follow.

The state of Tennessee passed a comprehensive vocational education act in the mid-70s to expand Vocational-Technical Education programs in every county in the state. Sumner County would receive a new vocational education addition at Gallatin, Hendersonville, Westmoreland, White House, and Portland High Schools. I came on board as the Vocational Director at the right time. Part of my job was to assist in locating qualified teachers to fill all of the new 50 programs throughout the county. During 1976, I spent countless hours scouring the area for the best instructors to meet the need. Basically, the principals, who actually made the final teacher recommendations to the school board, enlisted me to do the searches for qualified personnel.

I climbed on a roof top and recruited a building trades teacher, a highly respected home builder, Neal Dias, who led his students to build 11 nice homes in Gallatin and to build many other structures, like the clubhouse for the city golf course. His guys even built the emergency ambulance building as well as the local board of education building. I drove to area vocational-technical schools to snatch away adult instructors. I even called my friend, Dean Ward, Superintendent of the Hartsville Vocational School and told him that I was on my way there to steal his drafting instructor, Bill Hilgadiack. Dean was a great guy and told me that Bill would be perfect for Gallatin High School. Boy, was he right! GHS got a bonus. Bill's wife, Betty, became the GHS Cafeteria Manager and both were a big part of the Green Wave Pride for many years. Both have since passed away. I miss them both.

I met with local automotive dealers to find good auto mechanics, such as Hank Scott. I travelled to hospitals to find nurses like Susan Mozingo and Jenny Dowell, interested in teaching health occupations, meeting in restaurants to hire food service instructors, like Wanda Armstrong and Lloyd Owen, and many similar interviews in places I had never been before. Charlie Stieger became a printing/graphic arts instructor and a close friend for years to come. I was fortunate to find good administrators like LK Lannom, Tony Utley, Cody Richardson, and Ronnie Dowell.

At Gallatin, one of my good friends, Jim Spivey, a printer, left his family business, Quality Printing, with his son, and taught graphic arts/printing at the high school. That was just at GHS. There were over 50 such professionals we hired to work at our new vocational/career additions in Westmorland, Portland, Whitehouse, and Hendersonville. As hectic as it was, it was a joy and pleasure to get to meet and recommend so many great men and women to fill those new positions. I always referred to them as my "Vokie" army. Serving that outstanding group was an experience that I cherish to this day.

Hank Scott, auto mechanic teacher at Gallatin High School stayed for over 30 years and had a shop floor you could eat from. JoAnn Bates, teacher of consumer education, was one of my best advisors and friends. Who could forget Wanda Armstrong, her cinnamon rolls, and the cow pile cake she made especially for me? There were so many other fantastic staff members who committed themselves to a motto that we followed once the main army came on board. It was named after a poem I found and revamped it a little bit called. "Bloom Where You Are Planted." I don't know the author, but I credit the first two and last two lines to whomever wrote them. It is all about being the best at whatever you are engaged in any time in your life. If you chose to dig ditches, be the best ditch digger around. If you are employed as a cash register operator, be the best and in demand for the store's customers to ask to go through your line. Be the best in everything you do. We operated our vo-tech program in Sumner County with this goal in mind and drilled it in the minds of our students. If anyone forgot my name, they simply referred to me as the "bloom where you're planted guy." I was proud to wear the name. It just became our culture. Enjoy the message:

## Bloom Where You Are Planted

Your heart is the garden, your thoughts are the seeds.
When comes the harvest, will it be flowers or weeds?
When life seems hopeless with problems you find,
Remember, my friend, it's a matter of mind.

Hope never prospers where failures dim the thrill,
Of finding the treasure just over the hill.
No one plants your garden, it's yours to seed,
For you only are the sower and reaper of your deeds.

No guarantee of future, the time is now.
Bloom where you're planted. Put your hand to the plow.
Your heart is the garden, your dreams are the seeds.
When comes the harvest, will it be flowers or weeds?

First and last two lines: Author unknown.
Inside changes by Bob Lannom

Many of our "Vokie" teachers became team leaders in their respective schools. They volunteered or were asked to assume leadership roles in local teacher in-service training and professional growth experiences. We became a positive force in the county school system and were allowed to conduct our own school start up professional development workshops and training. We were fortunate to have some of the top principals and school administrators in the state to work with, which made coming to work a pleasurable experience.

I am still fortunate enough to remember the names of these dedicated and talented instructors. There are enough stories to go with each name that I could write more books just about their successes. New adventures lay ahead.

# Chapter 22

In New York City, in 1988, running back from Oklahoma State, Barry Sanders won the Heisman Trophy as the 54th recipient of the prestigious award. All Barry wanted to do as a kid was to play football. He actually rode the bench throughout his junior high and high school years,. He was overwhelmingly selected for the Heisman over USC quarterback, Rodney Pete, by a 2-1 margin of voting.

At Wichita North HS in Kansas, he was un-recruited. Oklahoma's Barry Switzer, saw him twice and wasn't interested. Dick Burkholder, Barry's high school coach sent videotapes to Tom Osborne, head coach at Nebraska. Osborne never acknowledged receiving them. Wichita State University, located just 200 yards from Sander's home, did not recruit him. At 5'7 and 175 pounds, Oklahoma State signed him, and, as they say, the rest is history! Barry Sanders was a "rock hitter."

Our kids were now at the age of getting involved in competitive sports. Julie was playing basketball and softball. Amy and Lee, now 7 and 8, played for the minor league baseball team I was coaching in the city recreation baseball league. As a parent and coach, I really had to be careful in handling the situation in a positive way. It wasn't easy but I loved every moment, especially watching them develop their skills and being able to suffer defeats without negatively affecting their competitive spirit.

I found out early that we had raised a bunch of sore losers. Loser's Balls were not on our agenda and thus not up for discussion at the dinner table. "Dad, talk about something else!" was the response from Amy. "I don't want to talk about it!" That was the way we handled it. No problem. All the time I am thinking, "They sound like me."

Julie skipped Little League and played softball for Coach T (Taylor) team. Amy and her classmate, Debbie Scott, were the first two females to play Little League baseball in Gallatin. Later, Lee joined the team I coached, sponsored by Haynes Realty. Amy hated it when I would give her the bunt signal, but with her speed and proficiency at bunting, she was almost an automatic base runner. Lee developed into a great pitcher and power hitter during his Little League years.

Brenda and I made sure that baseball never interfered with church. Often, they showed up for Wednesday night Bible study classes in their uniforms. We had fantastic kids who had their priorities in order.

Vanderbilt University in Nashville, hired a new baseball coach to replace George Archie in 1968. Larry Schmittou, who had been involved in Nashville baseball for years, was hired to lead the Commodores. Schmittou was what was needed to make a significant impact on the Commodore program. I had the pleasure of playing against teams coached by Larry in the Nashville Tri-State League for four years. His teams were always at the top in the league and won numerous championships.

During his ten years of coaching the Vandy program from 1968-1978, he won 306 games, compared to only 209 wins in the school's last 50 years before he took over the coaching job. He led his team to four Eastern Division Championships, two SEC Championships, SEC Coach of the Year in 1973 while ranked 8$^{th}$ in the nation. Larry Schmittou set the stage for the ultimate success of later coaches, Roy Mewbourne, and now head coach, Tim Corbin. Schmittou still ranks third in coaching victories at Vanderbilt. It was during this period of time that our kids became aware of the fun and successes that come to those who work hard and make a difference for their teams. They were smart enough to pick up the reason for mentioning these success stories to them during their growing years.

In 1978, fifteen years after no professional baseball in Nashville, Larry Schmittou and a group of Nashville investors built a new baseball field, Hershel Greer Stadium, home of the new minor league baseball team in the city, the Nashville Sounds. Farrell Owens, an outstanding baseball player at Lipscomb and in the Tri-State League, became the part owner and served as the team's first general manager. Farrell and I always played on different teams in the league while enjoying some competitive games at Shelby, Centennial, and other baseball parks in town. Farrell was a great leader and supporter of baseball in the Nashville area even up to his untimely death.

I still enjoy visiting his "office" at the Old Timer's Field at Shelby Park when I visit my friend Mickey Hiter, the field manager. I want to thank Bill Traughber, author of *Nashville Baseball History*, for his great book, from which I obtained much of the above information.

The coming of the Sounds was perfectly timed for taking a bunch of kids to a professional, family-oriented, baseball game where ice cream was served in small plastic batting helmets. I still have a drawer full of those multicolored helmets saved along with great memories at the ball park.

During that period of time, the middle school housed the $7^{th}$, $8^{th}$, and $9^{th}$ grades. Julie's $9^{th}$ grade basketball team won the District Championship. She excelled in softball as well as basketball, leading the way for Amy and Lee to follow. Soon, we found a small farm near Bethpage, Tennessee, that would be perfect to raise our little athletic family. It had a nice house and 12 acres on which to run and romp, plus with my addition, naturally, of a new basketball court. We were now getting ready for the big time of competing in high school as well as middle school sports.

Along with church, Brenda and I insisted that our kids maintain good grades and conduct at school. Lee got into the habit of carrying his football to school for the P E breaks for games outside. His teacher, Betty Bowling, called me one day and said that he was spending too much time during class playing with his football. She suggested that I let the air out of it and have him suffer the pain of having to do his work better for a few days. When he returned his grades back into "A"s, Betty said that I could air up his ball again. We still have a laugh about that little incident.

Once our school system completed all of our new additions containing the various shops, labs, and vocational programs, I felt that it was time to think about making another career move so that I could be closer to my family and more involved in their sports. Brenda had taken a job at the new vocational education addition at Gallatin High School as the secretary and bookkeeper for the newly hired Vocational Assistant Principal, L.K. Lannom, no kin. While I was at the central office, I was looking for a Consumer Education teacher for a middle school in Hendersonville. After my delightful interview with the most promising candidate, Susan Lannom, I asked her if she knew of anyone who had a degree in marketing. I needed a teacher for Gallatin High School. She smiled at me and said, "Yes I do, he's sitting in the car waiting for me to conclude this interview." I said to her, "Good, we're done, go get him." That was how the "other" Lannoms came to Gallatin, Tennessee. Two at the same time. Not a bad day's work of teacher shopping!

It didn't take long for L.K. to be promoted to assistant principal. After another couple of years, he left the school system to take a job in business. That' when I promoted myself with the support of Mr. Herron to his job as assistant principal. I liked the first three months in that role there because Brenda was officially working for me. That was the only three months in our married life that I was officially her boss. I guess she'd had enough of that arrangement and soon went into the main building to be the school secretary/bookkeeper for the principal.

Since Julie was four years older than her sister and brother, she graduated first from Gallatin High School, lettering in basketball and softball as well as being elected as President of the senior class. I had the unusual opportunity to be an assistant coach for her softball team in 1982, which was during her sophomore year. Her head coach, Sandy O'Neal, was expecting twins near the end of the season. I was an assistant principal at the time and wasn't permitted by board policy to coach any athletic sports teams. Our principal, Dan Herron, got special permission from the school board which allowed me to coach softball for only the remainder of the season.

Coach O'Neal basically told me to coach the team on the field and she would do all of the other duties like making out the lineup, handling the finances, and arranging for travel, etc. The first thing we did in my first official coaching practice was to teach those very talented girls how to bunt. We had a lot of speed on the team, but bunting was not at the top of their skills list. We also did a lot of practices involving base running, stealing, drawing throws, sliding drills, to name some basics in which they were not proficient. All of them were excellent hitters, fielders, and very competitive, just a dream team to be associated with.

This would be my only year to coach one of my kids in high school. Our girls won the district championship and was scheduled to play in the regional tournament. The regional championship game was played in Gallatin against Overton HS out of Nashville. Julie hit a game-tying home run in that game that helped our team win the regional, and send us to the sub-state to determine who would play for the state championship. After winning the Sub-State at home against Germantown out of Memphis, we were scheduled to play Knoxville Farragut in Knoxville, for the state championship. It would be a one game event. The winner would be the state champion. Coach O'Neal was near the date for delivery but she was a trooper.

We lost the championship game to Farragut in a very strange way. We were behind a couple of runs after the end of the fifth inning of a scheduled seven-inning game. There were no lights on Farragut's field and it was getting darker by the minute. I even tried stalling as I talked to the umpires several times to reschedule the rest of the game for the next day because it was getting dangerous to put our girls on the field. I was told, "Coach, get your team on the field or forfeit the game." We had no choice, even while pointing to all the surrounding fields that were in sight had their lights on.

The umps called the game after five innings, and let us know that it was called on account of darkness, but led all of us to believe that the game would be resumed the following morning. As we were watching the nightly sports, we got the news through the broadcast that Farragut had won the state championship. It was not a pleasant moment for any of us, especially the girls. It was a very poor ending to a great year, but should not have happened that way.

The authorities chose to play a championship game on a field with no lights with no provisions to permit both teams to play a complete game. Even our protests went unheard. Win or lose, it should never have happened. Thus ended my one and only softball coaching career! But, as is the case with Loser's Balls, that is just the way things happen occasionally.

I admired Sandy who had done a great job with her girls and never resented me being her assistant under very unusual circumstances. One of her sons, Corey, later signed with Auburn as a quarterback. Her other son, Kirk, served as a SEC football official for a number of years. Sandy had her two girls, and at a young age the Loser's Ball struck her family. Sandy developed cancer and passed away while her girls were young. Her son Corey and her parents raised those girls while Corey was in school at Auburn.

I had the pleasure to see Sandy's beautiful girls just a year ago at Gallatin High School, when Sandy was inducted into the Gallatin High School Athletic Hall of Fame. Her son, Kirk, and Sandy's mother were also in attendance. Corey had passed away several years earlier while still caring for his young twin sisters. I still have in my heart a place of love and admiration for this family and what they meant to all of us who knew them. Sandy O'Neal was a special lady.

Meanwhile at the ball park, both Amy and Lee started to shine as fierce competitors and teammates in leading their teams to a lot of wins. Amy played basketball at the middle school during grades 7 and 8 under her coach Gary Davis. It is amazing how things cycle in your lives and bring about results you would never have thought to happen. Coach Davis was a graduate of Mt. Juliet HS. He was a teammate of mine on our Bears championship football team. I had borrowed a pair of football shoes from him early in my senior year when I couldn't find new ones just like in the Hendersonville

"Shoeless Bob" game. Now here is this guy coaching my daughter in basketball.

Gary was special to all of us. Amy loved coach Davis. He and his wife, Linda, became very close friends later after she graduated from high school. Gary led that Junior High team to a district championship. A lot of old timer sports fans in town were calling them one of the best middle school teams ever at Gallatin.

Coach Pat Webb, my longtime friend and hunting buddy, had left his basketball coaching duties at Gallatin HS the same year Julie entered her freshman year. The job was held by Coach Richard Stephenson until Coach Gary Van Atta came at the same time Amy started her freshman year at GHS. Coach Van Atta was excited to see the new freshmen team show up his first year there. Lee made the Little League All Star team. They finally lost and were eliminated at a regional game in Cookeville. There were plenty of sports happenings at the Lannom household.

I had taken the GHS assistant principal job in 1980, just in time to watch Julie go through her sports career at Gallatin. The basketball team did not have the success as her softball team, but she had three great years there. In 1985, here comes our middle child, Amy, bringing with her a bright future for girls basketball at the school some called, Camelot on Main Street. Jerry Vradenburg, head coach, had won a state championship at Kingsport Dobyns-Bennett in boys basketball. Calvin Short, head football coach had previously won his first state championship against Chattanooga Red Bank. A cross country championship was soon to follow. It was a great time to be in Green Wave Country with both Brenda and me right in the middle of it on the school staff. I was there for thirteen years, enjoying every moment.

The football team was to play a big game on Friday night during my second year there, when I got an urge to write a poem and read it at the Friday morning pep rally. We went on to win the game that night and advanced to the Sub-State. Coach Short asked me to write another poem for our next game. For the next twelve years, I wrote a poem for many of the "big" football games Gallatin played. It was funny, but I wrote them early on the Friday of the game while sitting in the parking lot observing students arriving on campus, as part of my morning bus duty. What a fun time!

It was early during that time period when I celebrated the birth of Elwood P. Green. Elwood was a character I developed as a gimmick to fire up our student body, enhancing the poems. He was as country as a John Deere tractor and appeared just a tad on the red-neck side. I wore green and white striped pants, a Green Wave shirt with all kinds of football necklaces, and a funky looking straw hat, with green and gold pom poms sticking out of my pockets. I carried my trophy bag of tricks which could turn a pep rally into chaos. The first time I did this was in a pep rally.

Amy and Lee were both in school then, but didn't know about what was to take place in Elwood's first pep rally. Even Brenda did not know. My secretary at the time was Connie Kittrell. The pants were borrowed from her husband, Bruce. Connie had more fun fitting me up than anybody. I appeared during the pep rally after a glorious introduction by one of our teachers and got the crowd going. I had a blast, but after the pep rally was over, Lee goes into his mom's office and asks, "Mom, why did you let dad do such an embarrassing thing in the pep rally?" She told him that she didn't know anything about it and just shook her head. Soon, Amy came in with tears from laughing so much and had a bunch of her friends with her who wanted to meet Elwood and get his autograph. Lee later gave in to the majority of the student body.

Elwood made a few more appearances until I left the school. It was really a good way to let the kids know that teachers and administrators are human and can have a good time as well. Many of the students would often yell out to me at the Friday night games, "Hey Elwood, good poem!" It was all part of the spirit of the Green Wave during those great times. I really think that just a little of the Glade showed up in me and would always emerge when some stunt was needed to fire up the team. Life isn't meant to be lived with boredom!

*My older daughter Julie (3rd from left on front row) pictured with her sophomore teammates, were Tennessee AAA State Runner-up in softball in 1982 at GHS. That's me, the assistant coach in the middle of the back row with GHS Hall of Fame Coach Sandy O'Neal on the end.*

*Julie is crossing home plate after hitting her home run in the Region to put the GHS girls in the 1982 state semi-final game.*

*May I introduce, Elwood P. Green? This character, I developed, could turn an organized pep rally into chaos. I always had a trick or two in my bag. Elwood was a poet and usually had a poem to read to ignite the spirit of the Green Wave before big football games.*

*I spent 19 years as a teacher and administrator at Gallatin High School. My office was always a place for good conversation, the beginning of lasting friendships, and often the birth place of new adventures at GHS.*

*None of us at GHS will ever forget Wanda Armstrong. Nor, will we forget the day she made me a cow pile cake, after telling her my story of losing that championship baseball game caused by a cow pasture paddy. It was delicious but explaining this to the students was another matter.*

# Chapter 23

The 1970s started out with a dose of Loser's Balls for the Lannom family. My cousin, Raymond Bramwell, while proudly serving in the US Army as a Green Beret, was killed by a mine explosion in Vietnam. He and my brother, Larry, were very close and had agreed on a plan to tour the west when Ray got home. Larry, standing beside Ray's casket said to me, "Raymond is home, I'm headed west." He left his baseball career and headed out west. One year later, Ray's dad, my Uncle Charlie, passed away, some said more from grief from losing a son than anything. My mom's brother, James Eugene Comer, died of a heart attack at the age of 62, much too young to have lost his life.

It was a tough time for all of us, but with our faith, family, and friends, we made it through tough times. We were glad to see those years pass on by. Julie graduated in the spring of 1984, and began her college education at Middle Tennessee State University (MTSU). Her plans had been made earlier. She had hung up her basketball shoes and softball cleats and was determined to not only become a teacher, but the best teacher she could be. In fact, that was who she became in her 32-year teaching career in elementary school and middle school science and computer education. She always reminded me that the time that she had spent with me in my shop and ag classroom were just practice sessions for the real things to come.

She recently retired and went to work at a local garden center. With her plant knowledge she gained from lots of hours working in her MeMa's greenhouse, Julie became an associate on demand by many her customers. I had never heard of tips being given to a garden center worker before, but Julie was so good with her customers, taking the time to explain so much about the plants they purchased, she was rewarded for her expertise. It was also good when you got to hear former students say so many good things about their teachers. She was a favorite of many of them who had her in school. That is about the best references a teacher can have. Brenda and I were proud of her accomplishments.

It was 1985. Amy was in the ninth grade, which was located in the new addition at GHS. She was now a member of the varsity basketball team. She gained a lot of valuable playing experience as a freshman on the team during the year. On the night of the first game of the district tournament, during the playing of the national anthem, Coach Van Atta leaned over toward Amy who was standing beside him, and told her that she was starting at point guard that night. She handled her surprise start admirably, especially after just being told at the last minute about her start. She played the next three years as the starting point guard.

Coach Van Atta would later refer to her as his coach on the floor. Amy was blessed with great speed, talent, and team leadership skills, which her coach easily recognized, thus leading to her early start. She was fearless, never backing away from responsibilities, always wanting the ball in tight situations. The other members of her middle school championship team were soon in the starting lineup. That year the girls, actually with two freshman starters, won the district and regional championships, but lost to Pearl Cohn of Nashville in the sub-state championship game by only two points. These girls were well on their way to becoming one of the best girl basketball teams in the history of the school.

Lee, as a youngster, had won the punt, pass, and kick football championship, but decided that his sport was baseball. Gallatin was a football town and for a talented athlete not to play football was rare. Lee was somewhat apologetic to me for not wanting to play football. I told him that it was his decision to make and for him to just enjoy high school in doing what he enjoyed doing. I was fortunate to be one of his coaches for his Babe Ruth team and during those years watched him grow into his game of choice. He had a strong arm and had become a great hitter, bunter, fielder, and a possessed a lot of baseball savy. He was destined to be an outstanding first baseman with his quickness and range as well as his defensive talent. We looked forward to his high school playing days.

The Green Wave girls basketball team, went 23-7 during Amy's sophomore season in 1986, winning the district, regional, and sub-state championships. They were one of eight teams to play in the Tennessee High School state tournament at Murphy Center in Murfreesboro, on the campus of Middle Tennessee State University. Oak Ridge High School had an outstanding player by the name of Jennifer Azzi, who had committed to play for Stanford University. She was a highly recruited speedy point guard who lead the Wildcats to defeat Gallatin 49-47 in their first game of the tournament. She later played for the USA Women's Olympic basketball team.

It was a tough defeat for our girls, coaches, fans, and especially us as parents. There was not a lot of encouraging words that I could muster to sooth the depressing results of the abrupt end to Amy's goal of winning the state championship. There was never "coaching in the car" on the drives home from a loss. Having been through similar circumstances, and realizing that most of the team was just sophomores, the consoling words to my daughter still fell on a returned look of a determined "stare", which provided me the feedback that I actually grew accustomed to seeing.

The big Loser's Ball that she had just been thrown was turned into fodder for a resilient and determined mind-set that she initiated immediately into her plan to not let that happen again next season. Shelbyville beat Oak Ridge in "86 for the state championship and became the top ranked team in the nation by the end of the year. Amy also played softball and volleyball. She even participated in seven (7) basketball camps that summer at the end of the '86 season.

One of her summer tournaments while playing AAU Basketball, was held in the Bahamas. Amy and her team, consisting of her friend and teammate, Debbie Scott, and other talented mid-state players, headed to the beautiful Atlantic islands to play in a big AAU tournament there. After Amy and her team had gotten off of their vans and walked into the sports facility just prior to their first game, some staff member of the tournament made a big mistake by asking Amy if she was one of the ball girl or managers, and if so, she could put the equipment "over there", pointing in the opposite direction of her teammates. That was like throwing gasoline on a fire.

I suppose that since she was just 5'4 that could easily have been just a normal assumption for some folks. Her Tennessee CJs won the Bermuda AAU tournament. Incidentally, the little "ball girl" Amy, was selected as the MVP of the Bahamas tournament. I've always wished that Brenda and I could have been there! There's no doubt that all three of our kids knew their game, prepared themselves for combat, and had a strong will to win. Second place was like the "first loser" to each of our kids. I am so proud of them as I see them in their careers today, demonstrating the same drive for perfection, hitting rocks with a determined work ethic, and leadership skills that have elevated them to reaching their goals and fulfilling their dreams. I would gladly terminate my playing time in the game I loved, again, without any hesitation, to be able to enjoy watching them grow into not only talented athletes, but successful young men and women in their career professions of choice.

Without question, playing sports and their commitment to excellence, as well as their strong faith, spearheaded their growth to put them on top, while their parents were the proudest cheerleaders with the best view.

We sold our farm and bought a 5-acre lot, which was located only two miles from Gallatin High School. We rented a house from a friend while we were working on building our new home. I contracted out a lot of the work such as the foundation, framing, brick work, and drywall. Lee, who was 16 at the time, was playing on the GHS baseball team. Together, as my new and only construction partner, we worked many long and late nights doing the plumbing, electrical wiring, trim work, and installation of all interior doors.

In 1986, the Lannom family was thrown a big time Loser's

## The Loser's Ball

Ball, a "bean ball" that knocked us all in the dirt. Early on Sunday morning, October 12, 1986, my brother Larry's wife, Mitzi, called, and told us that Larry had just been killed in an auto accident. A few years earlier all of our families had suffered the loss of Brenda's sister, Donna's husband, Rusty Ferrell, in a plane crash while on a business trip. It just looks like Loser's Balls won't leave us alone. Larry was just 36 years old and had two children, Risha 5, and Micah 4. He had crammed a lot of living in those few short years, having worked on spectacular construction projects all over the world. When things were coming together for him in the infancy of starting up his own construction company in the Glade, his life ended. I still use the big welding table and radial arm saw that he hauled over to my shop all the way from Atlanta, Georgia, when he finished up a project there. It was his donation as my "shop warming" gifts. When he drove away from our nearly finished house that day; that was the last time I saw him before his death.

I realize as I write this book that I am not the only one who has suffered through grief of losing a loved one. Death is just the final extension of life to its end, but it's still so hard. Some deaths just seem to occur with bad timing, many much too early, especially, when positive changes lie only a short distance away. But, after all, our lives on earth are so short compared to the next life in eternity. James 4:14 says, *"Yet you do not know what your life will be like tomorrow. Life is just a vapor that appears for a little while and then vanishes away."* It therefore, behooves each of us to make more serious preparations for a longer life which far exceeds our time here on earth.

During those early trying days of Larry's death, a new family moved to Gallatin and started attending church at Hartsville Pike where our family worshipped. Garlin and Linda Farris, with their son Jeff, and daughter Kara, showed up with a cake and food to extend their sympathy to us. They, along with our current friends, JJ and Sharon Redmon, helped us to get through this horrible time. I will never forget when JJ went with me, during a rainy afternoon, to collect all of Larry's personal items from his wrecked Chevy Bronco at the lot where Brenda's cousin, Oko Hamblem, had taken it. Our tears were camouflaged by the pouring rain on our faces as we sorted through the wreckage recovering Larry's briefcase, sunglasses, cap, papers and other items. Our other friends at church were equally remarkable with their love and prayers of support. Our lifelines to recovery through prayer, friends, and family sure came in handy. We could not have asked for any better friends than the Redmons and the Farris families.

Jeff, Garlin and Linda's son, was the same age as our daughter, Julie. Jeff was a special gift to all of us. He was born with physical disabilities and was unable to talk and walk without assistance. Where ever Garlin and Linda Farris lived, they created the most positive outlook on life in each community than anyone could imagine. I learned so much from watching how they cared for Jeff and exhibited those bright smiles and positive influence on a daily basis. Linda wrote a book recently. The title is: <u>Lessons Learned On My Journey With Jeff</u>. It is a wonderful read for parents and caretakers of special children.

When they arrived in Gallatin, they had two lovely daughters, Jenny and Kara, that were great blessings to them and to all of us as well. I truly believe that God puts people in our lives just when we need them the most. I have no doubts that was what happened when our "best friend families" moved to Gallatin to help raise us from one of the lowest points of our lives. Garlin and Linda became more additions to our "closest friends" list along with JJ and Sharon and Elwanna Carpenter. Garlin's girls and Linda said that Garlin and I had to be twins separated at birth since we were both from the country and had such similar backgrounds. Ironically, JJ was raised on a farm also. Brenda always referred to Linda, Sharon, and Elwanna as her three Gallatin sisters. Great friends are better than gold, and we were rich, indeed.

Garlin was the new Production Manager at Fleetwood Homes Plant 26 in Westmoreland, just a few miles north of Gallatin. He would be instrumental in my life later by assisting me in making an unbelievable professional career move. My parents and sister were jolted to say the least. I don't think mom ever got over Larry's death.

All of us drew closer to them to help them to move forward in their lives. Our kids were great, volunteering to go over and stay with MeMa and PaPa on many occasions whenever they could get an opportunity. Healing just takes a lot of people pulling together to share in the grief and hurts of major Loser's Balls in our lives. Letting people share with us is a great way to successfully avoid those extended periods of suffering. It is no different than when I would strike out with the bases loaded and teammates meeting me on my way to the dugout to help me put it back together for the next opportunity to possibly get a walk-off base hit to win a game. Life works at its best when there is teamwork in action being displayed around us.

I was so glad that I had made the decision to change jobs and become an administrator at Gallatin High School. I would be fortunate to be a part of the sports history at such a great school with Brenda there to keep my feet on the ground, watching our kids do so well. From 1980 to 1993, during my time there as an administrator, the football teams would enjoy three state runner-up appearances in 1982, 1987, and 1991. They were also state champions in 1989, and 1992, to go along with their 1978 title. The cross-country team won state championships in back-to-back years of 1985 and 1986. The boys and girls basketball teams had a home sub-state record of 9 wins and 1 loss. A special season was in the making in the upcoming 1986-87 school year.

The Gallatin girls basketball team had a fantastic summer. Our girls were dominating every basketball team camp in which they beat several top state-ranked teams. They even defeated Shelbyville, a perennial state power, who had won the 1986 state tournament, was picked to repeat as state champions, and was ranked as the top team in the nation. Our bunch of girls were undaunted by fierce competition, and showed a lot of poise during tight games and situations. The team was composed of mostly juniors and sophomores. There were three junior starters, one senior and one sophomore. They were still a young team.

Once the season began, seats in the Gallatin gym for our home games were at a premium. Normally during most home high school basketball games, the crowd doesn't usually show up until the start of the boy's game. If a fan was not seated by the 6:30 starting time of the girl's games at GHS, they may be standing to watch both games. Having had great back-to-back seasons, the entire community was excited to see what was in store for the Lady Wave this season. The girls were undefeated leading into the district tournament. They extended their undefeated season by winning the district tournament and were scheduled to play in the Regional tournament at Vol State Community College in Gallatin.

The Regional championship game was against Dickson County. We were about to experience another Loser's Ball. Amy was driving for a layup and drew a hard foul that knocked her to the floor. She was rolling around on the floor grabbing her knee in pain. She was helped off the floor as I made my way down to see how bad she was hurt, one of the privileges of a school administrator. It was late in the game with Gallatin leading by a good margin when Amy came out of the game. We won the Regional championship, but our daughter's status was unknown as the team trainer, Brenda, and I followed our friend and family physician, Dr. Clarence Sanders, also the team doctor, to his office to check her out.

We were thankful that it was not an ACL injury, but was a deep bruise in her left knee that was very painful. Amy hates shots, but told Dr. Sanders that he could do whatever he needed to do to get her ready for Thursday's sub-state game. Doc gave her a shot that seemed to settle her down and relieved the pain. He also gave directions to the coaching staff and trainer on what to do to get her ready to play. Fortunately, she had a couple of days to rehab her injury before game day.

We were the host for the sub-state game with Pearl Cohn, the team that prevented the Wave from going to the state tournament Amy's freshman year. There was definitely a score to settle. Pearl Cohn had an outstanding point guard who was the leader of her team and was to guard Amy. The attendance for the big game was considered to be the largest crowd to ever watch a home basketball

## The Loser's Ball

game in school history. Our gymnasium had two levels of seating. Every seat was taken on both sides of top and lower levels with standing room only in many locations. Additional seating was brought in to go upstairs on the second level the entire width of the court on both ends. It was packed.

I normally stand at all of the home games, being on duty to monitor the crowd, my duty as an administrator. I don't think that I could have remained seated that night anyway. Lee had his gang of guys supporting his sister and led the GHS cheering section with style. Amy was able to play the entire game, and ended up scoring 19 points against the Pearl Cohn defense and her defensive guard. Near the end of the game you could tell that her knee was telling her that it needed to rest, but she kept going. Gallatin was now going to the Tennessee AAA State Tournament as an undefeated team with a record of 31-0.

My parents, lovingly known as MeMa, and PaPa, had attended the previous state tournament in 1986. Mom had made dozens of her famous "T Cakes" and passed them out to neighboring fans during the game. They were back with the goodies and sat in the middle of the Green Wave fans handing out more sacks full of her delicious pastries. Memphis Melrose beat Nashville's Father Ryan in game one by as score of 61-60. Our girls played game two against William Blount from East Tennessee. They proved to be a formidable opponent for our girls throughout the game.

It came down to the last possession. Gallatin was down 47-46 with 12 seconds to play when Amy brought the ball down the floor. She drove to the basket, but was fouled with just 5 seconds to play in the game and calmly made the first free throw, tying the game at 47. William Blount called time out as was expected. MeMa, who had her hands over her eyes, never saw her granddaughter's second shot rattle the twine for the game winner. William Blount didn't get off a shot as time expired with Gallatin winning 48-47.

Oak Ridge easily won their opener against Bradley Central of Cleveland, 73-56. The last Thursday game was a surprise defensive battle between top-ranked Shelbyville and Jackson North Side of

West Tennessee. Shelbyville squeaked out a win, 28-27. Fridays's two semi-final games featured Gallatin against Melrose and Oak Ridge taking on Shelbyville. We played the first game. Melrose was a physical team, but the Lady Wave were back in stride after a close encounter the night before and started pulling away in spite of some questionable no calls on some pretty hard fouls.

Just before the half, Amy got slammed to the floor and didn't get up. She had reinjured her knee and could hardly put any weight on it as she was carried to the locker room. I joined our training staff and followed them, again, this time really concerned about her injury. There was a medical doctor on duty at the tournament, who examined her and said that it would be best to take her to his office just a mile from Murphy Center where our game was played. Brenda, and I took off to his office with Amy in the back seat skeptical of her playing any more in the tournament. Amy seldom cried but her tears were more from probably missing the rest of the game or even the tournament than from her knee pain, knowing her.

Here we are again, same diagnosis, just a re-injury of the same knee, thankfully. Doc put an elastic knee brace on her knee, but insisted that she put one on her good knee to perhaps prevent it from being hurt. Our team held off Melrose to win the semi-final game 72-55. We missed most of the Oak Ridge/Shelbyville game, which Oak Ridge shocked the nation's number one team by a score of 44-40. It was to be a rematch of Gallatin and Oak Ridge for the state championship on Saturday.

It was a long drive back to Gallatin, not knowing if Amy will even get to play tomorrow in the championship game. I told Brenda before we went to bed to get some sleep, that unless a bone is sticking out of Amy's leg, she will find a way to play in that championship game! While we tried to sleep, we didn't know that Amy was awake most of the night keeping ice on her knee. I couldn't reach her the next morning or any of the coaches to find out her status for game time at 8 pm Saturday night. I tried to work on the house that morning to get my mind off of the situation when the idea hit me,

## The Loser's Ball

because if there was any way possible, we would see Amy dressed, and on the floor when we got to Murfreesboro.

Back during our high school football championships, there was a young man who made his mark as the most committed and confident believer our fans had ever seen. His name was Randy Moore, better known as Moon Pie. As Gallatin advanced in the playoffs, he would wear and hand out T-shirts after each game with the words reading, Gallatin Green Wave, "12 down, two to go", or the next game, "13 down, one to go". Our girls were now 33-0 with one to go. I could not let this opportunity slip by without adopting Moon Pie's T-shirt idea. I went to our friend, Bill Vandercook's sporting goods store and got all the T-shirts I could get, the quantity being limited by the available letters and numbers to stick on them. I left the store early that afternoon with 15 shirts that read on the front: "Gallatin Lady Waves 34-0", and on the back: "1987 AAA State Champs". I would have gotten more if the store had more "A"s. I never told anybody except Brenda what I had done.

I carried my sack of shirts to our seats in the gymnasium and hoped that I wouldn't be leaving with a bunch of car-washing rags. I kept them out of sight. I wouldn't reveal them until the end like Moon Pie. We didn't know until the girls ran out on the floor to warm up that Amy would start or even play. She was easy to spot with those two blue knee braces on going through her normal routine of getting ready. We were relieved. She was back.

The game with Oak Ridge was one of those classic girls basketball games. There were 16 lead changes with no team getting up by more than 4 points. There were 6,272 fans in attendance that night. It was coincidental that one of my former Nashville baseball buddies, Ron Bargatze, was the color analyst in the TV broadcast booth. Just like the first game, it went down to the wire. Oak Ridge led the Wave by the score of 61-60 when Amy passed the ball inside to our great center, Renay Adams, who turned and made the go-ahead basket to put the wave up 62-61 with 7 seconds to play.

Oak Ridge coach, Jill Pruden, called time out as the fans gathered their breath for the closing tics of the clock. Oak Ridge quickly pushed the ball down the court. One of their players took a long shot that missed everything, but another Wildcat player grabbed the rebound and put up another jump shot that also missed the hoop and backboard. They actually rebounded and bounced their third shot off of the backboard which fell into the hands of a GHS player wearing matching blue knee braces. She spread her elbows and kept the ball moving to avoid a tie ball from enemy hands. The next thing that we saw was that basketball being thrown by Amy about 30 feet in the air with the horn going off.

I then pulled out my supply of T-shirts and made my way to the floor. Gallatin High School's first ever girls state basketball championship, plus a bonus of going through the season undefeated. I was ready to pull off my "Moon Pie" celebration! Amy's teammates played like champions. Renay Adams had 16 points, including the game winner. Debbie Scott had 28 points and 13 rebounds. Sophomore, Lorie Hammock had 11. Without much sleep, Amy had 5 points, but her gutsy performance with steals and assists to her big girls was good enough to pull off the win. Debbie, Renay, and Amy were selected on the All-Tournament team, with Debbie accepting her trophy as the tournament's MVP.

MeMa and PaPa even drove back to Gallatin for the impromptu pep rally at the gym where the giant crowd of Lady Wave fans, led by our tournament award winning cheerleaders celebrated the end of Gallatin High School's most spectacular undefeated 34-0 girls basketball season.

# Chapter 24

My good friend, Ron Martin, who lives in Waco, Texas, sent me a copy of a prayer written by General Douglas MacArthur that had been paraphrased by an anonymous writer to apply to young athletes. It is titled: <u>A Coach's Prayer</u>.

Build me athletes, O Lord, who will be strong enough to know when they are weak and brave enough to face themselves when they are afraid; athletes who will be proud and unbending in honest defeat, humble and gentle in victory.

Build me athletes whose wishes will not take the place of deeds; who will know Thee, and that to know themselves is the foundation stone of knowledge.

Lead them not in the path of ease and comfort, but under the stress and spur of difficulties and challenge. Here let them learn to stand up in the storm; here let them learn compassion for those who fail.

Build me athletes whose hearts will be clean, whose goals will be high; athletes who will master themselves before they seek to master others; athletes who will reach into the future, yet never forget the past.

Give them, O Lord, a sense of humor so that they may be serious, yet never take themselves too seriously. Give them humility to always remember the simplicity of true greatness, the open mind of true wisdom, and the meekness of true strength.

Then I, their coach, will dare to whisper: "I have not lived in vain."

During the summer of 1987, following our exciting year of basketball and baseball at GHS, Julie was preparing to graduate the next year from college. Amy was getting ready to enter her last year of sports while Lee was welcoming his new head baseball coach for his final two seasons. Amy attended several basketball camps that summer. She was being recruited by several schools including Florida, Alabama, Tennessee Tech, Lipscomb, and others. Alabama was high on her list. Her teammate, Debbie Scott was also being recruited by a number of schools, including Tennessee. Amy decided she would seriously consider Alabama. She wanted to play in the SEC. After a couple of visits to Tuscaloosa, she decided to sign early and focus her time on the next season to defend the Green Wave's '87 championship.

After signing, her CJ AAU team played in a tournament in Georgia, where she was the tournament's leading scorer, very unusual for a point guard. She also joined the school's track team, running in the sprints and relay races. One of her relay teams broke the school record. She also set a new school record in the 100 meters and ran in the state track meet, finishing second with a time of 12.2 seconds.

Sometimes, things don't go as planned. The girls were well on their way to reaching their third state tournament by winning their fourth consecutive district and regional championships only to be defeated by Pearl Cohn in the sub-state. It was a disappointing time, but their records of accomplishments still stand as a great testimony to their dedication and competitive spirit they left for others to emulate. When Amy was a sophomore, she asked me, "Dad, if I get a college scholarship to play basketball, will you buy me a new car?" I sat there

## The Loser's Ball

looking at a 5'4 daughter that had already decided my fate. Amy left for Tuscaloosa in the fall of 1988, driving a new '88 Ford Mustang!

Julie graduated from MTSU and started teaching elementary school at Union Elementary at Gallatin. My job was to help her fix up her boards and build some small furniture for her room. She would begin what eventually would become a 32-year teaching career. It was reassuring to know that there would be a bunch of lucky students to benefit from her gift of teaching.

My mother, who was a good guitar player, encouraged Lee to learn to play. Lee, as I discovered early in his life, was a very disciplined and determined guy. He taught himself to play an old guitar that MeMa had given him. It wasn't long until Brenda and I bought him a new one for Christmas. He became a competent musician, even playing in his own band with a bunch of his buddies from school. Later, he learned to play the drums and was a gifted singer as well. Julie started singing with a group several years later.

Their talents encouraged me, along with friends who loved and played music, to produce a back yard event called, "Summer Celebration." Our kids now had a format to display their talents while enjoying their musical interests. We often had 250 or more friends and families to attend with pot luck meals and entertainment provided by our kids as well as several country and pop bands in the area, free of charge. We had a sound system furnished by Danny and Layna McCorkle, who usually closed out our shows with Elvis Presley songs by Danny, with Layna as his backup singer. I installed a light system in front of the stage, a 20' gooseneck trailer decorated with red, white, and blue patriotic banners and flags.

I was so pleased to provide my mother a venue for her to actually perform while singing and playing her guitar. She had a great voice and loved to sing. She told me after her last performance before she died, that she had always wanted to perform on stage and that I had made her dream come true. Blessings often come from sources that we never plan. I cherish that blessing. For 11 years, we enjoyed those concerts in our back yard. I could tell that Lee may have been looking further down the road, not so much as an entertainer, but as was his nature, the technical aspect of music and the business associated with it. That would come later.

In the meantime, he had a fun baseball season, doing a great job at first, and hitting over .300 at the plate. I could just see something good was about to happen during the next season, his final year. Julie is making money, Amy is on scholarship, and Lee is happy with his music and baseball. And, we are in our new house. Life is good at the homefront.

Amy got to start at point guard for Bama her freshman year. I had fun kidding her about how could she do this to her Tennessee daddy and go to Alabama? I made the mistake of telling her about a specific Bible verse found in Ezekiel 20:29, that read, *"Then I said to them, "What is this high place to which you go? So its name is called Bamah to this day."* Now it is used against me. My bad! She had a great season, being selected as a second team All SEC Freshman and leading her team in assists.

Amy spent all four years at Bama as the Lady Tide's starting point guard. She led her team in assists all four years. After her freshman year, Rick Moody became the new head women's basketball coach and led the team to the NCAA tournament her last two years. Amy enjoyed a spectacular senior year. She was invited to try out for the Pan Am Games at the US Olympic Center in Colorado Springs. She and her team were known as the "Long Rangers" since they led the nation in 3-point shooting. The 1992 team played 31 games of which they scored over 100 points in 14 of them, still a school record today. Amy was selected as one of eight women players in the country to participate in the first women's ESPN 3-point shooting competition in Minneapolis at the men's Final Four. During her home game with Florida, which Brenda and I were fortunate to attend, Amy set a new Alabama women's school record by scoring 38 points. She held the record set in 1992, until it was broken by another player in 2021, 29 years later. During the same game, she hit eight 3-pointers, which is still the school record shared by seven other players. She is still in the top ten of women's basketball records at Alabama in steals, assists, free throw shooting, points scored in a single game, and three-point shooting. She was selected as captain of the 1992 edition of the Lady Tide team.

Meanwhile, the Green Wave baseball team was enjoying one of its better seasons. We traveled to several games to watch Lee, our former Civitan Little League and Babe Ruth All Star, hit some booming home runs on his road wins as well as at home. Gallatin won the district championship and was host to the Regional game against McGavock High School. The team was coached by my friend Mel Brown, who was an outstanding baseball player and coach at Lipscomb University. It was one of the best baseball pitching duels I had ever seen, but unfortunately the Loser's Ball hit us with a 1-0 loss to the Nashville team. Lee's team fell two games short of going to the Tennessee AAA state championship that was played in Hershel Greer Stadium, home of the Nashville Sounds. Mel Brown won three state baseball championships at McGavock and became one the most respected principals of our own alma mater, Mt. Juliet High School.

When it came time for Lee to make his decision on where to go to college, he chose Tennessee Tech in Cookeville, which was one of the top engineering schools in the country. Lee decided to major in electrical/industrial engineering, which later would open up for him so many more opportunities. During that time of transition, he had trained to be proficient in his martial arts skills and had won a number of tournaments across the state and region including some major wins:

1st Battle of Chattanooga-Forms '91
1st Battle of Chattanooga-Fighting '91
1st Tri-State Championship '91
1st Mid South Championship '91
1st David Deaton Martial Arts '91
1st David Deaton Martial Arts '92
1st Volunteer Classic '92

Lee was well skilled in Tae Kwon Do as well as Kenpo martial arts, and won most of his katas, forms, and fighting competitions.

His decision to take a lot of early electrical engineering courses before switching over to industrial engineering, provided him a stronger background for his interest in sound engineering, which has become a large emphasis in his career.

Brenda and I spent a lot of evenings at Tech watching Lee play flag football, basketball and softball. It was great to see him enjoying the competition and the team atmosphere with his friends.

Though he was a standout, playing several intramural sports on campus, winning his best ever championship was when he found the love of his life, his future bride, Miss Julie Grace Peters. Lee graduated from Tech in 1995 with his degree in industrial engineering, and selected his first job with a company that assisted failing companies in developing strategies for reframing their companies for future success. He later worked for Duracell in Cleveland, as a plant engineer. From there, he started his own studio foam company, designed and sold acoustic treatment foam, specifically made for quality sound productions. Home Studio Foam became a brand name for him for a number of years until he changed the name to HSF Acoustics.

During his early years of starting his business, he produced and directed a late-night TV show in Chattanooga, Tennessee, *Chattanooga The Show*, that showed on Fox TV in Chattanooga for 13 episodes. The Mayor of Chattanooga opened up his last show at the Chattanooga Choo Choo. Lee's picture appeared on the front cover of a Chattanooga magazine highlighting his new business. He shifted his interest and attention to recording and sound productions being done in his home studio.

He grew his business and after 22 years, Lee is recognized as one of the premiere video producers and sound engineers in the area. Maybe that is another return on the investment of a back yard music production being the forerunner. He and Julie operate his company now called, Reel Rex Media (reelrexmedia.com).

His career has taken him to shoot locations like the Alamo in San Antonio, Boston, New York, Pennsylvania, Virgina, California, Wyoming, Washington DC, and many other locations. He has worked with Dirty Jobs TV host, Mike Rowe, Garth Brooks, Dennis

## The Loser's Ball

Quaid, Tim Tebow, Eddie George, Don McLean, Mary Lou Retton, Nancy Kerrigan, Amy Grant, Mike Huckabee, Larry Gatlin, Billy Ray Cyrus, T Graham Brown, Kid Rock, Alveda King, Little Big Town, Brothers Osborne, Jason Aldean, PBS show *Reconnecting Roots* streaming episodes, and many others, including commercials for numerous companies. Ironically, he does sound for the former tenor singer, Jimmy Fortune, of one of my favorite groups, The Statler Brothers. Jimmy's new group is called, Brothers of the Heart. Lee and Julie have three fantastic "grands" that I adore. All three, that were home-schooled by Julie, a certified teacher, their great mom. All three of them are talented athletes.

Camron, the oldest, who graduated Magna Cum Laude from Lee University in May of 2024, was an All-State track performer in high school, and is a talented guitar player like his dad. All of us attended his marriage March 11, to his long-time friend, Elleise Davies, who is to be a Physician's Assistant. He works for State Farm Insurance.

Liz, their daughter, is a speedy senior soccer player and track star at her high school, Walker Valley, near Cleveland, Tenn. She is a four-year Tennessee All State track performer, and in 2024, was selected to the All State soccer team. She currently holds six (6) track records at her school. During her final track season as a senior, she broke three of her own school records and is headed to the state track championships in the pentathlon and two other events. She recently signed a track scholarship at Lee University in Cleveland, Tennessee.

Cason, the youngest, is a committed athlete when it comes to playing his sports. He opted out of cross-country and, is now a member of the Walker Valley High School golf team. He finished his final match last fall by shooting 4 over par while making two birdies on his last two holes to end his season. We look for him, with his determined work ethic, to be one of the top golfers on his team the next two years. He has basically learned golf through videos, golf on TV, and lots of practice. He has only been playing golf for less than two years. He works at the Cleveland Golf Club, playing there as much as they will allow him to play. The passion is there. Cason has an outdoor set-up, including a battery-operated spot light, net, and mat, where he hits many balls almost daily in the back yard. Sounds familiar! He is a "rock hitter!"

I love to see any athlete commit themselves to excellence, always striving to work hard to improve their game. That same drive and determination carries over into their future as an employee, supervisor, business owner, or professional.

It's great when a plan comes together and kids do a "mind sweep", clearing out all of the "I can't.", "I'm not good enough.", and "What's the use?" trash-thinking, to reprogramming their minds full of "I can.", "I will.", and "Just watch me." inner-winner thoughts. Don't let the heights of your accomplishments be determined by any outside force or person. Do not give in to self-imposed limitations. That is probably the worst way ever to fail. It's like committing success suicide. Plan your work, and then work your plan. A little dab of passion goes a long way to reaching the top rung of your achievement ladder. Prepare to enjoy how to climb when you are still young.

You will learn one day that you must include everybody when bragging on your kids or grands. To omit anyone would result in me not getting any more Christmas or birthday cards, so I will make it quick. Amy's three incredible "grands" have grown up as athletes as well. Madison and Molly each won the state Middle School Basketball Championships while playing for their mother as coach for Ellis Middle School in Hendersonville, with a combined record of 65-5. Molly became an outstanding soccer player at Hendersonville High School.

Amy's oldest daughter, Madison, decided to pursue the academic trail and work to become a nurse one day, graduating near the top of her class at Hendersonville High School. They both started their college careers at Alabama. Maddie, graduated from there with honors and first worked as a pediatric nurse caring for babies with birth defects and other issues while at Children's Hospital in Birmingham. I asked her one day, "Maddie, how do you work with those babies who are so misfortunate to have such debilitating physical problems?" She smiled and said, "Poppa, somebody has to love them and take care of them. That's why I went to school." Wow!

## The Loser's Ball

and this is my granddaughter. Makes me proud. She works today as a pediatric nurse at the Children's Hospital in Memphis.

Her husband, Kevin, former Tennessee School Boy State golf champion, graduated from the School of Business at The University of Memphis on a golf scholarship, then graduated from the University of Tennessee Medical School in Memphis in May. He is now doing his residency to become a doctor. They are the parents of my one and only best great grandson, Ben Wallace Lee, who turned one on October 1, 2023.

Molly finally figured it out, leaving Alabama in the middle of her sophomore year and transferring to the University of Tennessee in Knoxville, where she majored in Supply Chain Management from the Jim Haslam School of Business. What a coincidence! Thank you again, Mr. Haslam. She is now employed at a Nashville healthcare company and still kicks a soccer ball, while playing great on her team, who recently won back-to-back city championships in a co-ed soccer league in Nashville.

Jack the caboose, who played baseball and football, just graduated in mechanical engineering from Baylor University in Waco, Texas, and is currently employed at an HVAC engineering company in Knoxville, Tennessee. Jack is a talented musician who plays the keyboard and guitar, sings, and loves hiking and camping in the mountains. He comes in handy when I need a buddy to take with me to a Vols baseball game.

Brenda and I never imagined that when we were football rivals with Hendersonville back in high school at Mt. Juliet, that both or our daughters, Julie and Amy, would one day teach and coach at Hendersonville schools, both receiving "Coach of the Year" awards. It was fantastic to have had three of my grandchildren play sports and graduate with honors from that great school. Small world! We were so Blessed!

There are just too many stories to share about Amy at Alabama, including all of the times her Lady Tide team rolled our motel room, and the pranks they pulled on poor old Vol dad and mom, while we were in Tuscaloosa, watching ball games. All three of our kids were just pros at making new and lasting friendships.

Amy was a classmate with Dabo Sweeney, who played football at Bama and is now the head football coach at Clemson University. They worked together in the Fellowship of Christian Athletes. Another of her classmates, Robert Horry, who was a star forward for the Crimson Tide, played on three different NBA teams (Rockets, Lakers, and Spurs) that won seven NBA championships. After one of Amy's games, while we were waiting for her to come out of the locker room, Robert walked up to Brenda and me and told us not to be worried about Amy while she was at Alabama, he would take care of little Amy for us.

As I write the Loser's Ball, I can't help but be reminded of the tragic story that happened in the life of another one of Amy's friends at Alabama, All SEC football running back, Siran Stacy. Siran was drafted in the second round by the Philadelphia Eagles. After one year he was released and tried out for the Cleveland Browns, but was not selected. He ended his NFL career hopes and played for the Saskatchewan Roughriders in the Canadian Football League. He later set the all-time rushing record for the Scottish Claymores in NFL Europe. A Loser's Ball of major proportions struck when on November 19, 2007, he lost his wife and four of his five children in a tragic car accident.

He remarried in 2013. He and his wife, Jeannie, along with their five daughters live in Franklin, Tennessee. Following his family tragedy, Stacy overcame his tragic loss, committed himself to Christ, and began a full-time ministry speaking everywhere about the love of Christ and his trust in Him. He made the decision not to spend his life in the loser's bracket, choosing instead to become a winner. He not only learned the importance of not letting outside forces plot his future, but chose to rise like the Phoenix and chart a new course. Student athletes all over the country now benefit by Siran's positive presentations.

Brenda, and I had the pleasure to meet and sit with Siran and his wife at a Vanderbilt women's basketball game when they hosted

Alabama a few years ago. He and Amy relived some old stories they shared together at the capstone. Amy says that he is an incredible motivational speaker and still keeps in touch with him today. To book or schedule Siran for your team, business, or group, you can reach him at SiranStacy.org What a great guy to bring the message of faith and resilience to any audience!

*Our son, Lee, was an outstanding baseball player for the Green Wave, hitting well over .300 and playing a great first base. GHS won the district and missed playing for the state championship by two games his senior year.*

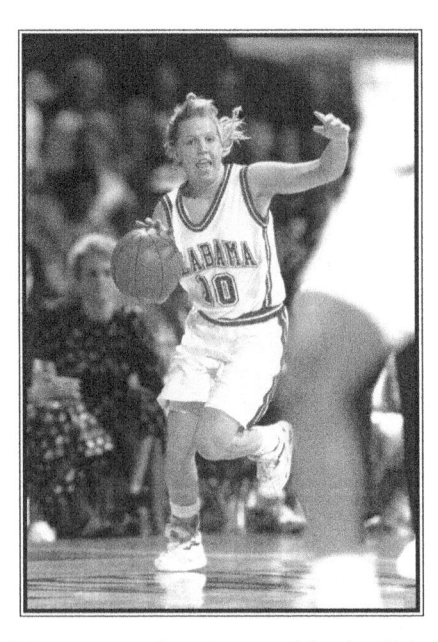

*Amy started all four years as the point guard for the Alabama Lady Tide. She was selected captain of the Crimson Tide team her senior year.*

# Chapter 25

*"Failure is not fatal, but failure to change might be."*
UCLA Coach John Wooden

Now, that the elation and pressure of getting our kids through high school and college has passed, I began to question my current position as a school vice-principal's role compared to fulfilling some possible adventures that I may be missing. For many years I have served as a school administrator, I was beginning to grow somewhat weary of the same old school opening routine, same old speakers at in-service education, and the same student problems from year to year, just wearing different faces. I am not saying that my job was boring, but like my son said about his "cubby hole" as an engineer at Duracell, "It limits your mind to expanding your talents in more places." I was at that point. There must be something that I can come up with to get myself motivated to improve my game. Finally, I made the decision that I was the one who had to make it happen, and not rely on some lightning strike.

When we had a faculty member to resign, Mr. Herron, our principal, asked me if I would take over the role of serving as the school's Key Club advisor. I actually agreed to do this without hesitation because I saw that I would be directly involved again in working with some of the best kids at school in developing their leadership skills and talents. I saw this opportunity to give myself a good kick-start to energize Bob to become a more positive administrator and at the same time feel that my time on earth was now more productive than hall duty or handing out detention slips.

The Key Club is an international organization sponsored by local Kiwanis International Clubs. Our Gallatin Kiwanis Club met for lunch every Wednesday in the basement of City Hall in Gallatin. One of my duties was to select two Key Club members each week and take them to the Kiwanis Club for lunch. That, alone, was a bonus, free food and get out of school for an hour.

The club consisted of many talented business and professional men and women who had established a fantastic organization in town, sponsoring the Kiwanis Little League program which I was pleased also to be a part of as well. There were other ministries that were sponsored and funded by the club's members. While I was there, I became friends with all of the members, but especially, spent a lot of conversation with one member by the name of Bob Atkins, who was the publisher of The Gallatin Examiner, our local newspaper. Bob was at the time the President of the Tennessee Newspaper Publishers Association. I think that was the actual name then of the organization.

At one of my Wednesday lunch meetings, Bob and I talked about the current columns that were printed weekly in the Examiner. It started out as just a casual conversation, but the more I thought about it, the more I thought about the possibility of writing a column myself, one to stimulate me, and also the readers. During the rest of the week, I decided to talk more to Bob about the opportunity of writing a column for the Examiner and the Portland Leader, the other paper in the county he owned.

The following Wednesday, after our discussion concerning this opportunity, Bob told me to write a column, giving me the guidelines about the space and size of the column, and to bring him a copy to look over. I spent the week making a decision on my topic and style of presentation. It was not hard at all, the more I wrote, the words just kept coming. When I read the finished product, I got a shot in the

## The Loser's Ball

arm, so to speak, and knew that I was on the right track. If it could do something positive for me, surely it could be of help to many more.

Bob read it, liked it very much, but said that I needed to do a couple of more things to get it published. I needed a column title and a picture of myself to complete the deal. I thought that the title made sense, but why scare away potential readers with my picture. Thanks to a photo in our church directory done by a professional photographer, I came up with one that may not drive the readers away.

I had heard that to do your best thinking searching for some answer, just sit down in a quiet room, preferably, your favorite chair and let your mind relax and focus on the answer you are looking for. That is exactly what I did. Finally after about 15 minutes I had it. The title of my column would be: "Your Dynamic Dimensions". My columns would be written to address the ever-changing and powerful (Dynamic) situations in our lives utilizing the best of what we have been given (our Physical, Mental, and Spiritual Dimensions). Bob got Steve Rogers, Editor of the News Examiner involved, who also liked the idea. The column would be devoted to motivating and helping readers to develop these inner dimensions to the fullest in overcoming obstacles and building better lives. I was to be the first reader! I was actually writing to myself. If I had a problem with the author, I would just take it up with him!

In March of 1989, my first column was printed in the Gallatin News Examiner. Bob and Steve informed me that they had gotten a lot of positive comments from subscribers and other readers. Since he knew the publishers and editors of other weekly papers across the state, Bob sent my first column to several of them to check out to include in their papers. It wasn't long before I was sending my column to six other papers in Tennessee. I wasn't getting rich at $5 per column, but the real payment was the feedback that I got from notes from publishers whose "letters to the editor" were copied and sent to me. I even received personal letters thanking me for my columns that they had even copied and sent to their relatives in the military and in other states and countries. I had no intentions of benefiting financially at all, but the payback from the readers made my day.

For your reading pleasure, I am including copies of a few of the original columns along with a brief introduction to give you an idea of the general reason for each one. I think that over the nearly two-year period, I wrote 87 columns before making another change in life's game.

Naturally the title of the first one was my by-line title, Your Dynamic Dimensions. I wanted readers to realize their own self-worth and to realize that their potential for success lies within them. Here goes:

Your Dynamic Dimensions by Bob Lannom

It has been said that, *"A man has to live with himself, so he should see to it that he has good company".* Although this sounds like a good reason for self-improvement, it is not the most important motive for making a careful analysis on one's needs to grow and develop.

The realization of your dreams and goals in life depends upon how your current output measures up to the actual potential of your three-dimensional self. You are endowed with three prominent and ever-changing dimensions—your physical, mental, and spiritual status. The development of these characteristics can be dynamic to your success. Dynamic means an energy, or force in motion. The secret to success is to get all three of these dimensions flying in a positive formation toward the achievement of your goals.

The Bible tells us in Luke 2:52, that Jesus developed the maximum potential of His dimensions as He "grew in wisdom and stature, and in favor with God and man". We are encouraged by this example to stimulate in our lives the fulfillment of our potential while living in a world where everything depreciates in value, except the human being. In order to discover greater success and happiness, you need to strive to unlock the potential within your tri-dimensional being.

Have you ever considered just how valuable you are from a physical standpoint? Before the age of the atom, chemists used to say a person's worth, from a chemical point of view, was about $32. Changes, however, occurred during the atomic age, according to Earl Nightingale in his cassette program. "Lead the Field". "In calculating the worth of the human body, scientists now have determined that if the electronic energy in the hydrogen atoms of your body could be utilized, you could supply all the electrical needs of a highly developed country for nearly a week."

In a nation where education is free to our young students and available to all, the development of our mental capacities is still lacking. Less than 5% of our population reads one or more books a year. Perhaps many are like the fellow whose favorite books growing up were daddy's check book, and mama's cookbook. We are told by psychologists that the average person uses less than 10% of his available mental capacity. They tell us that if only one-half of this available capacity was utilized, the average person could master forty different languages.

Daniel Webster said, *"If we work upon marble, it will perish. If we work upon brass, time will efface it. If we rear temples, they will crumble to dust. But, if we work upon men's minds, if we imbue them with high principles, with the just fear of God and love of their fellow man, we engrave on those tablets something which no time can efface, and which will brighten and brighten to all eternity."*

Development of your mental dimension is paramount in reaching your potential.

It has been said that we will be dead longer than when we will be alive. The third dimension, your spirit or soul, lives eternally. The greatest use of life is to spend it on something that outlasts it.

The outlook of too many people is gloomy, despairing, and agonizing. A story is told about an experience of a rookie sailor on his first cruise. A strong wind came up and the veteran captain sent the young sailor up the mast to lower the sails to prevent the ship from capsizing. When the rookie finally climbed to the top and looked down, he began to get dizzy. Sensing the danger, the captain shouted out to him, "Look up son, look up!" The young boy looked up and soon the dizziness disappeared. He again, regained his sense of balance and lowered the sails.

The lesson in this story is simple. When your "outlook" isn't good, try the "uplook". The best way I know to regain your balance in life. Helen Keller said, *"You see no shadows when you face the SUN"*. Develop your spiritual potential by facing the "S-O-N". Your dimensions are waiting to go to work for you. Energize these great gifts and become a dynamic you.

Here's one more. I wrote this one after Brenda and I got home from a scary drive in the fog coming back from watching Amy play a basketball game at Murray State University in Murray, Kentucky. The drive reminded me how life is a lot like a fog where we can't sometimes tell where we are and even where we are going. Sound familiar? Enjoy.

You've Got To See Beyond The Fog

Recently, my wife and I, along with some friends, drove to Murray, Kentucky, to see our daughter play a basketball game. On our return trip we had to drive through a dense fog. It didn't matter whether we used bright or dim lights. Our visibility was limited to only a few feet in front of us. The longer we drove in that fog the more I realized that life is a lot like our journey. Though you cannot see beyond the fog, you know that you have to set the correct course toward the destination you want to reach, and to feel some degree of confidence that your goal is somewhere beyond the fog. The idea of being able to never lose sight of your goals in spite of the obstacles is obvious in this story.

On the Fourth of July in 1952, the California coast was blanketed with a dense fog. On Catalina Island, 21 miles off the California coast, a thirty-four-year-old long distance swimmer by the name of Florence Chadwick, walked down the beach and into the water and began her swim toward California. Having already swam the English Channel in both directions, she now was determined to be the first woman to swim the channel from Catalina to California.

## The Loser's Ball

Chadwick fought the chilling waters, sharks, and the dense fog for hours. Fatigue never became a problem for her during her swim, but the cold waters numbed her into desperation. As she strained her eyes through her goggles, she could see nothing but the fog in front of her. There was no sign of the shore anywhere in sight. Her past swimming successes were an indication that she was as competitive as anybody could be, but she finally decided that it was no use to continue her swim. With assistance from her trainer and her mother, she gave it up and was lifted into the boat that was accompanying her on her swim.

She had been in the foggy waters for fifteen hours and fifty-five minutes fighting the chilling elements, but ended her swim attempt in failure of accomplishing her goal. Her feeling of failure was only made more devastating when she realized that she was only a half mile from the California shore. She later told a reporter, "Look, I'm not excusing myself, but if I could have seen land, I know I could have made it".

Two months later, Florence Chadwick swam that same channel, with fog that was like the one before, but this time the faith that she had inside kept telling her, "Somewhere beyond the fog is the California coast." She not only succeeded on her second attempt, but beat the existing men's record by two hours.

Seeing beyond the fog is not easy. As a matter of fact, it is nearly impossible when you have no specific destination as a goal. When we were driving home that foggy night from Kentucky to Gallatin, Tennessee, we had faith we would eventually get home because of several factors.

First of all, we knew our destination, our goal, our target. Even at various intervals we could get a glimpse of roadside signs giving us a mile marker or distance indicators on the interstate highway. Secondly, we were deliberate and confident that we were headed in the right direction toward our destination. The third factor that made our journey complete was that we had a purpose in mind, a reason to be moving toward our target, to return to our homes and families.

Travelling through life is a lot like our drive and Chadwick's swim through the fog. We must learn to "walk by faith, not by sight." 2 Corinthians 5:7. Set your course and choose the right road to a destination that will enable you to be successful. Choose the right direction, the right purpose, and look beyond the fogs that come your way in life in becoming a dynamic you.

In all of my columns I always found an appropriate Bible verse to go along with my stories. I ended each one with the challenge to become a Dynamic You. From the two columns just read, I think you can get the general idea of how they later became the foundation of The Loser's Ball that I finally took the time to write.

One of the most influential people in persuading me to write this book, other than Brenda, is Barbara (Barb) Walker. Her husband, John was one of my FFA students when I taught at Gallatin in the late 60's. For years, Barb would ask me every time that I ran into her at a restaurant or at the store, "When are you going to write that book?" Barb and John have a strong faith and love to do so many good things for others in our community. Encouragers are of such a great benefit to foot draggers who sometimes lag in their lope. Barb, as Phil Robertson of Duck Dynasty says, "I am now cooking with peanut oil!" You will receive one the first copies off the press. Thank you.

Also, in the summer of 1989, I started conducting business seminars presenting principles of supervision, leadership skills, and managing people in the work place. I came to recognize a need that I had to do something else than get in my 30 years of education, and call it quits, rusting away somewhere.

Our kids were now unrestrained, engrained and trained, headed for success in their careers. Now I felt a need to explore options where I could use the skills that I had learned in some other direction. Just because your compass always points north, that doesn't mean that your journey must be only north. I had my seminar information professionally done and advertisement flyers sent to local businesses, taking applications for the date of each event. Usually, I would fill up my spots for each seminar that I conducted. That was nice. There were 20 spots with a registration fee of $99 per person for a six-hour seminar.

I hired Carol Lyle, my school secretary to be the hostess. She helped me in setting up the workshops and assisting the attendees in their needs. It was a refreshing change from the school administration duties. One of my teachers told me that I did everything better at school, because I was in fact teaching again. I did love the teaching part, that's for sure. If it was that obvious, then I needed to take that to heart. Even Brenda noticed the difference. The best thing about being an administrator is the relationships with the teachers and how you go about serving their needs on a daily basis, plus the time you actually get to interact with the students. Local administrators are bound by so many extra-curricular activities that deprive them of the real pleasures of their jobs.

Dealing with discipline problems, supervision of parking lots, bus duties, crowd control at ballgames, cafeteria duty, and a hundred other jobs are not the most enjoyable. I was looking for something, but the only possibility of making a move would have to come at the next superintendent's election. I seriously started to think of running for school superintendent. I remembered an anonymous quote that said, "*Your talents are a gift from God. What you do with them is your gift to God.*" I accepted the challenge. It is time to do something.

In the fall of 1989, when school was starting back and all teachers had to report for their first day of in-service training, I received permission from our Director of Vocational Education to transport all 25 of our GHS career/vocational education teachers to the Fleetwood Homes Plant 26 in Westmoreland, Tennessee, to learn the quality process that Manager Bill Graves had instituted, which propelled his plant to the Number 1 Plant in the Fleetwood Housing group.

My friend, Garlin, the Production Manager there, helped in making this visit possible. I had already conducted a couple of management seminars at Plant 26 earlier. I was impressed and wondered if it would be worth the visit to see if we could adapt the quality process to our vocational classes at GHS. I was already familiar with what it had done for Fleetwood, and wanted the feedback from our team of teachers to see how we could put it to work for us.

Normally most changes are met with pessimistic reactions. That really did not happen with our group. Most of them were impressed with the quality process and how it could actually make their jobs much easier. The only skepticism was more about logistics than the actual specific changes. For example, teachers with six rows of typewriters had a problem with how to teach the skills using a team approach. Bill did an excellent job with the presentation as well as explaining the strategies of initial implementation. He answered a ton of questions, which showed me that my team was really interested. We had lunch, toured the plant, and returned to the school.

We decided to begin our new challenge and spend the entire first semester organizing and preparing to fire up the quality process to take effect the second semester. We had a number of meetings after school and checked off our list of all the necessary steps to get ready. It invigorated me to no end. I was flying high like the anticipation of waiting for Santa Claus to arrive on Christmas morning. Mr. Herron, our principal was 100% on board. We had the green light to make the biggest change in any instructional process that had ever been made in our school system. Our team worked tirelessly to make sure that we would be successful. I was so proud of them. They started involving the students in getting their shops, labs, and rooms physically ready for the change. The students liked what they had heard and bought into it as well.

The Quality Process that we implemented in January of 1990, was now a do or die situation. I know of no other high school that had made or has ever made such a change in the delivery of instructional information and skill development as we did. We saw how it had been proven to work in industry, and we felt a high degree of confidence that it would work in an educational setting. We established specific learning requirements for each of the lessons taught in each of our departments. Every department's teams established goals and problem-solving strategies as well as discipline and housekeeping requirements. Student and teacher hassle-elimination became a requirement. Goals and recognition boards were set up. Every job to be learned, had requirements of steps to complete each task to a standard that was in writing or shown in a picture. Deviations were not allowed. DIRFT (Do It Right The First Time) became our motto. Zero defects was our standard of conformance to the job requirements.

Even the typewriting/keyboard teacher, Donna Lain, who had attended MJHS with Brenda and me years earlier, had to start what her students came up with, a "100 and Up Club." She actually divided her room up into five clusters of six typewriters, three facing another three, which made up a team. The students learned from each other which freed up Donna to do other things. Her students finished the assignments so fast that she had to come up with more assignments at a higher level, for which they would receive extra credit, thus their averages surpassed a grade of 100. It was amazing.

This type of change occurred in all of our programs. At the end of the year, when we compared the top three categories we were tracking and measuring, we discovered that there were dramatic increases in the results compared to the first semester: Students grades for all of our programs increased by 25%. Student attendance increased by 30%. Discipline problems decreased by more than 40%.

As a matter of fact, the increased attendance achieved by our career/vocational programs made it possible for GHS to earn another teaching position from the State Department of Education funding formula. Mr. Herron told us, since our team earned it, to add another career program. That is when we added our Air Conditioning/HVAC program the next fall.

With each success, you can usually find related successes to follow. With 100% of our team headed down the "yellow brick road", our steps were quicker. Our heads were held higher, and our shoes were less worn out! As we concluded our second year of the Quality "Process", not "program", we hit a home run with the Recognition element of our process. Quality is a culture, a process. A program usually has a beginning and an end. Quality should never end, thus it becomes how you live each and every day performing your tasks to the perfect standard, "Conformance to Requirements."

The Rotary Club in Gallatin had for years sponsored a "Top Thirty" awards banquet and recognition program to honor, naturally, the Top Thirty academic seniors. Over 60% of the students at GHS were enrolled in at least one career education program, so we as a team felt like that it was time to come up with a comparable recognition banquet to present to our principal to honor and recognize our outstanding Career/Vocational seniors as well. Let me pause and just say a couple of things about recognition. If you cherish parental support for your school, the way to their heart is to honor their kids. I am not talking about "participation trophies" either. Real hard-earned achievements should be recognized in every kid when possible. When parents move from house to house with their kids, the trophies that the kids had won, always seem to show up in some box when it is unpacked.

Secondly, the most important need that every human being has, regardless of age or background, is the need to be appreciated. I have learned that from so many situations. I think my teachers would have walked on glass bare-footed if they were asked to do so by anyone who showed genuine care and appreciation for them. Remember, all of us walk around with an invisible sign hanging around our necks that if we could read it would say, "Make me feel appreciated." It works with students, athletes, teachers, administrators, ministers, everybody!

We conducted the first GHS Rotary Club Vocational Honors Banquet at the end of school, the following year. It then became a tradition at GHS, that bonded our entire student body where all student successes and achievements were recognized. I still remember that night as Brenda and I sat near her office in the main school office with our shoes off and feet propped up on the table in front of us. Most of the students and parents had already gone leaving us with the feeling of accomplishment of another dream that came true. My dear friend and Vokie teacher, JoAnn Bates, sat down and joined us followed by several of my other Vokie cohorts, soaking up the joy of the moment. It was like no other feeling that any of us had ever felt. Mr. Herron soon joined us and was as excited as we were. In just two and a half years, as JoAnn put it, "We did it!" It was a great "Tired".

But, again, find something higher to shoot for, set another goal, which we did the following year. Success begats success! There's nothing better than expanding your dreams to even higher achievement levels. If you happen to stand a long time in one place, I hope you get to hear an old baseball adage which I heard several times to wake up the outfielders, who have a tendency sometimes to "check out" of the game. Those words from their coaches were: "Move around out there, you're killing the grass!" We were ready to begin plotting some other plans to keep from killing the grass in Green Wave country.

The following year our programs reached their highest enrollments as we began our third year on the quality process. All of our class sizes were maxed out. The interest that resulted in an enviable situation gave us a warm fuzzy feeling, but placed a larger burden and responsibility on our staff to ensure that we were capable of providing our kids with work skills and advanced educational opportunities to give them the needs required to hit the job market or to continue their education. We decided to come up with a plan to help our staff to meet the challenge head on.

After talking with some of my friends at the state department of education, we applied for a grant to institute a new way of polishing up our students to hit the work force. We called our program, School To Work Transition Program, whose initials stood for absolutely nothing. Our application was approved and after interviewing and hiring our two new staffers we got started. It was the first of its kind in the state at the time. The state office sent out a crew to film a scripted interview to show the highlights to other school systems after our results started going off the charts. Kathy Pryor was hired as the receptionist and secretary. Bob Dyer, was hired as our Job Placement Coordinator.

This is basically how the program worked. All seniors enrolled in their career/vocational education class would be pulled out of their classes for a six-week class during the year. They were selected at random so as to leave the staff with enough students in their home class. Bob would spend the six weeks with them teaching job application and interview skills, how to dress for success, appearance, first two weeks behavior on their new jobs, personal leadership and team building skills, and other topics related to their potential success in getting placed in a job in their skill area. The quality process was integrated into the placement program as well.

Skill levels of seniors were charted such as meeting the requirements of interviews, job applications, and other skill areas. At the end of our first year, the statistics we kept showed that our programs had achieved a job placement or continual education placement of 98% of our seniors. We were somewhat disappointed not to reach our established goal of 100%. To most people, horns would be blowing and fireworks exploding over such a successful result. However, the quality process still proposes that we should achieve a perfect score.

Soon, Mr. Neal Dias and his building trades class, constructed our Vocational Education Hall of Fame which was mounted in the main hallway of the vocational education building. It was a great way to recognize our talented students and teachers as well as program successes with pictures, award charts, and banners.

To this day, I think that the quality process that our team implemented at GHS, patterned after the Fleetwood plant in Westmoreland, is the best kept secret in educational performance attainment ever. It is too bad that it wasn't incorporated in every school in the system and throughout the country.

# Chapter 26

### Keep On Kickin'

During an annual meeting of the Tennessee Farmer's COOP, several years ago, O. Glenn Webb, president of Growmark, Inc., spoke and presented the following poem to all in attendance to never give up, but to hang tough during challenging times. It was entitled, Keep On Kickin'. I also used this title in one of my weekly columns and included his poem:

Two spry young frogs one darksome night
come hoping home toward a light,
and passing by the milking shed,
One to the other, jokingly said,
"Let's have a look inside the can
left near the door by our milking man."

And accidents that happen still
befall those frogs. They take a spill.
And plop! The white whey pulls them in,
with just two choices, sink or swim.
They quickly find their breath will stop,
unless they swim upon the top.

They kick for life and kick and swim
until their weary eyes grow dim.
Their muscles ache, their breath grows short.
And gasping, speaks one weary sport:
"Say, dear ole boy, it's pretty tough
to die so young, but I've had enough
of kicks for life. No more I'll try it.
I wasn't raised on a milky diet."

"Tut, tut, my lad.", the other cries...
"A frog's not dead until he dies.
Let's deep on kicking, that's my plan;
We yet may see outside the can."
"No use, no use", the fainthearted replied,
turned up his toes and gently died.

The braver frog, undaunted still,
kept kicking with a right good will.
And soon with joy too great to utter
he found he'd churned a lump of butter!
So, climbing on this chunk of grease
he floated there in perfect peace.

Now when times are hard, no trade in town,
don't get discouraged and go down;
Just struggle still, no murmur utter
a few more kicks may bring the butter.

In the spring of 1992, just before school ended, I had made the decision to run for Sumner County Superintendent of Schools. I had the encouragement from our staff at GHS and many other teachers and administrators across the county. I would be running against a popular incumbent. I was completing my 26th year of service in the same county, and having worked 8 years in the school district's central office, I felt confident that I was qualified. I had earned all of the necessary certifications in administration plus my knowledge of the quality process, which I planned to implement at every level of schools and services with the approval of the Board of Education.

I just needed to learn how to conduct a successful election campaign and raise enough money to win. Brenda was so supportive, but often asked me, "Are you sure that you want to do this?" It was a great question, but I saw no other alternative within education that would permit me to be able to make the positive changes I was committed to making. My compass was pointing north, and I was too stubborn to head another direction.

My first step was to get my face in the newspaper announcing my candidacy. We had become great friends with a fantastic photographer, Hugh Counts, who did most of the senior yearbook pictures in the county. Hugh was aware of my decision to throw my hat in the ring, and told me to drive down to Fayetteville, Tennessee, where his studio was located, and he would take my picture. He said, "Just dress up but don't worry about the ugliness, I can do wonders with a camera." Brenda and I drove down and accomplished our first step with no charge from Hugh.

After my announcement appeared in the Gallatin News Examiner, I started receiving phone calls of support, which led to a number of generous financial contributions toward my campaign. Julie even had convinced her band she sang with, to perform at all of my campaign rallies. We were on our way and things were looking good, until we received a big Loser's Ball.

My plan and hopes were dashed, when it was announced by the Sumner County Board of Education early that summer, that they had received legislative approval to appoint a new Director of Schools instead of having a public election. That bubble didn't take long to burst, but I thought that convincing 7 board members may be better and less expensive than traveling all over the county to get 10 to 15,000 votes. I spent the next two weeks refunding donors and writing "Thank you" notes. There were six finalists approved by the board to be interviewed for the job. I had all of the required papers, but was the only one of the six, who didn't have a first name called "Doctor".

I spoke with candor and of specific changes I wanted to make during my lengthy interview with the school board, all of whom I personally knew. I probably said some things I shouldn't, imagine that, like requiring all elementary and secondary supervisors to gas up their tanks and be ready to visit administrators and teachers in the schools under their supervision, rather than operate behind their desks on Main Street. I also stated how the county maintenance program operated with nasty vehicles, grease everywhere in the shops, and leaving their trash after service trips to local schools. This was not true of all maintenance personnel. I knew many who were dedicated to doing quality work in performing their jobs. I have been told on numerous occasions to be more diplomatic in my assessment of things. I shared the positive results of the implementation of the quality process at GHS, and how I wanted to see it operated in all county schools.

At least the board now knew of my intentions if appointed the Director of Schools. Several days passed after the interview process was concluded. The school board's decision was to be announced at the next scheduled school board meeting on Thursday night. On the evening of the big board meeting, Brenda noticed that I was not getting dressed to attend the announcement. I think that I was still in my lawn mowing clothes. She asked, "Bob, aren't you going to the school board meeting tonight?" I just sat back in my chair and replied, "Nope, I won't get the job. I'm sure they'll call me if I do." Politics is a strange thing. I was not going to compromise my stand on improving our school system just to get a job as Director of Schools.

I discovered early that the school board was not ready for Bob Lannom, because of the responses and expressions exhibited by them throughout my interview. I wanted them, however, to get a clear understanding about the direction I wanted the educational programs in Sumner County to take. I did not get the phone call that night. The school board just readjusted my compass for me in another direction that resulted in one of the best "Opportunity Balls" that I had ever received.

Just before Christmas, my friend Garlin Farris, who was now the Central Region Director of Production with Fleetwood Homes, came over to our house with his wife, Linda and their son, Jeff, for dinner. Garlin had been encouraging me from the time he had been promoted to consider joining him at Fleetwood, but I just had to get it out of my system that I wanted to do for education what the quality process had done for his company. After dinner as we sat around talking, he finally said, "Okay Bob, now, do you want to come to work at Fleetwood? The timing is right. We are about to make a change at Plant 27, (the other plant in Westmoreland) and the Production Manager's job probably will be open. Are you ready to make the move?" I remember my exact answer, "Where do I sign?"

Two days after Christmas in December of 1992, and after a good luck kiss from Brenda, I boarded an early flight in Nashville, headed for the airport in Ontario, California. I left so early that I did not get to speak to the kids who were home for the Holidays. I rented a car and drove to the home of Fleetwood Enterprises, in Riverside. I was warmly greeted by the interview committee, whom I knew personally, since I had conducted numerous management seminars at the two plants in Westmoreland. They each had a portfolio containing everything about me that I had mailed them earlier. I made sure to include copies of some of my detailed presentations that I had made at Fleetwood, and highlights of our quality process results at GHS.

I got to meet a bunch of other folks, whose names I recalled Garlin mentioning in many of our conversations. One of those conducting the interview had actually attended one of my classes at Plant 26 on Supervision, while he was visiting the plant there. The interview far surpassed my last one on Main Street in Gallatin. We spoke the same language! Shortly following the interview with the selection management team at Fleetwood, they welcomed me to the Fleetwood family, and informed me that I would begin my new job as a Manager In Training (MIT), assigned to Bill Graves's Plant 26 in Westmoreland. It was cleared for me to give a required 30-day notice to the local school system.

I will never forget what greeted me as I arrived at home after my "red eye" flight that night. When I pulled into our carport just before midnight, I saw a large hand-written poster board with a message written by our kids, "Free at last, Free at last, Thank God Almighty, Dad's Free at last." At that point in my life, I remembered Dr. Martin Luther King's famous quote. When I read that, it made me realize that our kids were more perceptive of my struggles than I realized. It was the right time for me to head into a different direction. My family was there with me.

During the next month as GHS, I spent a lot of time saying "Goodbye" to so many of my friends in education, not only to those at the high school, but throughout the system. I could tell a good story about each one of them. I had been living a dream for 26 years working with some of the most fantastic students, teachers, and administrators anywhere. I hated to leave them, but I had a new directional heading on my compass toward achievement of other goals. I cherish the "Book" the school staff presented me on the day of my farewell at GHS. The old photos and letters that so many wrote about our experiences together, filled a 1-inch-thick album of memories.

I often open that treasured history book and recount many of the great times we had while I served as a teacher and administrator at GHS for 19 of my 26 years in public education. I certainly left a better person than when I arrived there because of the positive and long-lasting friendships, patience, love, and compassion of so many. I cleaned out my office and closed the door at 4 pm on Friday, January 22, 1993, met Brenda at the car, and together, we were ready to ride off into the sunset toward our next adventure.

Our exit, however, was blocked by a car coming directly toward us at the exit gate as we were turning on the street to leave that day. I had previously been involved in a nasty disciplinary problem earlier in the day and remarked to Brenda, "Now what?" When she stopped and got out of her car, I recognized her. It was Karla Beams

(Taylor), one of my fantastic Key Club students, struggling to get a large balloon out of her car while hurrying to stop us. She ran up to our car as I opened the door to see what was going on. Out of breath, Karla handed me the balloon and hugged me thanking me for being her advisor with the Key Club. She told us that she was so afraid that I would get away before she could get back to school to catch me before we left.

After dealing with the negatives, especially a big one on my last day at GHS, Karla Beams ranks up near the very top of my "Made My Day" list forever. What a great way to have washed away the negative! She and her family remain close friends with me and our friends JJ and Sharon Redmon's family as well. She is always in my heart for that great moment in my life. She and her daughter sent me a special box containing another balloon a couple of years ago that meant so much to me. Priceless!

I felt so welcomed by Bill, the managers, supervisors, and Fleetwood associates at Plant 26. It was like I was the "prodigal son" coming home. After all, we had spent many hours together during my management seminars there. I suspected that they were also anxious to find out if I would demonstrate the practices that I preached.

I settled in and started completing my Fleetwood Manager Training Manual. I was fortunate that the Production secretary, Charman Meador, volunteered to translate my hand-written notes and type my entire manual as I went through each section during my assignments. At least now, when I finished, I would have a ready-reference document that I could read! Charman saved my life. I will never forget her patience and skills in making my time there most productive.

Brenda remained at Gallatin High School, since we were not sure where I would be assigned after my training program was over. It just seems sometimes that when the future is charted and you feel good about where you are that out of the woods comes a big Loser's Ball. In spite of Garlin's confidence that the plant across town would hang on till my training was completed, it got so bad that after only two weeks, Tom Stoneburner, the Production Manager at 26, called for me to meet him in his office. "Bob, you may want to sit down," he said, "They just fired the Production Manager at 27. They couldn't wait on you, it had gotten so bad." He smiled and asked, jokingly, "Are you ready to take over at 27?" Both of us knew the answer to that. I had barely finished reading the front-page credits of the manual I was supposed to master the next four months.

Tom was already a great supporter of mine and was disappointed for me, but couldn't help but liven up the moment by asking me, "Think you and Brenda could live in Cushing, Oklahoma, as Production Manager of the unopened, recently built Fleetwood plant?" Boy, did this day develop into a bummer! That is the way Loser's Balls hit you. You are stunned, speechless, and feel that the rug under your feet was pulled so fast, you haven't hit the ground yet. The situation was made worse when in a couple of weeks, Fleetwood hired a 20-year veteran Production Manager from Redmond Homes to take over the job that was supposed to be mine.

I started looking up names of motels and their addresses in Oklahoma. I knew and did not expect Brenda to go with me and told her that I would come home every weekend. She was like the story of Ruth in the Bible and told me directly, no more questions, "Where you will go, I will go. Where you lodge I will lodge...." I now was convinced again that I had over married. She was my best fan and was there at every challenge in our lives.

I was soon told by Fleetwood executives that they did not plan on opening the Cushing, OK plant in the near future, informing me that I would remain at 26 working with Bill and his team until something else opened up. Brenda and I always prayed together at night, but felt that God's ears were burning from hearing so many more prayers, recently.

In 1986, I was selected to serve as one of the seven elders of the Hartsville Pike Church of Christ. Most church members always expect more from their elders and their wives than they expect of themselves and fellow members. It is a fact that becomes part of the life of a church shepherd. Our friends looked to us for help during

## The Loser's Ball

their problems and trials, and were now watchful in how we were going to handle our newest set back. We had a lot of discussions about the job change I had made, but never regretted our decision. We just added a new entry into our "Not Now" file.

I was about finished writing The Loser's Ball when my son, Lee, recommended a great book to me that fit in perfectly with my theme of overcoming losing and setbacks in life. The title of this fantastic book is *A Setback Is a Setup for a Comeback* by Willie Jolley. Willie's statement explaining the contents of his book tells it all.

> *In every life there comes a time*
> *A minute when you must decide*
> *To stand up and live your dreams*
> *Or fall back and live your fears*
> *In that minute of decision,*
> *You must grasp the vision*
> *And seize the power*
> *That lies deep inside of you!*
> *Then you will see*
> *That dreams really can and do come true*
> *And that all things truly are possible...*
> *If you can just believe!*
> *It only takes a minute...to Change Your life!*
> *It only takes a minute to learn that*
> *A setback is nothing but a Setup*
> *For a Comeback!*

—Willie Jolley

I highly recommend Willie Jolley's book as a must read. It is the closest book that I have read that presents many similar principles of success that I have included in The Loser's Ball. Willie shares numerous stories of many who struggled to climb out of depression and losses and found their trophies of success. I wish I had a copy of Willie's book as well as another one, *It Only Takes A Minute*, back then when I started at Fleetwood my first two weeks.

During this downer, Brenda and I talked about how the Providence of God had seen us through many other unknowns, but the outcome would always be on God's calendar, not ours. We needed to just put our trust in Him and move on. We maintained our faith because it is the substance of things hoped for, and if you have all the answers that lie ahead in your lives, it is neither faith nor hope anymore. We put it all in God's hands like I put that Loser's Ball in my pocket in Battle Creek years ago, and worked like a borrowed mule to be at my best for whatever lay ahead.

I had a fantastic training program. I spent over 9 months working at both plants 26 and 27 in Westmoreland, plus getting to visit many of the 40 other mobile home manufacturing plants in the housing group scattered across the country. I graduated from the Fleetwood Quality College held in Somerset, Pennsylvania, home of the Coleman Camper Division, that had just been purchased by Fleetwood Enterprises. On plant visits, I usually left on a Monday, and returned on Friday. I absorbed all I could, taking notes daily of the "how to" and "how not to" plant operations. Garlin went with me on many of the trips and meant so much to me in helping to decipher the whys and hows of many operations.

Bob, the teacher, became Bob, the student. I "hit a lot of rocks" during those times, hoping my chance would soon come. I was determined to effectively meet any challenge. Bill gave me some tough assignments, but was supportive in my analysis and problem-solving solutions. At that time I had over five years of experience working with the quality process, 4 at GHS, a year and a half counting my previous seminar training time at 26, and now a Quality College graduate.

Again, in my life, I was dressed up, but nowhere to go. About six months into my training, Plant 27 was relocated to Gallatin, Tennessee where Fleetwood had purchased the site of a modular housing manufacturing plant that had gone bankrupt. They had completely remodeled the existing plant there, and brought all of their plant associates and construction equipment to restart Plant 27. They kept their entire management team and spent a lot of time retraining their workers in the newer processes. Plant 27 had never bought into the same quality process that Bill's plant had mastered. The Plant 27 management team, apparently, had no notion to change anything except the address of their plant.

Dave Moran, who was the Central Region GM, Bill's and Garlin's boss, (He was the big cheese) asked me to meet with them in Bill's office one day. I immediately thought that this looked promising, maybe a job has opened up. Instead, Dave, with Bill and Garlin's support, wanted me to be temporally assigned to go to Gallatin and conduct an investigation for them on just what was happening with Plant 27. They had even heard about talk of a strike to occur. There were no unions in any Fleetwood plant anywhere, so this was of great concern. They had informed the GM at 27 of my assignment, so there were no secrets of why I would be in the plant for the next two to three weeks.

My job included making my report to Dave and Garlin first, then to the Plant 27 GM on the issues that needed to be corrected to get the plant back on track. I had never felt so in between a rock and a hard place before than during the next few weeks. Here I am, looking out of one of my daughter's upstairs bedroom windows in our new house, across the fields and seeing the new Plant 27 less than a mile away, being managed by the guy who, basically, has the job I had prepared to get. Now, my role is to let corporate know what needs to be done for the Production Manager to keep his job! How is that for a major dilemma?

I knew that it would be an up-hill challenge from the start when I met with the GM at 27 on Wednesday, my first day there. He told me that he would like my report on his desk Friday afternoon, only three days from then. As professional and calm as I could be, I said, "John, there is no way in the world that I can finish what I have been asked to do by Dave, and have a written report for him and you in less than three weeks. I suggest that you give Dave a call and discuss this with him." He told me that he would talk to Dave, which I found out later that he never made the call.

That plant reminded me of my worst day in high school during home room without teacher supervision. When a teacher leaves the room for a moment unsupervised, the kids go nuts. Management had left the room at Plant 27. I actually didn't have to "cook the books" in my report. I left management issues completely out of my report and did not attack anyone. I stuck with the mechanics of things like, un-trained associates, excessive re-work, tardiness, absences not being reported, abusive language, tearing up equipment, tool thefts, multitudes of infractions involving supervisor-associate conduct, drug use, etc. There was not much room in my report to even include an evaluation of management, which I was convinced was not the thing for me to do, considering my position. I assumed that Dave and Garlin were smart enough to see what was going on.

I believe that my report was just a step they wanted me to conduct to confirm a lot of their beliefs. It actually could have been an assignment where they could look at my perceptions and findings to evaluate my take on the matter. Associate moral was at a dangerously low level. Most were still fuming from having to drive further to work when the plant was relocated to Gallatin. It was literally like a disturbed fire ant hill. Tempers flaring, associates cussing out supervisors, and supervisors cussing them back, was just a part of the day's routine. I remembered Brenda's question to me about the super's job, "Are you sure that you want to do this?"

A couple of months later, on Wednesday morning, October 27, 1993, Garlin met me at the plant in Gallatin, and told me that we needed to go for a ride. I asked him if I could notify Brenda to make funeral arrangements before we left. We had a laugh over that. Our destination was to meet with Bill, who was waiting for us at his houseboat at the Gallatin Marina. That was when I found out that there was to be a major management change at Plant 27. I was told not to say anything to anybody about our discussion that morning. Bill told us that Dave Moran was going to arrive early at Plant 27 on Friday morning at seven O'clock, to fire the GM and the Production

Manager as soon as they arrived at work. Bill would be taking over the Plant 27 GM job as well as continue to be the GM at Plant 26.

Bill spoke the words later that I had waited to hear, "Bob, I want you to be my Production Manager at Plant 27." He said that on Friday, after break at 9:20, there would be a called plant meeting of all associates, office staff, and other departmental managers in the break room where he would introduce me as the new Production Manager at 27 and explain the new management changes.

I really never found out or asked about the standing ovation that occurred when Bill made his announcement. I was afraid to ask if the joy was about who was leaving… or who was coming. Anyway, that was one of the best days of my life. My first day as the new PM at Fleetwood Homes Plant 27 was on Monday, November 1, 1993. I now had a tiger by the tail. My "kickin" had lasted for over nine months. I was now floating on a chunk of grease. Ain't life good?

# Chapter 27

**A New Beginning**

A Short Course In Human Relations
(Anonymous)

The Six Most Important Words:
"I admit I made a mistake"
The Five Most Important Words:
"You did a great job"
The Four Most Important Words:
"What is your opinion?"
The Three Most Important Words:
"If you please"
The Two Most Important Words:
"Thank you"
The One Most Important Word:
"We"
The Least Important Word:
"I"

While growing up on our family farm in the Glade, I had the misfortune of getting right in the middle of swarming hornets, wasp nests, fire ants, and the attacks of those stinging bumble bees. I almost feel now, with my new role as Production Manager at Fleetwood

## The Loser's Ball

Homes Plant 27 in Gallatin, that I am engaged in similar swarming challenges. Plant 27 was currently ranked second from the bottom (41) of the company's 42 manufacturing plants in the Fleetwood Housing Group. Bill Graves, our plant manager, made it clear that he was there to support me and basically gave me the green light to make the necessary changes to get our plant out of the cellar. I counted on Bill's wisdom and guidance as we began together to make the necessary changes ahead. His leadership in the implementation of the quality process at Plant 27 was vital to any future success. Bill was always there for me.

It seems that every job that I had previously had was like starting all over from the bottom to get to the top. Some include my start at Tennessee with a new baseball coach, the Vo Ag teaching job that at first was not to be, the first ever county Vocational Director, and now a struggling plant that had been moved to a new location. This seems like the pattern for my life thus far. Each one of these renewed starts were successful, however, with the help of positive teamwork, a determined work ethic, a never say quit attitude, and paying attention to doing the right things. Establishing goals, involving team members, respecting the opinions of others, and focusing on the finished product, all were important choices and strategies to success.

Bill and I knew that it would not be easy. There were going to be many who would resist the changes that needed to be made. I felt confident in my management abilities, especially in the knowledge and application of the quality process, which was to be our salvation over time. Instead of the school system, I could now devote my abilities and energy to implementation of the quality process at Plant 27. We had a great upper management team when I started there as the production manager. Bill was the new general manager. Wes Chancy was our sales manager. Later, Larry Mathews came from Plant 26 and replaced Wes when he got promoted to the Central Region. Other managers were Mark Opitz, purchasing manager, with Troy Burrow and Leo Lundburg as assistants, Shorty Shockley, service manager, Dennis Lumpkin, quality manager, and Joe Owen as assistant quality manager. The supporting office staff, including Brenda Grubbs, Evelyn Oliver, and others were great.

My role as production manager consisted of staffing the production team of associates on the floor, training supervisors, setting up the production schedules, plant safety, maintenance of the plant facilities, purchasing production tools and equipment, keeping the tool room stocked, and work with the state and federal housing inspectors assigned to our plant. Other duties included: hiring and terminating associates, training new associates, responding to service needs on houses that had been sold and set up by customers, serving on the quality improvement team, and the least favorable one of all, responding to the plant opinion surveys.

All managers were responsible for improving our scores on the associate opinion surveys as well as our customer satisfaction index home owner surveys. When Bill and I started together at Plant 27, the CSI (Customer Satisfaction Index) was in the mid-80s, which was not good. Service costs were near the highest in the company. The cost and numbers of workers comp cases were much too high. The turnover rate was off the charts. Plant efficiency had dropped significantly, since the relocation of the plant from Westmoreland to Gallatin. The rating of the production team was horrible. Just about everything that was measurable was bad. The hornets and wasps were swarming, to say the least. Every associate conversation I heard was about money, low bonuses, and having to drive further to Gallatin. It seemed like that every direction we turned, we would find a new challenge.

Once we went on the attack of addressing some issues and making changes, it was only a short time when my welcome wore off. I was no longer the manager-in-training (MIT), the guys on the floor had known. I was Bob from the school system. I shall never forget the first associate opinion survey that Bill shared with me. Most of the comments were addressed to me, such as, "Bob needs to go back to the school.", "We don't need a school teacher runnin' this plant." I remember this one: "Any manager who hires a school teacher to run our plant needs to be fired." and of course, an often repeated statement, "Fire Bob!"

This was the first time that I had been openly torched so badly in my life. With 26 years in the school system, I had developed a pretty tough skin, but this topped it all. This reaction was no big surprise to me or Bill. Such was the treatment for five of the previous production managers in the last 7 years at 27. I remember telling my supervisors that getting run off by plant associates was not on my to do list and it would be others who would be leaving. Bill was a good manager who responded positively. He and I laughed about the survey and both agreed that we must be doing something right to solicit such responses. I have always appreciated his support. We had a plan and were determined to stick to it while digging this plant out of the hole it had gotten into.

After several months of maintaining a positive attitude and treating each of our associates on the floor with dignity, respect and appreciation, I began to see a positive change in a number of our production line workers. In the past 7 years, they had always been treated like dirt. I had spent almost 10 months seeing this. Previous production managers ruled with an iron fist telling the workers, "Look, It's my way or the highway. If you don't like it, there's the door." The plant associates simply backed off into a shell of insecurity and refused to say or do anything to agitate their boss. They offered no opinions or suggestions that needed to be done to make their jobs easier or to improve the homes being built. They just showed up for work, put in their time, and went home. The less time that they interacted with management, the better. It would take some time before they would learn to trust us and willing to emerge from their shells.

Management had refused to get any input from them, seldom recognizing or praising their performance. However, they always found time to criticize them, often in front of their peers. It was like, "How to destroy plant personnel 101." One of the best strategies I used was so simple and effective. While out on the floor, where I spent 95 % of my day, I would be talking to associates who were performing their tasks and would ask, "What do you think about (some procedure or tasks they were doing)? You could immediately see them try to put together a response because they were now feeling that their input was appreciated. Managers were actually asking for their ideas. That is one of the best ways to make someone feel important. That was definitely a first for them.... A manager was actually asking their opinion about something. Previous management did not feel that there was a need to ask for any associate's opinion. Evidently, they saw this as a weakness on their part or just didn't care.

As time went on, several associates would later seek me out and volunteer their suggestions. You just had to be ready to first listen and respond to about anything. Some ideas were not possible to implement. Some were just complaints, but many were good recommendations. Just by listening to them, however, and returning a positive response, made a big difference. Our supervisors and group leaders were also getting suggestions for improvement from their team members.

Several of our plant associates during that first year decided that Fleetwood was not the place for them, and walked out the front door to work elsewhere. I was concerned over how corporate would respond to the higher turnover rate that we were experiencing going into that first year, but both Bill and I were actually expecting it to get worse as we kept "hitting rocks." I admit that I even assisted a large number of our production team to seek employment elsewhere that year. I understood a lot of their frustration. I even made some phone calls for several of them, referring them to other companies in the area. We actually replaced 50% of our work force during my first year as production manager. It was very unfortunate, but a necessary thing to do. The culture could only change with new mind-sets, because so many who left, just could not adjust to the new plant standards for achieving our goals.

I started early doing all of the interviews myself, later training utility supervisors and departmental supervisors on interview techniques. We would occasionally sit in on each other's interviews, offering suggestions, in an attempt to develop their skills for that very

## The Loser's Ball

important job. We were winning over our supervisor team headed up by my assistant production manager, Pop Sizemore. Pop, also got into the interviewing process. He had been at 27 in the mobile home business for a long time and was a big part of our new team culture. He supported me from the beginning.

During my training time, Pop had been a big help in many ways, especially since he understood the history of the plant and the changes that needed to be made. He had a way of relaying what I wanted to communicate with a different style of his own that our supervisors understood, which generated a few laughs between us. They would tell me what Pop said to them in relaying a certain instruction from me, by often letting me know the interpretation of what I had said, using his "Pop" language. He was a great go-between in calming down issues in the plant. He was a perfect fit for our team. Pop remained my assistant for over 10 years at Plant 27. Oh, the stories I could tell. This one took the cake!

We employed several women in our final finish department. They were fantastic workers, several from the little town of Lafayette. One time a vacancy opened up and Pop suggested that I really consider hiring more Lafayette girls, because of their great work ethic. Some of the final finish girls came to me one day during the opening and complained that they had heard that Pop asked me to hire more Little Fat Girls. I said, "What?" When I finally figured it out, Lafayette girls does sound like.... "Little Fat Girls!" We all had a laugh over that one. There are hundreds more.

We needed two more important leaders to join our production team to achieve our ultimate goals. With the promotion of Murrell Whittemore and Danny Cates to utility supervisors, we now had the team to make a run for excellence. We had our team together, all singing from the same page of the song book and established goals posted on walls throughout the plant. There was no turning back. With Bill leading our quality improvement team along with the entire management team locked in, it was now up to the production team to "git er done." We were set to begin year two at Plant 27.

During that beginning year, Pop and I worked very closely with our supervisors and departmental assistants. We went through the previous supervisor training sessions that I had conducted at Plants 26/27, titled, "Supervising People". We discussed the negatives that had so profoundly diminished the performance of Plant 27. I was at a great advantage, having spent nearly 10 months in my training program. By spending that much time at 27 and seeing the new direction our supervisors were now heading, it was refreshing. All that they needed was support and a cheerleader to pull out the leadership qualities that had been tucked away for several years. Supervisors, like Greg Carter in walls, Neal Perry in floors, Roger Jones, and Tracy Wix, emerged as potential leaders and managers in the future. You could see it happening. Others were stepping up as well.

What Brenda and I thought about my extended training time being a negative during those long months, actually became the best thing that could have happened to me. I now managed a plant that if I went upstairs on a winter day with no leaves on the trees, I could see our plant less than a mile away with a newer vision than I had before. We made some rules of conduct that we required both our supervisors and associates to follow. Each would respect each other by refraining from cursing one another, as was the custom during the old days.

There would be open communications between them concerning hassle reduction, tool accountability, reduction of rework, voting on individual departmental awards by departmental associates (eliminate supervisor selecting their favorites like in the old days), and reporting promptly any injuries that may occur. We made it a point to basically treat each other like we would like to be treated. I believe that's called, "The Golden Rule." Matthew 7:12. It's for sure that using the Bible will work for a number of good management principles.

Mary Crowley was the founder and CEO of the Texas-based Home Interiors and Gifts, Inc., which became one of the largest direct sales home furnishing operations in America in the 1970s. She was considered to be one of the leading businesswomen in the United States during that period. She stated in a speech she was giving at a conference that she used the book of Proverbs as the primary information in her company employee training manual. The Bible is packed with great management skills that I have found to be presented by many professional business trainers and motivational speakers throughout my life. Naturally, they come from the best Master Teacher.

It wasn't long until our entire plant was trained in the Fleetwood Quality Process. Our QIT met twice a month, recognizing our outstanding associates, departments, and recognized success stories that were being generated on a regular basis. Every department had their Performance Center constructed and in place in their department location. There were a number of required pieces of information that were displayed and kept current on a weekly basis; production efficiency, job requirements and audits, associate recognition and awards, production goals, success stories, Corrective Action Reports (CAR), problems selected to be solved, safety reports including accidents and lost-time accidents, and the Four Absolutes of Quality. Basically, if it happened in the plant, we measured it!

A general plant floor meeting was conducted each Tuesday morning after break to communicate with our associates plant efficiency, recognize associate and departmental performance, and make any other necessary announcements. Near the end of our first year, we began to have a quarterly plant-wide cook-out for everybody at lunch to celebrate some of our improvements made during the previous quarter. Danny, Curtis, and Jim, our plant maintenance guys prepared the grills for Chef Bob, who did the cooking along with Pop and others on the management team.

As more improvements were made, we graduated from hot dogs and hamburgers to steaks. It was good to see smiles and our associates celebrating some positive accomplishments for a change. Recognition was so important to everyone. Trophies at Fleetwood were definitely earned. You could tell that as the second year began that there was a feeling of trust beginning to emerge as well as less negatives ruling the roost. We were not there yet, but progress was being made. Bill began to start challenging us to go up in production. He would meet with me and ask me if I was ready to go up another floor. A floor was one half of a house, since we were building double-wide homes. Going up in volume meant perhaps the need to hire several more associates, depending on the department needs. It didn't take long for us to figure out to the man just what we needed each time to increase our production.

Each additional floor built in a day meant more money to each associate. It didn't take long before some associates were telling Pop and me before Bill; "I think we are ready to add a floor, let's do it." That was my hope from the beginning, letting our team tell us when they were ready, which was a long way from how it was back when.

One Monday morning before the shift started, my supervisors, Pop, Murrell, Danny, and I were getting ready to begin our day, I presented a challenge to them. We had increased our overall plant efficiency up to around 165%, which was good in a way, considering where we had come from. It had seemed to have leveled out the last few weeks, hanging in the mid to upper range of the 160s. Something needed to be done.

Pop and I decided that it would be fun for the two of us to put on a two-man concert and sing a song in the floor meeting to our General Manager, Bill Graves, if and when the plant hit 180% efficiency. Pop was a gifted singer and musician. I was our church song leader. I definitely needed his singing to override my attempts for sure. We announced our challenge at the next floor meeting. We were told during the week by several associates to pick out the song, because 180 was about to happen! A year and a half ago that challenge would have been received only with negative feedback from the associates on the plant opinion survey.

We didn't have to wait long. Two weeks later, the production team ran 181% efficiency. It was time to put up or shut up. The day came for the concert. Joe Owen, one of our quality managers, who was our "tech" specialist, was set up and prepared to film the Big Show and have it for "posterity", he said! Bill spoke first to the associates, congratulating them on their recent accomplishments and the steady progress the plant was making in reaching so many of our goals. He set the stage for the concert stars with a great and grand introduction. The plant associates couldn't wait for the show. Pop and I had promised that if we hit 180% efficiency that we would dress up as Tammy Wynette and a friend wearing dresses and wigs and sing to Bill. My friend Norma Hyre was there to see me in the slinky red dress she made for me and my long blonde hairdo. Pop wore a mini-skirt and blonde wig with a "Miss Fleetwood" beauty pageant banner.

After an associate welcome of yells and whistles, we began our tribute to Bill. We had him come back up front and stand between us as we sang our rendition of Tammy Wynette's hit song, "Stand By Your Man." Bill, being a great sport, even joined in with us while singing the chorus. Brenda was in attendance to again watch Bob at work doing another one of his stunts. It must have been received well. At the conclusion of our number, the entire group of plant associates, service, sales, purchasing, and office teams gave us a standing "O". Joe commented to us as we went back to work that, "The filming went so well that I am sending it to Corporate." "Joe, you didn't tell me you were going to do that." I spoke up in surprise. He went on to say, "By the way, the name of the album is, "Plant 27, the Duds in Concert." We were nothing like Wynonna and Naomi Judd, but Pop and I had our first album out now.

It may have been an unusual thing to do, but everybody had a great time together. It also let our production team know that we could have fun while reaching and achieving higher goals if we decided to do so. It was a good thing. It was always fantastic seeing the entire group of once unhappy associates finally having a fun time at work. Corporate even followed up by sending copies of the album with an attached message to the other 41 plants, suggesting, "Something to do to increase your efficiency".

I don't recall that performance ever being performed at another plant. From that point forward, Plant 27 began to shine like it had never done before. We began to raise production to more floors per day about every six weeks.

Since I had come from the education sector, I had noticed, especially during the interview process, that too many of our employees were not high school graduates. I had almost decided to not hire anyone without a high school diploma. I asked Bill what he thought about our plant setting up a plan to help our associates to get their GED (General Educational Development) or as it was called, high school equivalency diploma. Bill saw it as a great opportunity. I contacted my central office education buddies and arranged for the prep classes to be conducted at Fleetwood one day a week after the work shift. I had one of my supervisors ask me prior to setting up our plan, if I was going to fire him because he did not graduate from high school. My answer was simple. If you don't get your GED, I just might!

Plant 27 actually paid for all graduate caps and gowns to go through the graduation ceremony. The supervisor I mentioned, told me later that he no longer felt embarrassed about his situation and what it had meant to his family. I believe that decision to conduct GED classes did more for associate relations than anything we had done for them along with the quality process. We were told before we did this that we would see an exodus of associates leaving for other jobs. It never happened! We were now close to having 100% of our workers with high school graduates in our plant.

At the annual Fleetwood Housing Group Leadership Conferences, held in Dallas, Plant 27 started bringing home some hardware, winning various production, sales, purchasing, service, and quality awards. I believe while in Dallas at the Leadership Conference that year, we went to the podium six times to be presented championship plaques, the most coveted one, the 1998 Fleetwood Housing Group Production Team of the Year. It took us a little over three years to accomplish that goal, climbing from being ranked 41 to Number 1, actually beating out Bill's former Plant 26 in the process. What a great feeling!

Our plant was further recognized when the founder and CEO of Fleetwood Enterprises, John Crean, paid an unexpected visit to our Gallatin plant soon after our Dallas awards. I have included a picture showing John meeting with us in our break room expressing his

## The Loser's Ball

sincere thanks to us for sticking to the quality process and personally congratulating us for our accomplishments.

Soon, we were building 20 floors a day with just over 300 associates. Wages were at a record high with associate bonuses at an all-time level. Some days we would build 21 or 22 floors just to see if we could do it. No more hot dogs. All of our plant cook-outs consisted of steaks. At our quality celebrations, we often had a local band to play and at times on Saturdays, on "Zero Defects Day". We invited associate families to join the party. Julie and her band often performed for us. We celebrated a lot and presented tons of awards to many outstanding deserving associates.

It was about time for another challenge. We were at the production rate that was best for us, considering our manning and facilities, so it became a challenge again of raising efficiency. After a major regional reorganization, Plant 27 was assigned to the Eastern Region management team. The original Central Region Division was no more. Garlin, our Central Region Production Manager, in fact, took a General Manager's job at the Fleetwood plant in Benton, Kentucky.

My new Regional Production Manager was now Jimmy Phillips. I can talk about Jimmy because we are best friends today, but our first meeting when he came to Plant 27 for his plant visit was short of encouraging. By the time lunch was over, Bill asked me to come upstairs to his office immediately. When I went inside, I was asked to shut the door. Hmmmh, this is serious. Sitting beside Bill was his new boss, Buddy Ryan, the Eastern Region Vice President. Bill asked me to sit down and explain what was going on between Jimmy and me. He had gotten the word that we were not getting along too well that morning.

The whole deal originated when some of our plant associates went to buy their lunch from the lunch truck at 11:45 instead of 12:00. We were rocking along with a production efficiency of 195% or better. I had not given much thought to our production team going to lunch a few minutes early. I had told Jimmy that if he followed them, almost all of them would be back at work by 12:15. We had gotten to the point of trusting each other and felt that I, nor our supervisors had to ring a bell for them to go to lunch. It was just a way of showing confidence in our team for the great job they had done to earn that trust.

Jimmy had a lot more experience in the business than me. I respected that, but felt that I owed him a better explanation other than just a disagreement. I told Buddy and Bill that all I said to Jimmy in our last discussion in my office before lunch, was for Jimmy, as my new regional supervisor to just tell me the final results he wants in product quality, efficiency, service costs, and worker's comp cost and other measurables, but to leave the nuts and bolts on how to achieve them up to our 27 team. I couldn't resist so I asked Buddy, "Buddy, are you more interested in how Bill and I run the plant, or more interested in our meeting the division objectives and goals?" Buddy answered the way I had hoped.

It was no big deal, but could have escalated to one, if we had too many ducks out of line. I still had my job when I left that day. Jimmy and Buddy spent the week with us. By the end of the week, Jimmy and I got to know and respect each other more. Before he left our plant, he asked me to come down to visit the three Georgia plants to pick up some ideas, and when I packed up to come, throw in my deer rifle. He said that he would take me deer hunting after work on his farm. One of my best plant visits ever was to Georgia a couple of weeks later.

Communications are so important between individuals. Jimmy and I would never have grown to become the best of friends if we had not just sat down and leveled with each other. I learned a lot from his experiences that were valuable to me during my stay at 27. Jimmy and his wife Marion, welcomed me into their home. Jimmy and I turkey hunted together on our family farm and even took a week-long deer hunting trip together to Kansas one fall. We still talk to each other about once a month. Jimmy lost his lovely wife, Marion in 2023 to cancer. I have an open invitation to visit him anytime.

At one of our floor meetings I again challenged our team to go for the platinum. We had done so well in improving plant efficiency. We were currently at the top of the other plants with an efficiency of around 198 to 200%, unheard of numbers. I did not plan on conducting any more stunts to go after our next goal. I had earlier made a call to corporate in Riverside to find out what the Housing Group plant record was for plant efficiency for a week's production. We were close, but it would take a 205% week to break the record. After hitting 205 a couple of weeks later, I called in our efficiency report, but was informed that a Georgia plant had run 208% the same week. It had to be one of Jimmy's old plants. I soon expected a phone call rubbing it in.

When I announced in the next floor meeting what our two plants had done, there were "boos" and a number of remarks mentioning cheating, which was not the case, but that announcement hit a nerve. One of our associates stood up and offered the next challenge to beat the Georgia record. It was well received. I felt like a football coach who had said the magic words during a half-time speech to his players, and watching them run over each other to get to the field to smash the opponent. Another associate stood up and told me and Pop to set the production schedule so that they could go after the record. Pop and I made some changes in the production schedule that would give us a chance. Two weeks later we ran 213%. I called the corporate office and informed them. The championship belonged to Plant 27 and as far as we know, that record was never broken.

Plant 27 continued to hold on to the Number one spot for the next five years. We even surpassed any previous plant records by achieving a 98% CSI (Customer Satisfaction Index). We fell just short of our goal of 100% but our score was recognized by corporate as an outstanding achievement. That always meant a visit from Glenn Kumer, President of the Fleetwood Housing Group to our plant where he instructed our payroll department to award a new crisp 100-dollar bill to every employee in the plant on another steak cook out quality achievement day.

Showing up at work every day took on a new meaning. Because of our quality process, our plant developed an unmatched culture. Quality was a process, not a program with a beginning and an end. When we started training and awarding all associates with certificates of certification in their job requirements, the process actually ran itself. There was a process for every activity involved in the production process on the floor, in sales, service, purchasing, quality assurance, and in the office operations. Everybody that had a job had job requirements in writing and in production, thanks to Joe and Dennis, pictures of what the finished product looked like. Hassles were virtually eliminated. We even held our suppliers to higher standards by actually giving them written requirements/specifications for the supplies we purchased.

Another great recognition came to Plant 27. During one of our QIT meetings, Bill informed us that Fleetwood Homes Plant 27 had been recognized by the Phil Crosby Associates as the winner of its 1998 prestigious National Beacon of Quality Award. Our quality process was patterned after the Crosby model, and to be named its annual winner was just incredible. We were the first and only Manufactured Housing plant to ever be presented the Crosby Beacon of Quality Award.

Shortly after having received this great award, we were informed by corporate that the team at Plant 27 was selected to train all other 41 Fleetwood Housing Group management teams in the quality process. This was to include all general managers, production, service, sales, purchasing, and quality assurance managers in the Quality Process that we were using in our plant. What a surprise this was, as well as a humbling experience, to see our corporate managers select us to train the entire housing group. What a long way Plant 27 had come!

Joe Owen began putting it all together into presentations for use by our production team to lead the way in accomplishing this task. We even used some of our departmental group leaders to make presentations from production. We felt like that it would be an effective way for all of the plant managers to hear from actual associates on the floor, who were involved daily in the manufacturing process. It took the better part of a year to rotate all of the plant managers across the country to complete the training. To all of us at Plant 27, it was the ultimate recognition of a job well done. Our only disappointment was that actually just a few plants took quality seriously enough to implement the process.

Plant 27 produced something else of great value to the Housing Group. With new orders increasing from sales, we got to the point that we found ourselves with more than a six (6) month backlog. Even though our volume of homes produced was the highest, not only in our company, but among our competitors, we found ourselves in an enviable, yet, helpless position. Corporate made a quick decision, however, and purchased the needed property. They soon built a new manufactured housing plant, our sister plant. Thus, Fleetwood 27-2 was born in Lafayette, Tennessee. So, now there are two of us, 27-1 and 27-2, with Bill as the general manager of both plants.

Once 27-2 got into full operation, the combined daily production rate of the two plants was at 33 floors. To be a part of a plant that was once in big trouble and then reach the level where it had to reproduce itself because of its success, was one of our greatest and most thankful achievements. It even surpassed any grand slam game winning home run I could have ever hit. It was a remarkable demonstration of a solid team effort by the management team, but mostly by those dedicated associates who built our quality homes.

I retired from Fleetwood Homes in January of 2003, having spent ten plus fantastic years working with some of the best men and women on the planet. During my last day there, during the Tuesday floor meeting, Bill presented me the Fleetwood Homes Plant 27 Beacon of Quality Award. Few people saw it, but Pop did, when my eyes watered as I accepted this great award. Having been involved in this phenomenal process for a total of almost 15 years, it was tough to give it up, but it was time to move on. Pop nudged me when the presentation was over and said, "Kinda got to you didn't it?" I was glad that they had invited Brenda to be with me that day. She was as much a part of the Fleetwood story as anyone else. Great things do "kinda get to you."

When you set and reach your goals, develop an unmatched work ethic, never give up, refuse to settle for mediocrity, and form positive hard-working teams, you stand a good chance of becoming a champion. I could not have been more blessed. When I need a transfusion today, I dial up the old familiar phone number of our old Plant 27-2 and hear the answer, "Fleetwood Homes of Tennessee, May I help you?" I hop in my truck and drive to Lafayette, and visit the only operating Fleetwood plant in Tennessee. I can proudly spend the day visiting with so many of my former friends and coworkers at 27 before they moved to Lafayette to operate their successful plant, now under new ownership, but keeping the name Fleetwood Homes as their label.

In a recent conversation with Greg Carter, now the Safety and Maintenance manager there in Lafayette, he informed me that the plant was now adding a $5 million expansion project. Many of my former friends are now managers and valued associates there. Neal Perry is now the Production Manager and Tracy Wix his assistant. Roger Jones is now the Service Manager. All four of these guys helped make the remarkable success of Plant 27 possible. God truly guided me in the right direction and to work with such fantastic people. He helped me to adjust my compass toward the brightest stars. Many of them still shine today on Highway 52 in Lafayette, Tennessee.

*At the 1998 Fleetwood Homes Leadership Awards Convention in Dallas, Plant 27 carried home six of the top championship plaques. Left on the front row is my friend and Regional Production Manager, Garlin Farris. Next is Glen Kummer, Fleetwood President, Bob Lannom, Tom Stoneburner, Plant 26 Production Manager, and Ron McCaslin, Director of Sales. Plant 27 was the recipient of the Production Team of the Year award.*

*The happy guy with his hand on my shoulder is John Crean, the CEO and founder of Fleetwood Enterprises. To his right is Bill Graves our Plant 27 General Manager. Behind are Dennis Lumpkin, Quality Manager, Chris Rossous, Manager-In-Training, and Shorty Shockley our Service Manager. It was nice to have an unexpected visit from our CEO to show up and congratulate us.*

# Chapter 28

Someone said, *"You may not be able to change the direction of the wind, but you can always adjust the sails."*

The temperature in the huge exhibition tent where I was sitting in my woodcrafts booth was hot! Really hot! The outside temperature at the Fairgrounds was 94 degrees. It was in late August, just two days into the 2004 Wilson County Fair in Lebanon, Tennessee. I was literally getting "burned out" by watching the fair-goers walk by my well-stocked, displays of quality made wooden toys and other crafts. During my first year of "freedom", I had set up my booth in many craft shows in the area, barely making enough money to pay for the cost of the booth rental at the shows. A couple of my friends at church, Nick and John, joined me for a couple of shows with a similar lack of success. My Loser's Balls were coming at me faster than my customers.

One of my friends passed by early that morning and asked me. "Hey Bob, having fun yet?" That wasn't funny! There was one advantage to boredom. I had a lot of time to think. My new business that I had named, "Woodel Toys For Woodel People", was either inappropriately named, or just doomed for failure. Brenda let me know that is was simply "Poor management." That hurt! I sat on my stool trying to come up with a plan to adjust my sails into a different wind direction when an old friend, John Leeman, and his wife Kathy, walked up to my booth. John's first words to me were, "Bob, what in the world are you doing here at the fair sweating in this hot tent?"

John and I had taught Agriculture years earlier in the 1960's, when I was at GHS, and he was at Goodlettsville HS. We spent a lot of evenings at Camp Clements FFA Camp during the summers on the back porch of the old administration building solving many of the world's problems.

Several years ago, John was appointed the Assistant Commissioner for Vocational/Technical Education for the state of Tennessee. He tried to persuade me to join his staff while I was the Vocational Director in Sumner County. I always told him, "I didn't want to fight the Nashville traffic every day, besides, I am looking forward to following our kids' sports at the high school. Thanks anyway." Since business was slow, I told him and Kathy to pick out something they liked at no charge, just to make me feel better. John went on to say, "You don't need to be doing this. Did you know that our buddy, Ralph Barnett, is now the Assistant Commissioner, and that the state office has announced that they are reopening the position of Tennessee FFA Executive Secretary, and taking applications?" That was the job John had tried to persuade me to take when he was there, years earlier.

Ralph, who was one year younger than me, served as an FFA Camp officer with me in 1961. Both he and I had served as Tennessee Association State FFA Officers one year apart. Ralph taught Agriculture like me and was one of the West Tennessee State FFA Supervisors before moving to the state office. Actually, when John stopped by, he was working at the time in Ralph's office in another position. If it had not been for John coming along, I probably would have never gotten the word about the opening.

When I got home that night, I discussed the situation with Brenda. She was always supportive in whatever I chose to do, except for a few stunts I would resort to pulling sometimes. She helped me make the decision when she laid out the facts, "Bob, you've loved the FFA, since you were in high school. It probably was not just an accident that John showed up today, you know? You already know just about everybody down there at the state office. The kids are out of school now. I think you should call Ralph and talk to him about the job." That was basically the message Brenda told me. She then asked me, "If you get that job, what are you going to do with all of your toys and things you have made?" Good question. I would have to think about that.

After talking with Commissioner Ralph the next morning, we worked out a date and time for me to meet him in his office in Nashville for an interview. I stuck to my commitment to finish the week at the fair, barely covering my booth cost. I boxed up hundreds of toys and wood products, and bid farewell to all the "woodle" people at the fairgrounds. My "re-wirement" was not going so well. If you know anything about electricity, when I left Fleetwood, I was wired for 330 volts, three-phase current, and now I'm reduced to a 110 volt single phase circuit, literally, with output no more than a gentle "shock". I needed a recharge!

When I arrived for my interview a few days later, it was like old home week with the family. Of course, Ralph and John were there. Dan Covington, my former buddy from Metro Nashville Schools was working there in the office. Then, in walks my friend, Will Lewis, a former Ag teacher and state supervisor. Steve Gass, a former state officer and Ag teacher, also sat in on the interview. I had met Steve before at various FFA events. He would be my partner working with the Ag curriculum and me with the FFA, if I got the job.

We all sat around a conference table and talked about old times more than engaging in a formal interview. Ralph, being the consummate professional asked a few "interview" questions to make it official, I guess. Ralph told me that they had to interview a couple of other candidates and that he would get back to me in a few days, but he wanted me to go to work for the department if it worked out okay.

When I was with the local school system, especially as an assistant principal, involved in many discipline problems, our home mailbox was usually attacked by some of my rowdies, who were not happy over their "sentences". Every time it happened, I just went to Wal-Mart and bought a $4.59 cheap mailbox, stuck on my address numbers, replaced the posts with two $.99 cent studs nailed together, stuck them in the ground, and waited for the next event. After each mailbox incident, I would record a damage score on an index card I had bought for the occasion, and stapled it to what was left standing. My scores ranged from a 6 to a 9.5 depending on the severity of the damage. It was the Olympics of mailbox destruction. If they knocked it completely down, I drove a stake nearby with my card on it and gave them a perfect score of 10. Brenda told me that I was asking for it and advised me not to be doing that.

Once I left the school system, I had no more issues with our mailbox. While at Fleetwood, I built a nice woven lattice frame and even put a blooming clematis climber vine growing up the painted white frame. The very morning that I headed out of my driveway to start my new job reentering education at the state office, I noticed something was missing at the end of the driveway. My mailbox, nice frame, clematis, the post, everything…….was Gone! All that was left was a hole in the ground. I saw what was left of my masterpiece, piled up in the ditch down the road about 50 yards from our driveway. I could only guess by the vehicle tracks that a Loser's Ball, disguised as a Mack Truck, had wiped it out. That was my "Welcome Back to Education." I replaced it with a 15-inch round cedar tree in 3 feet or concrete. I named it "Timex". Hopefully, it can take a lickin' and keep on tickin'. So far, so good.

During my first month working with the gang at the state office, Steve and I made a visit to Van Buren County to Camp Clements, our state FFA leadership camp. We acquired enough historical documents that were needed to confirm that Camp Clements was the oldest State FFA camp in the nation. The old Administration Building on the campus was built in 1929. It was no longer in use, but with the growth in summer camp attendance, it had become a fire hazard and a safety issue. It was definitely in bad shape.

I told Steve that in order for that building to still be standing, the termites had to be holding hands. We decided on our visit that the old historical structure had to come down. Dale Bray was in charge of the maintenance of the camp complex, cabins, landscaping, swimming pool, staff lodge, and just about everything above and below ground there. Brenda, his lovely wife, was the camp Director, and handled all of the summer camp reservations, finances, and all special meetings that were held there. Dale and Brenda became dear friends to Brenda and me as soon as we met.

The two Brendas worked at the state convention registration counter together for years, occasionally being assisted by Dale and Bob. Camp Clements was in great hands with the Brays in charge.

A few months later, plans were made to raise the old structure. Dale agreed to save as much of the good oak flooring and other wood structures such as the steps, stairs, paneling, windows, and doors. We even bought a big covered trailer to store the items until we could find a use for them. I finally figured out how to adjust my sails. I began taking some of the oak flooring and making gavels for use at our state FFA Convention in 2004. I also started making ink pens out of the camp flooring as well. The pens were sold at FFA events or by special order. The FFA received a major portion of the sales.

I was also commissioned to make many presentation gavels and plaques. Each year, since 2004, I have made the Official Tennessee Association FFA State Convention gavel. It is used only at the state convention, returned to the FFA Alumni, who sells the gavel at their annual auction with the total sales going to the FFA Alumni Scholarship Fund. The gavels usually sell for around $400 at the auction. Amazingly, the 2024 convention gavel was sold at auction for $2,000. I also made the stage podiums which are still in use at the state conventions. They are also made from the wood from the old Camp Clements Administration Building. Looking back at my failed attempt to sell toys and crafts, it just had to be a big reason. I soon found out what it was. I was charting the wrong course. Now, what shall I do with all of those woodle toys?

Another opportunity was being formulated that I had no idea was waiting for the right moment. I again, took some vacation time one summer and along with about a dozen of our Hartsville Pike Church of Christ members, made our second church building trip, headed for the Mexican border to meet up with other groups at Laredo, Texas, to help a small Mexican village build their church building just northeast of Saltillo, Mexico. The little village was two hours from our hotel in Saltillo. We were there for a week and made the drive to and from each morning and afternoon. It was a fantastic adventure. The small village was virtually in a desert setting. Donkeys and carts were their means of transportation.

We laid blocks for four days and finally topped off our construction of their block church structure on Thursday afternoon. Earlier in the week, our team built a concrete volleyball court for the locals. We had a devotional meeting with the families there, their minister, small children, and a few donkeys looking on.

Following the devotion, we went to one of our vans and unloaded two huge Wal-Mart storage bins about five feet long full of "Woodle Toys", and presented them to the "Woodle" children gathered around us. The feeling that afternoon far exceeded any of all my best sales days combined at the craft shows. To see those kids on their knees rolling little wooden trucks, cars, tractors, and buses on the ground was a sight I shall always remember. Maybe my business wasn't that big of a loss after all. God provides.

I worked with four state officer teams while I was at the state office as the FFA supervisor. Steve and I were very fortunate during that time to have the first ever all Tennessee FFA female state officer team. Those girls were amazing. We found that out after our first executive committee meeting when we met at our house at our big conference table in our den addition that it was going to be a great year. Most of them were Valedictorians of their senior classes. The others were in the top ten. I had a small strawberry patch behind the house where we picked strawberries for our family and friends. After engaging in a state officer strawberry picking exercise, Brenda made two delicious strawberry pies for them. We were fortunate to have the cream of the crop in several other fantastic state officer teams to work with during my service with the state.

I developed eternal friendships with so many great educators, students, and state office staff members during my stay. I could not have made it without fantastic people like Ralph, Dan, Will, Steve, Joyce, Iris, Dale and Brenda, Martha Hix, and so many dedicated advisors and FFA volunteers. Thanks is not enough for the job done by Kim (Newsome) Holmberg, who virtually produced and directed the state FFA conventions each of those years. There is no telling how many midnight emails we conducted getting our plans for convention finalized. I am glad Brenda was a trusting wife, because Kim and I spent many nights up after midnight on the computer finalizing our convention plans. Kim was a state officer from west Tennessee when her dad, Bill, was an ag teacher in Dyersburg.

I could never pay back the loyalty and support that I received from my FFA right hand man, Steve Gass. He retired his position in April of 2023, leaving a legacy of excellence for others to follow. If you are a part of the FFA, you are surrounded by a team who cares about your success. People like my friend, Wayne Walker, that spent over 35 years at GHS, is a testimony to the diligence and determination to be successful by giving all during their work careers to students and their peers. Terry Shartzer, and his wife Marie, have both dedicated their entire work careers in education. Marie makes good tomato juice, too. Other Ag teachers like the Glade McDonald boys, Dale and Benny, Jerry Cooper, JJ, Dan, Jim, Jill, Doc Ricketts, Pete, and so many more who made great memories for me. Hopefully soon, our proposed Tennessee FFA Archives/Museum will showcase the contributions of many men and women who have made the Tennessee FFA tops in the nation.

I could make a giant list of so many former friends and teammates in the Ag-Ed programs, who are still remembered and appreciated by their former students and fellow teachers. The FFA, is by far, the best youth leadership organization in the world. Many of the leadership principles I learned in the FFA carried over to my career in education and later throughout my tenure in the corporate world. I also learned so much during the years that I spent in competitive sports, both in winning and through the defeats suffered by my Loser's Balls.

During my last year at the state department of education, I had the golden opportunity to do a pay-back, something most of us either don't take the time to do, or cannot do because of circumstances. It was during the year that we were having a state FFA Board of

Directors meeting. One of the tasks on the agenda was to nominate the recipient of our annual Tennessee FFA Distinguished Service Award. I nominated my Ag teacher, William H. (Bill) Coley, who was retired at the time from serving as the Middle Tennessee FFA Supervisor.

He was also, as most retired FFA folks did, volunteering to work at our state conventions helping in the state officer election process. It was a unanimous decision. Mr. Coley was selected. When I notified him of being the recipient of the award, and that it would be presented to him at the National FFA Convention in Louisville, Kentucky, he put it on his schedule to attend.

You may recall in one of the previous chapters when I was a high school freshman, that I had to room with Mr. Coley at my first state FFA convention in Memphis, where he basically planned my life the next three years. He asked me if I had him a room. I said, "I have you a room..... mine! You are rooming with me." We sat up that night till midnight not planning anyone's future this time, but letting him know how much he had meant to Brenda and me throughout the years, as well as still being my "advisor" in career decisions. He truly was like a second dad to me. I got to complete the cycle watching him receive the top FFA award given at the National FFA Convention. It was perfect timing for his award.

I had seen his health begin to deteriorate very rapidly, caused by an advanced stage of cancer. He was living in Knoxville with his son, Bill, who called me and gave me the news one afternoon I had dreaded hearing. Bill and his sister, Catherine wanted me to do the eulogy at their dad's funeral in Mt. Juliet later that week. It was tough, but with God's help, I made it through in the presence of many former FFA members, state staff, advisors, family, some current state FFA officers, and a host of friends. Bill Coley was indeed a special man. I wrote a poem for the occasion, entitled, "Here By The Owl", which was the advisor's first response in the FFA opening ceremony of our meetings. I wanted to do more to honor him if I ever got the chance. Bill Coley was always by the owl for me every time I called on him since 1958.

Steve and I had noticed that the National Officers opened and closed the National FFA Convention with a huge gavel over three feet long so it could be gripped by the six national officer team members to open and close the national convention. Steve asked me if I would like to make a gavel just like the one used by our national officers for our state officer teams. I agreed and that I would get on it.

Following a severe wind storm in Sumner County later, a friend of mine said that she had a big cherry tree to blow down. She said that it was very old and could be cut into useful lumber if I wanted it. I never turn down a good cherry tree. I hooked up my trailer, gassed up the chain saw, and loaded it up and brought it home to my shop. A friend of mine came with his portable lumber mill saw and did the honors. It did have some beautiful wood that would make a perfect gavel. I made a large gavel just like the National FFA Organization gavel, and dedicated it to the memory of William H. Coley. His son, Bill, came to the convention for the dedication, where we presented the memorial gavel to the state officer team for their use at the state conventions. It has an engraved brass plate on the gavel head, and is protected throughout the year in a case made from the flooring and walls of the old Camp Clements Administration Building.

It is stored at Camp Clements and is taken to each annual Tennessee State FFA Convention in Gatlinburg, Tennessee, for use by the state officer teams. It is taken out of its case, tapped twice by the current state officers to open the convention, and tapped once by the newly elected state officers, to end the convention. After that, it is returned to its case ready for the next state convention. It should last forever since it is only tapped three times a year.

I am so blessed that John Leeman came into my hot tent and stopped by that day in Lebanon. Just like Brenda had said, "It was not an accident that John showed up that day." I am a firm believer in the providence and care of our Heavenly Father.

Brenda and I have experienced too many unexplainable events in our lives to convince me otherwise. It seems that very often our happiest moments, however, are interrupted by a direct knock-down pitch called the Loser's Ball.

We had already experienced the loss of my brother in 1986, just 36 years old, my cousin, Raymond and coach Lumley, in Vietnam. My mother died in 1997. She was only 72 years of age. My dad lived a full life before a stroke hit him and resulted in his death in 2009. Brenda's oldest brother, Gilbert, died in a tragic farm accident in 2017. Brenda's brother in-law, Rusty, died in a plane crash years earlier. We knew what "bean balls" were. We had a bunch to come our way. It was so hard on Brenda, though, when her brother, Gilbert, was killed.

As we often did, we were sitting in our swing under a shade tree behind our house one day following a photo shoot of all the family members taken by friends of ours, Scotty McCullough and his wife, Donna. Soon after talking about our family, the great times we had raising them, and being with our parents and families for so long, Brenda suggested to me that since I liked to write about things, that I should write a book about our relationship, my baseball career, our kids, their sports, and our lives together in sports, our time together in education, my experiences in the business world, and leave it for our kids and their kids to remember us by. At the time I just took her idea as more of a suggestion during our casual conversation that evening. I didn't give it much thought at the time.

Years later, Brenda and I were driving home from church one Wednesday evening, when a lady ran a stop sign and T-boned us in our Ford Explorer, flipping us upside down. As we were skidding down the street in our car, we found ourselves hanging upside down strapped in our seatbelts. Our only escape route was to crawl out the rear hatch window which was completely shattered. Brenda sustained a nasty cut on her left hand. I picked glass off of me for an hour at the hospital but was unhurt.

After that incident I began to think more about the book, but soon, my compass was redirected. A couple of years later Brenda began to show symptoms of dementia. She was having a lot of difficulty getting over our accident and the death of her brother, Gilbert, a year later. We worked in a couple of return trips to Alaska with our kids and grandchildren, once with her brother and sister, their families, and some friends, but it kept getting worse. We had a life of travel visiting almost every state in the nation with friends and during our kid's ball games, but on our last trip with our kids and grands to Jackson Hole, Wyoming, and the Grand Tetons, all of us noticed that she was really struggling to get through each day.

The dementia slowly changed to Alzheimer's. I read up as much as I could about this horrible disease. With such deterioration of the mind, yesterday became our best day. It was the worst possible Loser's Balls ever to come my way. Several of our church members and friends were also going through the same battle as Brenda with members of their families. The last six months of Brenda's life were so bad. I felt so helpless. To see my high school sweetheart, my best fan, the love of my life, my precious wife and Nana to her grandchildren slip so fast, was so hard to bear. I thank my God above for the strength and stamina to care for her as long as I could. When she quit eating and drinking and began to try to get out of the house at night, I had no choice but to get her the best help I could at a nearby memory care unit close to our daughters, Julie and Amy, who lived nearby. We took turns spending the nights with her.

One afternoon, I was told by the Hospice nurse that I should stay with her that night, which would probably be her last night. I watched over her all night, but while I was sitting at her side of the bed holding her hand at 5:30 am on Friday, June 18, 2021, she took her last breath. She was now present with the Lord and absent from that horrible physical condition which took her life. She was there only 24 days. She was 76 years old. We had been married 58 years and 11 days.

I now faced the challenges ahead in adapting to a new world without my best friend. I had resilient children, mature and strong, as well as tremendous grandchildren, all of whom are Christians and faithful to their Lord. I could not have been comforted and supported any better because of the bond that we shared. Brenda had led the way in showing our kids what actions to take to comfort and support others in need.

She was a Ruth, a Martha, a Lydia, and a Mary wrapped into

one Christian lady. Her life of service to her Lord and church family will never be forgotten by any of us. I knew that I was going to make it through the period of grief that lay ahead because of my faith, my family, and my friends. I thank God and all of them daily for such great gifts of love, comfort, and prayers.

It had been exactly two years since her death when I started on "her book". She wanted me to tell my baseball stories so that the young people could gain the confidence in spite of limitations, so that they could be successful. She wanted everyone to know that our kids worked hard, loved their friends, and respected their teachers and coaches. She wanted a way for our grandchildren to better remember their Nana and Poppa and what they stood for in a cruel world. I was to make sure that in spite of negatives in her life, she would want all or us to be positive and set goals for our futures.

Her desire was for me to write about how we can be thrown the meanest and nastiest Loser's Balls and still emerge as winners and champions. She would want me to show what friendships really mean, how devoted close friends are to each other. She expected me to write about those of us who must fulfill the needs of those less fortunate than us. It would be terrible if I didn't prioritize the love of family, brothers, sisters, parents, children, and of course, cousins, she exhibited throughout her life.

One of her top requests she would want me to mention was that it takes three to make a marriage; the husband, the wife, and God. If she was writing her book, she would want you to do something good for somebody every day of your life, especially for a little child. She would want you to go to the Dollar Tree (her favorite store), and buy boxes of cards to mail someone when they were sick, had lost a family member, or just on their birthday or anniversary. She would ask you to learn how to make a special recipe and take a covered dish to someone who is confined at home.

If she could, she would encourage you to be at your best at your place of work, to do everything right the first and every time. One of her best pieces of advice would be to never spend beyond your means, and examine your checkbook every time your husband writes a check, making sure he wrote everything down. She would strongly suggest that you get what it takes to decorate your house for every occasion and holiday of the year and get your husband to buy you a barn in which to store and organize everything for each seasonal use.

She would make sure to find out the children and grandchildren's favorite dessert and have one made ready to serve when they came for a meal. She would ask that you make sure to tell them, "I love you with all my heart", every time she gave them a goodbye hug. She was always the first to show up for special "Graves" dinners and get-togethers, plus to be among the last to leave. As an accountant and bookkeeper, she would never end her tasks until everything balanced to the penny. Brenda ended her life with everything in balance, all debts were paid, all credits accounted for, and all preparations made. She had a well-earned appointment with God in eternity to welcome her home at last.

I still miss her so much. She left me more than memories, however. She showed and demonstrated before me what life is really about. I have been entrusted with making sure that my life is more of service to others, just as she did. She never took the last piece of cake from the platter. She gave of herself and her talents to the benefit of others. I hope I can measure up to her great example and leave our children, grand, and great grand-children an enviable "Nana" example. Proverbs 31:10-12 describes Brenda perfectly, "Who can find a virtuous woman, for her price is far above rubies. The heart of her husband doth safely trust in her, so that he shall have no need of spoil. She will do him good and not evil all the days of her life." I was and still am so blessed!

# Chapter 29

### Met at the Milk Barn

All of us have gone through many hardships in life. Most of us know the sadness of losing our friends, relatives, and even our spouses to death. God doesn't expect us, however, to live our lives in the loser's bracket. We must emerge with new beginnings, new hopes and a sense of positive endurance and motivation.

I have discovered that life beyond the hardships is just waiting for you to begin new and exciting adventures. Seeing my children's successes in their careers, grandchildren excelling in sports, completing their educations, and to hold a new born great grandson in my arms, add so much encouragement to modifying my status and excitement of climbing out of the hole of knock downs and bruises of depression. I love what Paul said in Philippians 3:13, *"Brethren, I count not myself yet to have laid hold: but one thing I do, forgetting the things which are behind, and stretching forward to the things which are before..."*

So many new adventures, friendships, opportunities, untraveled paths, and discoveries lie ahead to those who are willing to take advantage of their past and utilize them as foundations for future successes. I am fortunate to have had a great foundation on which to build and chart a bright future as well as a loving and supportive family with whom I intend to share together the riches of not only my reshaped goals, but theirs as well. The anticipation of new challenges overwhelms all the negatives that have come our way. "I press on", as Paul summarizes his decision in adjusting his sails. Full speed ahead!

Developing new friendships is like finding gold nuggets. This story relates the beginning of a new relationship with my new friend as I began to write my book. I never knew that baseball was a common denominator in both of our lives. It started out with a phone call from a close friend of mine, who asked me a simple question to see if I could help him out with a special request. My friend, Ray, wanted to know if I knew anybody who had a bunch of dairy cows. I said, "Ray, half the people I know have cows, why do you want to know?"

He answered, "Bob, you are not going to believe this. I have a friend who has something on his bucket list. He wants to pet a cow and a calf." This was highly unusual, since I grew up on a dairy farm and spent many days and nights caring for and milking cows as well as raising and feeding their calves. I didn't know many people who had not petted a cow or calf. "Who is this friend of yours and why this request?" I asked. Ray let me know what was going on. I'm thinking, "Boy, this ought to be good."

Ray told me that he had met a man by the name of Roger, who had moved to Tennessee, with his wife, to live a "higher quality of life" in our beautiful state of Tennessee. He said that they often had breakfast together and had become great friends. He told me that Roger had never been around cattle and wants to actually put his hands on a cow and calf as a part of his wish list. Ray said that he called me, because he knew of my agriculture background and by growing up on our dairy farm that I may know of someone who could help Roger out.

I knew instantly who I wanted to contact to ask to help out with this unusual request. Roy, a friend of mine and a local dairy farmer, whose farm was not too far away, agreed to let Roger come to his farm and fulfill his goal. The closest that Roger had been to a dairy cow was a picture of a beautiful Jersey cow, given to him by one of his friends. I think Roger had done some financial work for a member of her family who owned a milk company in New York. Roger grew up with a daughter who is still a personal friend of his.

## The Loser's Ball

I set up the date and time with Roy, for Ray, Roger, and me, to meet him at his milk barn about two hours before milking time. Roy was milking over 200 dairy cows twice a day, at the time. We didn't need to interfere with his valuable work schedule. We arrived one afternoon well in advance of the regular milk time. Roger was going to see more than one cow and a calf on this visit. When we arrived at the farm, Roy greeted us and introduced us to his granddaughter, Addison, who was active in 4-H at the time, and had her best show cow with her. She even had a rope halter on her cow so Roger could lead her around the barn lot. Addison even gave Roger some tips on showmanship as he led that big Holstein cow around. For Roger, it was like being in the show ring at the State Fair. He was all smiles. There was no doubt that he was enjoying every minute of this adventure. It was a big bonus having Addison to be with Roger for his bucket list event.

Once the first half of Roger's request was completed by "petting" his first cow, we walked over to the calf corrals, where Roy had his baby calves contained in their hutches (outside houses). It was time for the calf petting. The normal practice for dairymen once a calf is born, is to permit them to nurse their mamas a couple of days, and then separate them to individual hutches. Each calf has a small wire fence around the hutches to contain them. They are fed milk replacer and started on grains as soon as they can handle it. This process allows Roy to get his cows in the milk parlor early to start milking them, which is what dairy farming is all about. The calves are fed their milk from oversized milk bottles with long nipples on them to simulate their natural nursing process.

These facts you need to know, because, Bob has a plan to make sure Roger gets the most out of his next experience in petting a calf. Roy explained all about the calf pens to Roger while we looked on as hungry calves moved closer to us at the fence. I suggested to Roger that it was time to pet a calf, so I told him to let them get use to him by sticking his finger through the fence and touch the nose of the calf looking up at him. Our kids grew up on our little Gallatin farm mixing and feeding many calves that we had on bottles, so I was familiar with what was about to happen. If a calf sees anything approaching them that even resembles a nipple of their milk bottle, look out. As soon as Roger's finger went through the fence opening, that calf engulfed his finger and began to sucking so hard that Roger jumped back but the finger stayed there because the calf did not want to let go. I wish I had captured that moment on video. It was priceless. We had a great laugh in welcoming Roger to the calf barn. After getting his finger freed up, he finished petting the calf.

We made a couple of pictures with Roy and Roger and thanked Addison and Roy for their time and kindness, in welcoming a New Yorker to a Tennessee dairy farm. Roger talked about his experience all the way to another surprise I had for him. One of my other dairy friends, the Turners, owned another dairy farm a few miles from Roy and even used the fresh milk from their dairy to make ice cream that was sold at their ice cream store on the highway to passing customers. The three of us went inside the ice cream store, sat down, and enjoyed some delicious ice cream cones to celebrate Roger's introduction to the dairy business.

I soon joined with Ray in making Roger one of my new found friends. He even attended my 12$^{th}$ annual Bob's Buck Breakfast that I have for many of my friends who have meant so much to Brenda and me over the years. We provide breakfast for nearly 100 buddies each year just before Christmas. When Ray found out that I was writing a book on baseball, he called me and told me that I should give Roger a call. Ray insisted by saying, "Trust me, Bob, you need to give him a call." I didn't hesitate so I called Roger the next day. He told me that he wanted me to visit him at his home, and that there was something he wanted to show me. We set a date, and I drove to his home, meeting his lovely wife, Alicia, and their dog, Tee Tee. That Boston terrier was all over me like I was a lost son or relative returning home. Roger and Alicia, were the consummate hosts. We sat down at the kitchen table where I found out who Roger Freedman really was. He handed me a six-page brochure of pictures of his New York Mets baseball collection.

There were pictures of baseballs signed by former Met players, autographed baseball bats and pictures, caps, banners, medallions, and many other items in his collection. I asked Roger how he came to have such a great collection of New York Mets memorabilia. He went through an extensive explanation, but I will summarize what he told me.

After the Dodgers and Giants left New York, the city was looking for a new team to replace them. The Payson family obtained a major league baseball franchise and started the Mets in 1962. They played their first game, on April 11th, on the road in Busch Stadium in St. Louis, losing by a score of 11-4. Coincidently, their lead-off batter was Richie Ashburn, whom they had acquired from the Cubs. It would be the Hall of Famer's final year in professional baseball. Richie was the first New York Met player to lead off at bat with their new franchise. The Mets that year, set a major league record by losing 120 games, still the record for most losses in a single season. Another connection I have with the Mets is that in addition to trying out with the Cardinals, I also tried out with the Mets in 1961. If I had been blessed with more talent, I may have had a chance to be in training camp with Richie Ashburn who was in the line-up with the Mets the next year. That really would have been the chief of ironies!

When the Paysons, the previous owners of the Mets, passed away, Roger told me, the team was inherited by a niece, Linda de Roulet, who knew very little about running a baseball team and decided to put the Mets franchise up for sale. Because Roger's occupation was in the financial consulting business, he said that he was contacted to develop the infrastructure necessary for the sale of the Mets. The $23 million dollar sale was finalized in January of 1980. The team was purchased by the Doubleday family of the Doubleday Publishing Company.

Once the sale was consummated and Roger was to be paid for his services, he simply told the attorneys who were ready to discuss money, that what he wanted, "Money couldn't buy." Once they found out what he was talking about, he was rewarded. His request was that he would be given the previous owners's four reserved seats in Shea Stadium, and own those seats until Shea Stadium was no longer the home of the Mets. The seats belonged to Joan Payson, the previous owner, and were located directly in line with first base. The sports writers and photographers were situated in a dug-out area in front of Roger's new seats.

Roger and Alicia saw many great games, sitting in the first base line seats behind photographer's row near the Mets dugout until September 9, 2008. Shea was replaced by the new stadium, Citi Field, which opened in 2009. Roger and Alicia gave up their seats by choosing not to pay the high price to retain them in the new ballpark. Roger explained that an advantage of sitting next to photographer's row was that the photographers gave him so many pictures of not only Met players, but opposing team players. Many of the players were kind enough to autograph the pictures. I saw in his collection, autographed photos of Gary Carter, Nolan Ryan, Bud Harrelson, Davey Johnson, Dwight (Doc) Gooden, Keith Hernandez, and others. I held bats autographed by Pee Wee Reese, George Foster, Daryl Strawberry, Willie Randolph, and a host of other Met and visiting players. Roger pulled out boxes of autographed baseballs and Met jackets, caps, etc. I was like a kid in a candy store. I asked Roger what he was going to do with his collection. He said that he was looking to sell the collection to someone who would not start selling portions of it just for money. I even suggested that he contact the MLB Baseball Hall of Fame in Cooperstown, and maybe they would love to have this history of the Mets. He was not in favor of that.

Several months had passed since I last talked with Roger about his collection. We had met for breakfast and lunch a couple of times but not really got into the baseball collection much at all. Recently, at breakfast one morning, he finally told me that he had sold his collection to someone he trusted to keep it in tack and keep passing it on. I soon learned who that someone was who purchased Roger's great Mets memorabilia. It was our mutual friend, Ray, who started this whole thing with a phone call to me about going to a milk barn to pet a cow and calf. I was thrilled to see that Ray now owned such a great collection. Ray's interest in baseball is centered around his very talented 13-year-old grandson, who has the potential someday, just maybe someday, to perhaps wear a New York Mets uniform and have access to a lot of Mets history. We shall see. I was so glad to have met my Met at the milk barn. Thank you Roy and Addison Major. Thanks also, to my friend Ray, who made this whole thing happen and of course, to two delightful new friends, Roger and Alicia.

*My Met, Roger Freedman, right, at Roy Major's milk barn. Roger got more than a "bucket list" petting of a cow and calf, thanks to Roy's hospitality and help from his granddaughter, Addison. Roy and his wife, Diane, manage their large dairy operation on their family Century Farm.*

# Chapter 30

## It May Look Like Failure

Since the first part of the Loser's Ball is about baseball, I find it appropriate to end with a final admonition to everyone who believes that perfection is the only level of achievement to be the standard of success. It is okay to have that target as a goal, but when reality stops you in your tracks, it's nice to have a recovery plan. By now you should realize that perfection left you a long time ago. Failures are just as much a part of success as the wins that come your way. It's what you do in time of failure that makes you destined for success. Both coaches and players who are often crowned with honors for high achievement would never have done so without failures along the way.

I want to rewrite for you a column that I wrote in 1992 about failures in the lives of some of our most lauded professional athletes that maybe you never heard about.

Ty Cobb is remembered as one of the greatest major league baseball players in the history of the game. His record for stealing bases stood for years. He set a record in 1915, by stealing 96 bases. He did it in 134 attempts, a 71.3% success rate. Max Carey, playing for the Pittsburg Pirates, stole 51 bases in 53 attempts, a 91% success rate. But, who ever heard of Max Carey? The point is that in order to be successful and legendary, one must be willing to fail more by attempting more. Playing it safe and conservative won't get you the gold! You must be geared for success by eliminating your fear of failure.

Ty Cobb's career stolen base record was 897 out of 1112 attempts. (80.9%)

Max Carey's career record was 738 out of 865. (85.3%). They both made the Hall of Fame but it appears that if Carey wanted to be remembered, for his higher success rate, he should have attempted more steals.

Maury Wills broke Ty Cobb's stolen base record by stealing 104 bases in 1962. Lou Brock broke Maury's record with 118 steals in 1974. Brock's career record is 938 out of 1245 attempts for a success rate of 75.34%. Basically, Brock was a failure 25% of the time.

Ricky Henderson currently holds the MLB season stolen base record and career steals. He erased Brock's record when he stole 130 bases in 1982. He also holds the career record with 1406 steals out of 1741 attempts for a success rate of 80.76%. He was a failure 335 times. But here are the facts about failure and success.

First of all. None of these players were perfect.

Failure was a part of their success. The worst thing for them to do after failure was to stop trying. Currently in the majors, there are 61 players with a higher stolen base success rate than Ricky Henderson. Who are they? You probably have never heard of most of them

Ever heard of Byron Buxton? He has the current MLB highest stolen base success rate at 89.58%. He plays for the Minnesota Twins, but he has only 86 stolen bases in 9 seasons! I suggest that Byron make more attempts with that high of a success rate. The more we try, accept it, the more you will fail. Also, the more you try the more you succeed. Learn to live with failure, but never fear to fail.

Let's look at another famous Yankee by the name of Babe Ruth. All of us in baseball know about the great Bambino. The Babe set a major league record by hitting 60 homers during the 1923 season, and 714 career homers. Hank Aaron of the Atlanta Braves, broke the Babe's career record by hitting his 715$^{th}$ home run in 1974.

The Babe also set another career baseball record most people have never known. He struck out 1,330 times during his career, the most of any player in baseball history. But what is Babe Ruth known for? His home run record.

The career strikeout record of Babe Ruth, set in 1935 when he had retired, was finally broken by another Yankee great in 1964, another player known for his home runs and his 1961 home run chase with his Yankee teammate, Roger Maris. His name was Mickey Mantle. I bet that you didn't know this. Two records belonging to the Babe were broken by former Yankees like him in the span of four years, Maris hitting 61 homers in 1961, and Mick's strikeout record in 1964.

There is not one baseball fan that I know of who claims that any of these players were failures. They just accepted the fact that failing is a big part of success. Enshrined in the MLB Baseball Hall of Fame are the best of the many players to wear a uniform. The majority of the players who have been voted into the hall have failed as hitters in their careers 70% of the time. They make 7 outs in 10 at bats.

They just learned to take their Loser's Balls and turn them into "Opportunity Balls", which made them successful. You can do the same thing.

It's time for you to step up to the plate...... Play Ball!

# Reviewing Some Interesting Ironies . . . . . . .

1. The new baseball glove that I got for my 12$^{th}$ birthday was a Richie Ashburn autographed model. I got to see Richie while playing for the Chicago Cubs at Wrigley Field against the Dodgers and Giants in 1960, during my Bramwell summer vacation to Chicago. Who was Richie Ashburn? Thanks to Wikipedia.org, I found out some facts that are incredible. No wonder my daddy bought me that glove with his autograph on it.

   Don Richard Ashburn was born in 1927 on a farm in Nebraska. While playing center field for the Philadelphia Phillies from 1948 to 1959, he was a four-time NL All-Star player. He was a two-time NL batting champion and finished his 15-year MLB career with a .308 batting average. Richie was a left-handed hitter with blazing speed, He was a prankster and lovable teammate. He is still ranked third among all MLB center fielders for most put outs. He is only behind Willie Mays and Tris Speaker. He ended his career, playing with the Cubs in 1960 and '61, when I got to see him play in Chicago. He was the first batter in the lineup for the new expansion club, New York Mets in 1962 who, unfortunately, set a major league record for most season defeats, by losing 120 games. He retired after that horrible year and became a Phillies broadcaster for 33 years.

I was never in the class of Richie, but some things were just coincidental. I hit left-handed, played center field, had good speed, hit over .300, suffered a number of defeats, liked to pull pranks, and became a speaker of sort. Such a headshaking moment to be given that particular glove on my 12$^{th}$ birthday! My glove was eventually stolen, and I had to replace it, but not with one like the prized Richie Ashburn model.

2. I chased down a foul ball one Sunday afternoon at a Glade baseball game and instead of returning it, I hid it in our truck. My daddy made me give back that ball to the Glade manager, Van Dobson. Four years later during my first year of playing for the Glade, Van gave me a new baseball for my own to take home for practice. He told me, "This one is yours. Next Sunday you are pitching for us." Van was a special guy.

3. My childhood baseball idol was Buddy Gilbert, who I saw in person, playing center field for the Nashville Vols in 1959. In 1965, while playing the second year with my summer team, the Knoxville Prospectors, we needed a catcher, and Buddy Gilbert joined our team. Buddy and I played together that year. We won the Tennessee State Championship in amateur baseball as well as the Regional Championship. We played in the Stan Musial Amateur Baseball World Series and each of us had three hits in winning our first game in Battle Creek. We placed 3$^{rd}$ in the national tournament. An article on the win appeared in the Battle Creek Enquirer that highlighted our performance. How often does that happen?

4. My Knoxville Prospectors coach was Sid Hatfield, who played for the Tennessee Vols, who won the SEC Baseball Championship in 1951. The Vols lost in the finals to Oklahoma 3-2 in the College World Series. Sid was selected as the MVP of the series. Sid coached our Prospectors team to a National Championship in the 1964 Amateur Baseball Stan Musial World Series that

was played in Battle Creek, Michigan. His son, Bill, a former Vol baseball player, told me that his dad once told him that national championship was one of his best baseball achievements. I couldn't have been playing for anyone better at the time.

5. One of my Uncle Charlie Bramwell's best friends was kind enough to write a letter on my behalf to the coaching staff at Tennessee to inform them of my intent to play baseball there, and if there was any scholarship assistance available. His name was Kirby O. Primm, Vice President of Third National Bank in Nashville, who also happened to be a member on the University of Tennessee Board of Trustees. Stuff like this just doesn't happen often, does it?

6. My freshman baseball coach at Tennessee in 1963, was Don Lumley, a former Knoxville Smokies first baseman. I had the fortune to play with Coach Lumley on the 1964 Knoxville Prospectors team that won the state, regional, and the 1964 National Championship Stan Musial World Series of Amateur Baseball. I have a championship black bat with our names, as well as all of the names of the other team members engraved on it. How often do you get to play with your mentor?

7. Even though Hendersonville High School was one of our biggest rivals while I was playing football at Mt. Juliet, both of our daughters, Amy and Julie, were selected as Coaches of the Year, while coaching middle school teams in basketball in Hendersonville. Three of my grandchildren graduated with honors from Hendersonville High School. I have breakfast with old retired HHS faculty and coaches once a month now. It is unreal how things change over time, opening up great opportunities.

8. During my first regular season baseball game as a freshman at Tennessee in 1963, I hit a home run against Hiwassee College. In

1966, at my last at bat in our last regular season game at Vanderbilt, when the count went to 3-0, I backed out of the batter's box and told the catcher, "I am not going to walk, especially with my entire family watching from the stands, so throw me something I can hit." He replied, "Get ready, here it comes." I got one down the middle and hit it over the right field fence for my last regular season game home run for the Vols. It was retrieved by Larry, my brother. That still amazes me to this day. What a thrill!

9. My FFA advisor and agriculture teacher at Mt. Juliet was Bill Coley. Mr. Coley was like having a second dad. We became even closer over the years. I always wanted to thank him in so many ways for all that he did for me. After he died of cancer, I was asked and accepted the privilege of conduction the eulogy at his funeral. I later made a large ceremonial wooden gavel that was presented in his honor to the Tennessee FFA. It is used to open and close every annual Tennessee FFA State Convention. What can I say? He was the best!

10. In 1961, our Mt. Juliet football team lost one game. It was a blowout by Greenbrier. They had a beast of a fullback named Ronnie Walton, and a star guard named Terry Gann. During my freshman year when I moved into my $7^{th}$ floor dorm room located at 1720 Melrose Ave on the UT campus, two rooms down was a room shared by Ronnie Walton and Terry Gann. We became the best of friends the rest of my time at Tennessee. All alone was I, but they pulled me through that first year. Great memories.

11. After searching several days for a job for Brenda in Knoxville, in the fall of 1963, she was employed by Pilot Oil Company, owned by Jim Haslam. Mr. Haslam was the captain of the Tennessee Volunteers National Championship football team in 1951. He was also the President of the Orange Tie Club. Brenda did all of his correspondence for the club as well as the accounting duties for the then fast-growing Pilot Oil Company. Mr. Haslam is

still one of the University's chief financial donors. He provided funds for the Haslam School of Business. Several years ago, our granddaughter, Molly Claire, graduated from Tennessee with her degree in business from the Haslam School of Business. God provides!

12. While competing in many FFA activities at Mt. Juliet H S, our Parliamentary Procedure team won the Tennessee FFA State Championship. Years later while I was teaching FFA and agriculture at Gallatin High School, our Parliamentary Procedure team also won the state championship. I just taught it like Mr. Coley taught us.

13. My brother, Larry, and I, while playing baseball in Nashville on two different teams in 1970, were both selected to the Nashville Tri-State League All Star team. I am just glad that I never had to face him while he was pitching against my team.

14. My long-time friend, Ralph Barnett, and I were both FFA Camp Clements Officers in 1961. I later worked on his staff when he was the Assistant Commissioner of Career Education in 2004. I completed the circle in the FFA from; an FFA student, chapter officer, regional officer, state officer, teacher/advisor, and Tennessee FFA Executive Secretary. Not many get a chance to do that. I was so blessed. What great friends and teammates at the state office! Thanks, Ralph.

15. When Uncle Charlie took me over to visit Coach Jim Turner's baseball museum, I found out more about him than having just retired as the New York Yankee's pitching coach. He, actually, on a number of occasions had come with Uncle Charlie to rabbit hunt on our family farm when I was very young. His brother Bryant, had also accompanied him a few times. While I was at the Tennessee State Fair about a year later, showing my Guernsey cows, Uncle Charlie came by with guns and shells, picked me

up, and drove me to a dove shoot at the farm of Bryant Turner. I always said that I had three dads; Daddy, Mr. Coley, and Uncle Charlie.

16. The Fleetwood mobile home plant where I received a lot of my manager's training was relocated from the small town of Westmoreland, 17 miles away, to a site only 1.7 miles from our house in Gallatin. That plant (Plant 27), was the plant where I was hired to manage the production department in November, of 1993, and remained the Production Manager there until 2003. That timing just couldn't have been by accident.

17. My last Mt. Juliet H S football game was played in Joelton, Tennessee. We won the game 21-6, which resulted in our winning the first football championship title in our school's history. After sticking together for four years, going our first two years without a single win, the boys from the Glade hung in there and never gave up. I am proud of that season and our guys, but especially proud that during our last game on that night all three members of our backfield, Doyle Sanders, Ray Underwood, and Bob Lannom, were from the Glade. So many more, who were key starters: Tommy Knowles, Hilton Hamblen, Billy Pickett, Eddie Foster, Jerry McDonald, and Butch Martin. Hatton Wright, who was our quarterback, lived elsewhere, but ironically, he now lives on a farm near the Glade that he purchased from the heirs of one of my uncles. He is now definitely a Glade boy!

18. After playing so many years on different teams, three of my best baseball buddies and I finally got a chance to play on the same team one year. I was given a copy of the official score book page listing the four of us as the first four hitters in the line-up. We were playing for Walter Nipper's Nashville Sporting Goods. Leading off was my good old base stealing buddy and left fielder, Boots Kirby. I was batting second and playing center field. Hitting third was our shortstop and one of my best quail

and deer hunting pals, Pat Webb. Hitting cleanup, which was his natural position with his great hitting skills, was my friend from Ray Batts Furniture fame, Belmont University star, and a TSSAA Hall of Fame basketball coach, Jerry Vradenburg. I am deeply proud of this score sheet because it also has listed, Donnie Fortner as our pitcher. I played with and against the late Donnie Fortner, who was a super baseball player and teammate.

The score sheet was copied out of the official score book kept by Donnie's brother Dudley Fortner, where he and his wife, Sue, worship with me at our church. Dudley and his wife Sue, also shared with me a copy of the scorebook page when the Prospectors were playing Ray Batts in the state championship in 1964. Donnie and Jerry were both members of that team. Dudley attended all of his brother's games and was their score keeper.

All of us suffered a great loser's ball when Donnie, a remarkable baseball talent passed away from cancer several years ago. Small world! The Fortners are special folks.

19. Even though my cousin, Charles Bramwell Junior, was almost 8 years older than me, in later years, Brenda and I would visit Charlie just about every time we went to Knoxville. We would often meet at the Cracker Barrel restaurant at the interstate exit and join him either for breakfast or lunch. He, like his father, my Uncle Charlie, was one of the most giving individuals I ever knew. He was devoted to his church and his passion for his Camp Wesley Woods youth camp.

He would often drive down to our farm and bring some of his buddies to dove hunt. By meeting them, I developed a friendship with them as well. Charlie needed some help in building another log cabin at the youth camp. I introduced him to one of my friends, Paul Gentry, owner of Old Timer Log Homes. Paul is a special Christian man. He has donated finished logs to many churches in our area to build churches and camping cottages. Charlie worked out a deal with Paul for logs to build his cabin. Paul donated the logs and had them hauled to the site near

Maryville. He took me along for a week's work to lay the logs and build the walls of the cabin.

Paul and I stayed with some of Charlie's friends. We had a great week working together to get the cabin walls completed. Charlie worked his magic and got his cabin built with free logs and labor. That was typical of how he worked, but you could never out give him. My home is filled with wildlife prints and art that he gave us over the years. There will never be another Uncle Charlie, nor another "Charlie Junior." I was asked to speak at Charlie's funeral in April of 2019. It was one of the hardest things I have ever done. I loved him like a big brother.

20. By attempting to attend Lebanon High School and not going as zoned to Mt. Juliet, I would have missed out on the best thing that could ever have happened to me in my life. If I had stayed away following that morning's send off, and never returned, after I made my puny pitch to that pretty basketball player, sitting on the bleachers waiting to go to class, I have no idea what my future would have been like. But, since that didn't happen, I can attest to the fact that my life was completely transformed into an exciting, wonderful, successful, and joyous 58 years of marriage bliss. Brenda was my rock, my best fan and supporter, my faithful Christian mate, and the mother and grandmother of a bunch of extra special kids. It is no doubt that truly as some of our best friends, who have known us for a long time, have said, "You and Brenda's marriage had to be made in Heaven." I believe that, and have never been in doubt.

# Acknowledgements

Brenda and I had so many friends and supporters. It would take another book just to name them. Sorry, I couldn't include them all. I do, however, want to acknowledge some of the following individuals who made so many great things happen in our lives.

Thanks to our parents, our children, Julie, Amy, and Lee, as well as our brothers, sisters, and cousins, who knew and demonstrated the bonds of family love and care for one another. A special thanks to my dad, who was my coach, inspiration, and friend. To mom, who showed me how to become a better person. To Mama Pearl, who helped to raise me and was one of my biggest fans. Thanks to my sister, Lugene, and brother-in-law, Eddie Snipes, who made our world such a fun place. Thank you, Whitney, Taylor and Mackenzie. I am grateful for the full support and great times together with my brother, Larry. To his children, Risha and Micah. The great love of our grandchildren and my daughter-in-law, Julie Grace, means so much to me. To my grandson-in-law, Kevin, and my first "great grand", Ben Wallace Lee, who already at age one, loves his Poppa. In spite of his parents making him wear crimson occasionally, he is still destined to become a "Winner".

To Uncle Charlie, Auntie, and the Bramwells, Charlie, Ann, Earl, and Raymond, who never stopped supporting me. To Bill Coley, who was always there for me, always! To Coach Agee, who showed up in my life at exactly the right time our team needed him. To the rest of my teachers at the Glade and at Mt. Juliet HS for keeping this country boy focused on the important things of life. To my Glade baseball coach, Van Dobson, who replaced my literal Loser's Ball with a new one.

Thanks to O.E Willie Co. and superintendent, Darnell Burgess, for giving me my first construction job during the summer after Brenda and I were married. Thanks to Donna and Rusty for providing us a summer "honeymoon" cottage, as well as Oko and Betty Hamblen. To Mr. Kirby Primm and Mr. Jim Lancaster, for writing those letters for me to UT. Thanks to Coach Lumley and Coach Wright, who made me a better ball player at Tennessee, and to all of my Vol teammates and fans. Thank you, Pilot Oil and Jim Haslam, who gave Brenda the best job ever, and supported us all the way through graduation. And to Mr. and Mrs. Haynes who provided us a place to live.

I acknowledge my special coach for two fantastic seasons with the Knoxville Prospectors, Sid Hatfield, a Volunteer legend. To all of my Prospector teammates for making a country boy's dream come true.

To Dan Herron for giving me my first job in education at GHS, and later hiring Brenda as the school accountant. A special salute to all of my "Vokies" at GHS and all the other schools in Sumner County, as well as my office buds, Connie and Carol. To Gene Brown, my long-time friend and superintendent of schools, for a great promotion. To our dear friends, Garlin and Linda Farris and Jeff, for our road trips, kindness, and endearing friendship. A giant thanks to JJ and Sharon Redmon, and Pete and Pat Carpenter, for long-lasting friendships. To my Fleetwood manager and friend, Bill Graves for taking a chance on me. Thanks goes to all of my former associates and friends at Fleetwood Homes, including: Pop, Neal, Danny, Murrell, Joe, Dennis, Larry, Troy, Leo, Mark, Wes, Shorty, the Brendas, Evelyn, Shawn, Ginger, and James, plus about 300 more too numerous to list.

To my friend, Ralph Barnett, who gave me some extra innings working with the Tennessee FFA. To John Leeman who stopped by on a hot day. To my Ag partner, Steve Gass, for putting up with me while trying to learn the high-tech computer stuff. To all my other buddies at the state office and ag teachers across the state for their kindness and support while there. Thanks, Martha Hix. I am forever indebted.

A special thanks for my friendships and support from my Nashville baseball buddies: Jerry Vradenburg, Pat Webb, Boots Kirby, Simon Dickerson, Perk Williams, and all my teammates from Nashville Sporting Goods and Ezell Dickerson Realty.

To the Tennessee Association FFA for presenting me with the 2022 Lifetime Achievement Award, Honorary State, and American Degrees. A special thanks to all of the Tennessee FFA state officers that Brenda and I had the pleasure to work with throughout the years. A special thanks to a great cheerleader, Barb Walker and her husband John.

Thanks for the support of Bill Broderick and Stephanie Angel, of the sports department at the Battle Creek Enquirer, for giving me permission to use several pictures, articles, and box scores displayed in the picture section.

Special thanks to Bill Traughber, whose book "Nashville Baseball History", provided me with a lot of local history of Sulphur Dell and related stories. Thanks goes to my baseball old timers, former Nashville Vol, Cincinnati star, and Prospectors teammate, Buddy Gilbert, and former Tennessee Vol great, Bill Hatfield, son of Coach Sid Hatfield. I cherish the visits I made to their homes, listening as they shared their fantastic baseball stories with me. Thanks to UT Sports, and the Tennessee Baseball Archives for providing information on past scores and records of our games. Thanks to Chris Landers and CUT 4 by MLB.com, for his research on the history of the MLB rulebook on stealing bases and other strange stories. Of course, to Google, Wikipedia, and articles available on websites, I am grateful.

I want to express my appreciation to my editor, Eva Jane Johnston, one of our kids favorite English teachers at GHS. I was with EJ for most of the time I spent there as a member of the Green Wave faculty. Eva Jane is a super baseball fan who understands the game. Her biggest challenge was to keep me from striking out during the writing of The Loser's Ball. Thank you, Joann Bates, one of my best cheerleaders and heroes, for recommending EJ and being there with me as well.

Thank you, Janice Garrett and Charlie Brown Co. for everything.

Without the love, devoted companionship, and support of my wife, Brenda, our stories would have probably just remained memories, rather than recorded events in our book. To our friends in Gallatin and members at the Hartsville Pike Church of Christ, and to the Lord and Master of our lives, our Savior, Jesus Christ, I submit my deepest and most sincere appreciation for supporting us as we turned our life's Loser's Balls into "Opportunity Balls", which insured us of such a wonderful and blessed life. And thanks to all of you who took the time to read our story. God bless.

# CREDITS FOR: REFERENCES AND RESOURCES

### Quotes:

Michael Phelps, World class Olympic swimmer
Charles Barkley, NBA All Star and Hall of Fame
Tommy Lasorda, Manager Los Angeles Dodgers MLB Hall of Fame
Sidney Howard, American playwright
President Calvin Coolidge
Branch Rickey, Owner of Brooklyn Dodgers MLB Hall of Fame
Lou Holtz, Football coach and author
Derek Jeter, New York Yankee shortstop MLB Hall of Fame
Kobe Bryant, Los Angeles Lakers and NBA Hall of Fame
Jerry Rice, All Star Receiver, San Francisco 49ers.
Helen Keller, American author, disability rights advocate
John Merritt, Head football coach Tennessee State University
Zig Ziglar, Author and motivational speaker
John Maxwell, Motivational speaker and author
Babe Ruth, New York Yankee, MLB Hall of Famer
Yogi Berra, New York Yankee, MLB Hall of Fame
John Wayne, American patriot and actor
President Abraham Lincoln
Tom Landry, Head coach for Dallas Cowboys, NFL Hall of Fame
Mike Ditka, Chicago Bears player and head coach, NFL Hall of Fame

George Barnard Shaw, Irish playwright and critic
Michael Irvin, Dallas Cowboys receiver, NFL Hall of Fame
Deion Sanders, Colorado head football coach, NFL Hall of Fame
John Wooden, UCLA head basketball coach, Naismith College BB Hall of Fame
Daniel Webster, American lawyer and statesman
Bible: Matthew, Galatians, Philippians, James, Isaiah, Ezekiel, Proverbs, Luke
President Theodore (Teddy) Roosevelt, The Man In The Arena, The Strenuous Life
General Douglas Macarthur, A Coach's Prayer
O. Glenn Webb, Cooperative Educator Poem: Keep On Kicking
Walter Wintle, Author, The Man Who Thinks He Can
Bob Lannom, The Loser's Ball, Extra Innings, Your Best

**Books/Resources:**

Paul (Bear) Bryant, I Ain't Nothin' But A Winner
Earl Nightingale, Lead The Field
William Danforth, I Dare You
Zig Ziglar, See You At The Top and Top Performance
The Battle Creek Enquirer, Box scores and sports articles from archives
Wilson Sporting Goods, The Will To Win
John Maxwell, Team Work Makes The Dream Work
The NFL Pro Football Hall of Fame and the MLB Hall of Fame
Jim Abbott, Olympic Champion, MLB Hall of Fame
Wikipedia.org and Google
William Gibson, The Miracle Worker, movie of Helen Keller
Linda Farris, Lessons Learned On My Journey With Jeff
Pat Summit, Reach For The Summit
Willie Jolley, A Set Back is Just a Set Up for a Come Back
Tennessee Volunteers baseball archives
Phil Crosby, Quality author, Quality Is Free, Quality Without Tears

Gale Sayers, I Am Third
Bobby Richardson, Impact Player
Bill Traughber, Nashville Baseball History
Ken Dugan, How To Organize and Coach Winning Baseball
Tammy Wynette, and Billy Sherrill, Stand By Your Man
Chris Landers, CUT4, 7 Strangely Specific MLB Rules. Google 8-23-2017

**Related foundation resources:**

Empowering Teams, Richard S. Wellins, William C. Byham, and Jeanne M. Wilson
Making It Happen, by Bob Alexander
How To Cultivate the Habit of Succeeding, by Mack R. Douglas
How To Win Friends and Influence People, by Dale Carnegie
Psychology of Winning, Seeds of Greatness, The Winner's Edge, by Dennis Waitley
How To Get What You Want and Want What You Get, Willard Tate

# Courage and Strength

I sat among members of my family on the front row watching and listening to our two talented grandsons, Jack and Camron, playing musical tributes to their "Nana" during her funeral at Hartsville Pike Church of Christ that afternoon. We were surrounded by a large crowd of family and friends. Brenda would have been so proud of her boys. Jack played "Great Is Thy Faithfulness" on the keyboard. Camron played his rendition of "Amazing Grace" on his guitar.

My heart was moved by their courage, love and devotion that day. They never missed a note! The encouraging words by our two ministers, Brian and Doyle, as well as some stories told by two of our friends, Tom and Doug, helped me to make it with dignity and grace. Those present joined in with the singing of Brenda's favorite little song, "Thank You Lord" as we exited the auditorium.

I reflected back to that afternoon when we sat in our swing with her suggestion that I write a book about our lives together. I had some grieving to go through first, but I never dismissed that idea at any time. All of us first had to learn an adjustment to a new way of life without our wife, mom, grandmother, sister, and friend. Her story was finished. She had shown us by example her own personal book for us to read and from which to live by.

Once it finally sank in and I could eventually muster the courage to recall and put in print so many events in our lives, I was ready to begin writing about our story together. I knew that I would be writing and crying at the same time, but, I was determined to never permit a Loser's Ball to interfere with the great and meaningful stories that I wanted to share with so many people.

When I began our story, I found it hard to stop writing. I got to relive many of the great times and adventures of our lives. I had never really considered just how many times our lives had interwoven with so many others, who seemed to always be there in our time of need. I am delighted that I had the opportunity to share them with you. I hope that you found some encouraging words to help you to one day, write……….. "your book" of life.

*Following our family photo shoot, while Brenda and I were "just a swinging", she suggested that I write a book about my baseball, our lives together, and the successes of our kids.*

*This book is for you, my greatest friend and companion for 58 years. You still keep me going. I still love you with all my heart. Bob*

# Your Best

Your best dreams are the ones you live.

Your best gifts are the ones you give.

Your best deeds are the ones just done.

Your best days are the ones to come.

What would life be without fulfilling your dreams? I can't even imagine living a life without hope for the future and doing the things I dream of doing. The most successful people on the planet are those who dreamed of a better life and way to do things. Our best inventors were first dreamers. Dare to live your dreams. Don't be sorry and live to regret it. Dream big!

All of us love to receive gifts for birthdays, at Christmas, and on other occasions. Unfortunately, however, the joy is really not in the receiving, it is in the giving. Jesus taught us that it is more blessed to give than to receive. Givers are special people and much more in demand than the takers or receivers. If you want to get more, give more. It's a Biblical principle. It comes back pressed down and multiplied. You cannot out give God. He beats you every time.

You know what really makes you feel good? It is a deed done to or for someone who least expects it and can in no way return the favor. The ones done without the recipient knowing who did it are the best.

Deeds done for you cannot come close to the impact deeds performed by you make in your life and the lives of others. What would our world be like if everyone lived to serve? Jesus told his disciples that the greatest among you is the one who serves.

There is not a sweeter word than hope! Without hope for a better tomorrow, how can we live to our fullest? Storms of life are brushed away just like a thunderstorm followed by the sun and blue skies. If we live our lives with a faith that our best days are yet to come, just imagine the courage and strength we have to endure and press on for a brighter day. Knowing that the treasure just may be over the next hill gives us the perseverance to move forward with a peace and determination unmatched by the doubters and skeptics. Enjoy your best days ahead.

Bob Lannom

Galatians 6:9

# The Loser's Ball

You step into the batter's box,
So confident you'll hit the ball.
No matter what the pitch may be,
Just hit it over the wall.

You're now prepared to be the best,
No fear while at the plate.
The work, the sweat, the price you've paid,
Are enough to make you great.

But, there's just one thing you don't control,
It's the pitch that comes your way.
The one you least expect to see
May take you down today.

Why is it when, all the time you spend
To avoid your grief and fall?
You should have known that just in life,
You're thrown a loser's ball.

A sinker, a slider, a change-up, or curve,
All designed to make you lose.
So, how much time do you endure a loss?
It's time for you to choose.

Don't waste away in the loser's bracket,
Push on for you're not done.
Losses will come as foundations you see,
Disguised as victories soon won.

So brush off the dirt, step back in the box,
A loss is not your end.
Since you are made to never quit,
Life's game is yours to win!

Bob Lannom

# My Walk Off

I must admit. My timing for completing **The Loser's Ball** couldn't have been any better. Days before all my final edits had to be sent to my publisher, my Tennessee Volunteers baseball team made it to the finals of the Men's College World Series in Omaha, Nebraska. Busy work schedules, house renovations, and planned family vacations prevented my former traveling buddies from going with me to Omaha. I decided to stay home. Once the Vols made it to the championship finals to play Texas A&M for the title, my daughter, Amy, said, "Dad, you are going to the World Series and I am going with you. Pack your bags, I have our flights scheduled and hotel reservations made. Your job is to get tickets."

My son, Lee, is responsible for the cover photo of my book. Julie, my oldest, has been helpful in the editing process. Now, Amy, is making sure that I will be in attendance at the historical Volunteer Baseball moment. We left Gallatin with a lot of faith that we would find tickets for an almost sold-out event. A lot of faith! My friends from Knoxville came through with great tickets, located behind the Tennessee dugout in the shade, for all three games. Thanks guys! Amy made sure that we attended the pre-game Vol Walk as well as the Vols Alumni Tailgate Party. As a former Vols player, I even got to speak at the tailgate party.

Tennessee was handed a big Loser's Ball the first game by losing to A&M 9-5. It reminded me of the birth of my Loser's Ball back in 1964 in Battle Creek, Michigan, when we lost 5-4 in our first game. I like to refer to this 2024 Vol baseball team as a bunch of "Rock Hitters". In game 2, they proved to nearly 25,000 fans in attendance that they refused to give up, tying the series by a score of 4-1. The championship game, winner take all, was to be determined by which team could turn their Loser's Balls into "Opportunity Balls" to win the title. Heros are not always the fan favorites, not the highest rated draft pick, nor always the most experienced senior. They emerge because they are part of the TEAM, that at the most needful period of competition, do their part to make a victory happen. Sometimes it may just be a sophomore left fielder.

The 2024 Tennessee Volunteers became the Men's College World Series National Champions. During the celebration, Amy was thrown a game ball by one of the officials. She caught it and immediately handed it to me, "Dad … (hug)… now you have a **Winner's Ball.**"

Made in United States
Orlando, FL
23 July 2024